INTEGRATION
IN
CHRISTIAN HIGHER EDUCATION

Integration

IN THE

CHRISTIAN LIBEI

Foreword by
SIDNEY FRENCH

Preface by
CLEMENS M. GRANSKOU

Edited by
HOWARD HONG

ST. OLA

L ARTS COLLEGE

BY THE

ST. OLAF COLLEGE SELF STUDY COMMITTEE

CLARENCE CLAUSEN *(Social Studies)*

HAROLD DITMANSON *(Religion)*

ALBERT FINHOLT *(Natural Sciences)*

NORA SOLUM *(Humanities)*

ORIN LOFTHUS *(Dean of the College)*

HOWARD HONG *(Chairman)*

OLLEGE PRESS, NORTHFIELD, MINNESOTA

Manufactured in the United States by Augsburg Publishing House

CONTENTS

Volume I

PART ONE

EDUCATIONAL FRAGMENTATION AND INTEGRATION IN PERSPECTIVE

PART TWO

CHRISTIAN HIGHER EDUCATION AND INTEGRATION

PART THREE

INTEGRATIVE MEANS

Volume II

APPENDICES

(separate supplement)

"In the early days even one of our present problems would have been enough to take up all of our time. Now we are required to bring to some common denominator such varied problems as war, marriage, the Church, profession, housing, the danger and death of our nearest and dearest, and as if all that were not enough, my imprisonment here. No doubt most people would regard these as quite separate problems, but for the Christian and the man of liberal education that is impossible: he cannot split up his life into water-tight compartments. The common denominator is to be sought both in thought and in practical living in an integrated attitude to life. The man who allows himself to be torn into fragments by events and problems has not passed the test for the present and the future. It is related in the story of young Witiko how he set out on life with the intention of doing everything there was to be done. In other words, it is a question of *anthrōpos teleios* (the primary meaning of *teleios* is 'whole,' 'complete')—'Ye therefore shall be perfect *(teleios)*, as your Father is perfect' (Matthew 5:48), in contrast to the *anēr dipsychos*, the 'double minded man' of James 1:8."

Dietrich Bonhoeffer,
Letters and Papers from Prison
(London: SCM Press, 1954), pp. 97-98.

Foreword

WHEN I was first invited to serve as a visiting consultant by the Self Study Committee of St. Olaf College, I accepted with pleasure both because it would give me an opportunity to get better acquainted with a fine college I had known about for a long time and because it would serve as a valid excuse to re-visit the country of my childhood and young manhood. I was not prepared, however, for the virtual avalanche of mimeographed materials which shortly thereafter arrived on my desk to be pre-digested.

As I settled myself dutifully to read these many materials, however, any irksome reaction I might have built up vanished. I discovered a new approach, one which I believe no other college has yet taken in so full a measure, to the study of itself and to the problems of the meaning of a liberal education.

We are prone to think that the present uneasiness about our fragmentized curricula in the liberal arts colleges is something new. We tend to go about the solution of the problem by introducing *more* courses, courses of generalized character, while retaining all the others. We hope, thereby, that the student will achieve integration; we feel thereby that we have done our duty. Perhaps the student does achieve better integration, incidentally, but there is little of it apparent in the program itself and we have certainly stopped considerably short of our duty.

The St. Olaf Committee has done several things in this study which are unique and which should prove most helpful to others engaging in similar future studies. They have deliberately taken as their theme the examination of all the possible integrative factors which may latently exist in a modern liberal arts program, and then have traced the history of integrative efforts in education down through the ages from ancient Greece to mid-twentieth-century America. The emphasis, for example, on "citizenship" in Sparta and Athens, though quite different each from the other, had most *practical* objectives. Only with "good citizens" was survival possible militarily, on the one hand, and essential cultural supremacy on the other.

The medieval period "aimed quite deliberately at synthesis in terms of authoritatively given goals and techniques. . . ." But man was on the move; new ideas were creeping in and there arose "a steady process of disintegration and fragmentation." Revolt against authority, political, religious, social, and financial, saw the rise of new societies of men and the creation of a "world-wide mechanism of production and exchange." Belief in reason, in God, in the dignity of man, in the search for truth and knowledge, and in the development of natural laws and natural systems, all represented efforts to generalize and integrate, but the tide of movement was running strongly against the effort.

So it has gone down through the ages, the forces of disintegration and fragmentation arrayed against those of integration. As knowledge has accumulated in accelerating amounts the trend toward disintegration has become more tangible, and the attempts at integration more difficult. The modern flood-gates to fragmentation were opened wide when we had to abandon the classical curriculum because of the onslaughts of psychology and admit, perhaps prematurely, that mental discipline and transfer of training were unattainable myths.

One finds in these several chapters an excellent, well documented account of man's efforts to pull his educational thoughts, processes, and materials together in the face of continuing disruptive factors. Nowhere else has this story been traced against this particular kind of background.

Another unique aspect of the study, whether it can bring about the desired results or not, is the effort to get each department, each teacher, in fact, to examine carefully all the integrative aspects of a field of study. It is quite possible that a suitable remedy for fragmentation will eventually come not from introducing a host of additional so-called integrative courses but rather from trying more intelligently and persistently to re-integrate those courses and areas already in the curriculum and to bring them together especially in the senior year.

As those concerned with higher education well know, it is common practice today for departments and teachers to "ride off," each in his own direction. Relationships to other departments or courses become casual at best and are seldom even pointed out— usually because the teacher is too intent on "covering" his own subject and has been prepared for his assignment by the narrowing rather than the broadening process. There is a tremendous amount of valuable and important history of science, for example, which could re-set science in the proper context of a liberalizing study, but science teachers complain that there isn't even time to teach all the modern concepts of science, let alone add the history.

The attempt to bring about greater integration through thoughtful examination of the liberal integrating factors in *each* field or department of study is a courageous step. Too often in similar self-studies this effort is side-stepped for fear of arousing certain fears or antagonisms on the part of established interests. In the final analysis, however, real integration must be achieved through such a re-synthesis. What happens, all too often but not necessarily, in the attempt to gain integration through a series of new generalized courses is the establishment of a new set of vested interests. This in turn sometimes results in a new type of fission within the institution arraying the old set of interests against the new, the specialists against the generalists.

There are, of course, numerous types of efforts today at integration between departments and courses. Usually they are of limited nature, involving a few courageous and like-minded teachers within an institution who are willing to experiment with new ideas. Seldom, however, has this movement gained overall institutional support. There are also programs of general education which have many fine integrative qualities, but, again, these are usually of limited scope and seldom attempt to do the job on an institution-wide basis. We have in this study an example of pioneering along new and different lines which could very well blaze a new trail for future efforts to restore many of the liberalizing qualities to a liberal education.

It is a curious anomaly that the serious effort to secure better integration by examining the potential integrative qualities of existing programs should be regarded as something new. For, after all, most of our many diverse programs have stemmed from a few common ancestors whose qualities and quantities are quite well known historically and whose boundaries and unities were clear. But it points out again how far we have gone down the line of evolution into specialties. We have gone so far that we have ceased to regard our specialties as having any common ancestors; the resemblance to anything else, living or dead, becomes purely incidental, and without roots into a common past.

So, we view the problem of integration as something new, which, in fact, it is to us, for we cannot go backward to achieve it. We must go forward. As this study indicates so well, however, we cannot attempt to go forward without first looking backward.

The third aspect of this study which deserves special attention is the Committee's proposal to start with an integrating course in the *Senior* year. Too often the Senior year becomes a year of aimless wandering for the student who has largely completed his requirements. Or it may become a "Senior loaf." The Committee proposes making this a time for careful examination of, and a synthesis of, what has gone before, based on the concept of Christian civilization and ideals.

Most programs of general education have started with the Freshman year. Many end with the Sophomore year; while a few extend through all four years. The emphasis upon achieving unity has been in the lower years, with the idea that specialization would largely consume the upper years. This has not worked out as well in practice as in theory, and the need for integration at the upper level is certainly great.

By starting at the top rather than at the bottom the Committee hopes to achieve and *retain* integration through the *four* years. Having *well* defined the objectives of a Christian liberal education and having established the capstone of that education in the Senior year, it should be possible to re-build the supporting areas of the lower years in harmony with both the objectives and the capstone, taking full advantage of all existing studies re-oriented toward these ultimate objectives.

Under whatever guise they may take in the future, attempts to restore the liberal qualities to the so-called liberal arts programs will continue. This must come in terms of genuine integration of subject matter. But this alone is not enough. The one integrating *quality* which should pervade all such subject matter is that of the thoughtful approach designed to produce better thinking. Whether or not this generalized process can ever be a successful outcome remains to be seen. It is, in a sense, the modern interpretation of the older concepts of mental discipline and transfer of training, which concepts we have never really abandoned in spite of all the evidence against them.

The effort to find integrating *qualities* as well as integrating *materials*, to examine the past for its bearing on the present, to start at the top, and to start with existing programs as a basis for seeking both these materials and the qualities marks this study as unique and auspicious. It will probably not solve all the problems before us, but it does open new doors which may well lead to eventual solution. For such reasons I am grateful that I was invited to participate in a small way and had the opportunity to urge that the Committee's materials be made a part of the public record so that the many others also concerned with the problem of restoring liberality to the liberal arts could profit from such experience and start from a new base.

SIDNEY J. FRENCH,
*Formerly Professor of Chemistry
and Dean of the Faculty,
Colgate University
Dean of the College, Rollins College*

Winter Park, Florida
August 2, 1955

Preface

I
N THE Prologue to his translation of the Bible into English, published in 1535, Myles Coverdale wrote these words: "Sure I am, that there commeth more knowledge and understandinge of the Scripture by their sondrie translacyons than by all the gloses of our sophisticall doctours." Thus the English divine set himself to the task to introduce the Bible to his world in the conviction that it was more important to proclaim the Truth than to defend the Truth.

No doubt the same spirit has animated the many studies and surveys of Christian Higher Education which have flooded the market in recent years. These studies affirm the role of liberal education in a democratic society in the hope that the American public might awaken to a deeper realization of the rich storehouse of "knowledge and understandinge" which is the claim made for a Christian Liberal Arts education. These books go beyond a mere delineation of what makes a particular type of education tick. They affirm a philosophy of education that is fundamental to the democratic process: an education which makes sense in a troubled and confused world. Christian Liberal Arts education does not need to be defended; it needs to be proclaimed.

The present study is thus one of many attempts of a small Christian Liberal Arts college to interpret its program to the immediate college community. It also may be of special interest to a wider circle of friends who still believe that this type of education is the open way to the fulfillment of the American dream—the development of a free being.

A number of studies of the aims and objectives of St. Olaf College have been inaugurated by the faculty in recent years. These statements of policy have brought to a focus many educational objectives and problems which needed further clarification and implementation. They have been of great value to the Self Study Committee 1954-55. The grant from the FUND FOR THE ADVANCEMENT OF EDUCATION, COMMITTEE ON COLLEGE SELF STUDIES, has enabled the committee to devote more time to the present study and has provided the means for securing competent advice from educational experts outside of the faculty circle.

"He who would succeed," said Aristotle, "must ask the right preliminary questions." This report purposes to ask questions relative to the success or failure of our students to acquire the kind of education which leads to the pursuit of truth and to propose basic changes in our current program which may be required to meet these needs more adequately. Perhaps the most significant contribution of the study is to bring to a focus the distinction between training and education, between the search for knowledge and the pursuit of truth, between acquiring specific skills and developing an appreciation of values which lie beyond the things that can be measured by the material yardstick.

All through my ministry as college president, which covers a quarter of a century, I have carried conflicting dreams on what to do to stimulate the faculty to productive scholarship. An outstanding southern educator, Henry Nelson Snyder, former president of Wofford College in South Carolina, defined productive scholarship as *"the biological capacity of repeating itself more richly in other minds."* The great teachers I have known had this capacity. They were conscientious scholars who looked upon the exercise of intelligence as a sacred trust. These great teachers inspired in me a faith that knew no fear of truth because it was grounded in the conviction that man is accountable to God for his thoughts and his actions. Being abreast of the thinking of their day, they refused to make a virtue of credulity. They clarified my thinking about the things that matter most by helping me to face my intellectual difficulties honestly and squarely. In humbleness of spirit they communicated confidence and hope by the dedication of their minds as sacred instruments to tne glory of God and the welfare of the student community. At the heart of their creative scholarship there was (to quote from a recent statement of the Department of History) *"sufficient room for imagination, intuition, the role of imponderables, the sudden flash of insight, and the creative commitment of the professing Christian."* Education under these great teachers was coherent and integrated because they saw life, and saw it whole.

On several occasions when I met with the Self Study Committee, the hope was expressed that the report and the proposals to be submitted would lead to a cooperative effort on the part of the faculty and administration for the improvement of teaching. We can all concur in this hope. For one of the most perplexing questions confronting a college president is "dying at the top." The process by which this insidious atrophy takes place is so subtle that the victim is scarcely aware of anything happening. Almost unnoticed he finds himself at odds with the academic community. Faculty meetings bore him, and his classes become dull and uninteresting. Good students avoid his courses. He wonders, "Why?" He is not too concerned about his reputation on the campus for "snap courses." It becomes noised about that he does not prepare his assignments, nor does he put much stock in examinations. Why should he? He professes to know his students' capabilities without the use of tests and measurements. Furthermore, according to his opinion, examinations at best are very ineffective tools for determining academic progress. The tragedy is that this familiar figure on the average college campus has all the potentialities of a good teacher. He earned his PH.D. under the best authorities in the field. He is congenial, affable, and in a way popular with the students. His main difficulty is that his spirit has been blunted by a false sense of arrival. He may continue to live and even render valuable service to the college community, but he has ceased to grow.

What shall be done about this all-important problem to preserve the sensitiveness of mind and spirit which alone make great teaching possible? Now there are some very specific reasons which justify the dismissal of a teacher from his post. He may be discharged for lying, stealing, drunkenness, immorality, or any other gross breach of conduct. But what of academic laziness? What of the teacher whose pride of opinion has closed the door to his curiosity, sympathy, initiative, and sensitivity to spiritual realities? What is immorality if it is not a failure to sense the obligation to be the best kind of teacher he is capable of becoming? What is immorality if it is not a refusal to live up to the high expectations of a productive scholar? The world is heavily in debt to the scholar who has met new possibilities of life with eager spirit and open mind.

Fragmentation, unrelatedness—and the more positive concepts— coherence, wholeness, and integration are some of the key words in the report. What can be done to gain greater coherence in the college program? This is perhaps the focal point of the report. Cicero defended the studies which had enriched his life. Said he: *"These studies nourish youth and delight old age . . . they travel with us."* Do they? What kind of studies travel with us? Are there some subjects which are more weighted in this respect than others? How can the students be made aware of those values which really remain behind when all the details are forgotten? Is there any way of planning more intelligently what the student should take with him after four years of academic life? Or, must his educational development be left to chance? How can the faculty and administration cooperate with one another in bringing about the right kind of educational experience? Obviously, there will be some disagreements as we grapple with these problems. For there may be honest doubts relative to the pattern which should be set up to bring about an integrated learning experience. However, there can be no division of opinion concerning the objective of the study: to create and stimulate the kind of atmosphere on the St. Olaf campus which will be conducive to the development of the student as a thinking being.

Sure it is, any academic progress in an institution is dependent on the initiative and the performance of both its faculty and administration. For neither the faculty nor the administration can answer the above questions alone. Administrative leadership is stymied when faculty enthusiasm lags. Progress then usually comes at the costly price of a crisis. It is equally serious when the administration holds back. For with administrative lag the faculty finds it necessary to hurdle barriers which are almost insurmountable. No doubt the proposals of the Self Study Committee will stimulate considerable discussion relative to what constitutes the core curriculum of a liberal arts education. Nevertheless, it is our hope that the faculty and administration may find common ground in coming to grips with the important issues at stake. The strategy of the report is that the task of working out the specifics for implementing the basic proposals of the committee is left with the faculty. The faculty is thus charged with the responsibility of facing the issues and doing something about them.

We are indebted to the St. Olaf Self Study Committee for the dedication and enthusiasm with which they accepted this assignment. Thanks is also due to the faculty who responded so generously to the requests for information. The value judgments submitted by the departments were particularly enlightening and helpful. These replies indicated the keen desire on the part of all concerned to appraise the work of the College objectively and constructively. Something is bound to happen on the college campus when faculty, students, and administration are animated by a positive concern for academic enrichment. The development of students who are intellectually alert, morally responsible, and spiritually dynamic is the central task to which we are all committed.

CLEMENS M. GRANSKOU
President

St. Olaf College
Northfield, Minnesota
October 12, 1955

Acknowledgments

ALTHOUGH the St. Olaf College Self Study Committee is responsible for the final form of this report, the major substance of the study consists of valuable contributions from many quarters. Members of the St. Olaf College Faculty and Administration, through discussions, questionnaires, and writing, participated significantly in the study. The experience and judgment of Senior students have also been of importance.

Indispensable criticism and educational wisdom were shared by consultants who spent long hours with the Committee and in many instances with Departmental Chairmen, Faculty Divisions, and the entire Faculty. We are deeply appreciative of the visits of Edward Dirks (Yale), Sidney French (Rollins), John Gaus (Harvard), Arnold Graeffe (University of Florida), Julian Hartt (Yale), Carroll Hinderlie (Youth Director of The Evangelical Lutheran Church), Robert Hutchins (Fund for the Republic), Alvin Rogness (Luther Seminary), and Joseph Sittler (Chicago Lutheran Seminary), and also to colleagues in numerous other institutions directly involved in self studies. Dean Sidney French and President Clemens M. Granskou have provided this volume with a Foreword and a Preface which in themselves make rewarding reading. Throughout the year great help has been given by the St. Olaf Library staff, by Print Shop personnel, by George Nordwall and co-workers at Augsburg Publishing House, and by faithful typists.

Few available publications deal directly and extensively with the specific problem of educational integration. Nevertheless a large number of books and articles were found to be prerequisites for our information, stimulation, correction, and orientation. Full footnotes in the text constitute specific acknowledgment of our great indebtedness to these sources and give complete bibliographical data.

The study as a whole was made possible by a generous grant from the Fund for the Advancement of Education.

PART ONE

Educational Fragmentation
and Integration
in Perspective

Chapter One

Contemporary Concern
Over Fragmentation
in Higher Education

SOMETHING which may fairly be characterized as revolution
has been taking place in the underlying philosophy of higher
education in the United States," says Henry P. Van Dusen in an
article called "Conversion in Education."[1] That a revolution in
the philosophy of higher education, together with a nationwide
revolution in practice, has been gaining momentum since the first
decade of this century is attested by the amount of penetrating
scrutiny to which the dominant educational philosophy, practice,
and results have been subjected, as well as by the extensive literature it has provoked. A felt need for scrutiny derives from what one
educator describes as "the eroding soil of education."[2] Expressed
in general terms the conclusion is this that "We have lost our
grip on education."[3]

The many ways in which professional educators and laymen alike
observe a shortsightedness in our thinking and practice in higher
education may be deduced from a number of critical phrases and
statements, such as: "aimless wanderings in the mere bypaths of
knowledge."[4] "Our university graduates have far more information

---

[1]*Christianity and Crisis,* April 26, 1946.
[2]L. Thomas Hopkins, *Integration Its Meaning and Application* (New York: D.
Appleton-Century Company, 1937), preface, p. vii.
[3]Sir Richard Livingstone, *The Future in Education* (New York: The Macmillan
Company, 1945), p. 126.
[4]Alexander Meiklejohn, *The Liberal College* (Boston: M. Jones, 1920), p. 49.

1

and far less understanding than in the colonial period."[5] "The history of American education illustrates among many other things that pre-occupation with the practical may in the long run, be dangerously impractical."[6] "We need to decide whether we want a nation of merely well fed, clothed and housed individuals. . . . And unless our schools re-establish courses in other than immediately practical fields . . . our long-range society will be impoverished in thought and feeling if not in merchandise."[7] Because of shortcomings in our education Professor Henry Margenau finds educators in the Western democracies noting a loss of cultural values and sensing a danger to the moral character of the coming generations.[8] "This [the enlightenment of human beings completely viewing their human situation] is no longer an academic matter. It is of crucial concern for our common life."[9] "The time would seem to be at hand for institutional self-examination in order that the quality of education may be elevated."[10]

The curricula of higher institutions of learning and their administration of graduation requirements have been especially subject to attack because of their centrality in determining the kind and the quality of the educational product. The curriculum is seen to be a great and growing aggregation of courses, a thing of "shreds and patches," of "this and that," of "academic islands." "Learning," says the Harvard Report, "is now diversified and parceled into a myriad of specialties. Correspondingly colleges and universities are divided into a large number of departments."[11] "That our universities have grave shortcomings for the intellectual life of this nation," says Felix Frankfurter, "is by now a commonplace. The chief

---

[5]Robert M. Hutchins, *Education for Freedom* (Baton Rouge: Louisiana State University Press, 1943), p. 25.

[6]Clarence H. Faust, "The Problem in General Education," *The Idea and Practice of General Education* (Chicago: University of Chicago Press, 1950), p. 3.

[7]James B. Carey, secretary-treasurer of the CIO, in an address at Antioch College, "The Antioch College Institute on Conditions for an Enduring Peace," quoted in Ralph Tyler, *Cooperation in General Education* (Washington, D. C.: American Council on Education, 1947), pp. 10-11.

[8]"Integrative Education in the Sciences," *Sixth Yearbook of The American Association of Colleges for Teacher Education—1953* (Oneonta, N. Y.: The American Association of Colleges for Teacher Education, 1953), p. 132.

[9]Howard Lowry, *The Mind's Adventure* (Philadelphia: The Westminster Press, 1950), p. 35.

[10]Melvin E. Haggerty, *The Evaluation of Higher Education* (Chicago: The University of Chicago Press, 1937), III, p. 8.

[11]*General Education in a Free Society* (Cambridge, Mass.: Harvard University Press, 1952), p. 56.

source of their inadequacy is probably the curse of departmental-ization. Among students, as well as among teachers, there has been a tendency to regard courses as something which exist in nature, instead of artificial simplifications for the mastery of what are complicated organisms, whether of nature or reason or Society."[12] "Why is it," asks Robert M. Hutchins, "that the chief characteristic of the higher learning is disorder? It is because there is no ordering principle in it . . . . it must be clear that if each person has the right to make and achieve his own choices the result is anarchy and the dissolution of the whole."[13] Protest is also raised at the failure to recognize any hierarchy of values. " . . . it means abandoning the usual attitude of regarding 'distribution' as a sphere in which the student exercises a virtually untrammeled freedom of choice . . . . there are truths which none can afford to ignore if one is to have that wisdom through which life can become useful."[14] It is further contended that no more fallacious tendency has plagued American higher education than the notion "implicit in the unit and credit hour system, that discrete units of knowledge, however well mastered, will automatically mold to produce the liberally educated graduate."[15] The committee which drafted the Harvard Report expresses the view that "a supreme need of American education is for a unifying purpose and idea."[16] Thus far, however, "Purpose has been defined only in the most general terms. There is a grop-ing after some unifying conception, but the goals suggested are usually vague and uninspiring."[17]

The recognition of fragmentation is widespread, and the most arresting conclusion to be drawn from the foregoing strictures, in-sofar as they describe the liberal arts college, is that the educa-tion it offers needs to be re-located within a context which is at once organic and supremely significant. The rectifying word is

[42]From a letter "Alfred North Whitehead" appearing in the New York *Times*, January 8, 1948, and reproduced as a special introduction to the Mentor edition of Alfred Whitehead's *The Aims of Education.*

[13]*The Higher Learning in America* (New Haven: Yale University Press, 1936), p. 94.

[14]*General Education in a Free Society,* p. 57.

[15]Oliver C. Carmichael, formerly president of the Carnegie Foundation for the Advancement of Teaching, in "Strengths and Weaknesses in American Higher Edu-cation," *Association of American Colleges Bulletin,* XXXIX, 2 (May, 1953), 241.

[16]P. 43.

[17]Carmichael, *loc. cit*

integration, seized upon because of its basic meaning of *relatedness within or with reference to a whole.* Having become a "big word" in American education, it has shared with other big words the tendency to lose its specific meaning.[18]

That a clear, stable, and optimum meaning of the term *integration* is not common may be concluded from a sampling of its narrower or very limited applications. It has, for example, been used to designate a device among a number of devices employed within a single course, as in the statement that "Integration of memory work with written reproduction can accomplish results hard to equal by any other method."[19] In principle it is observed, although narrowly, when a specific course is recommended as an aid in some vocational or professional pursuit: "they can relate their subjects to the trades, can show how botany will serve the grower of food, how physics guides the engineer, how economics helps the business man. . . . Yet this is not the learning that we seek, but only some fragments of it."[20] And it is a result hoped for in the so-called block or survey types of course which cut across departments and range over a wide area, bringing together something of this and that on a purely additive basis.

The concept of integration in higher education is so difficult of comprehension and the discovery and right application of an integrating principle so baffling that in actuality, say Paul L. Dressel and Lewis B. Mayhew, it has been little observed in learning experience in spite of the "verbal tributes" to it.[21] However, by deducing positive characteristics from a typical sampling of adverse descriptions of our curricula one can arrive at some characteristics of it. An undesirable opposite of integration, namely, *separatedness,* expressed in such criticisms as "discrete," "splintering," "undigested lumps of information," "this and that," "islands," "unconnected phenomena," "parceled into specialties," implies the positive characteristic of *connectedness,* of a *hanging together.* There is also, concomitant with *connectedness,* the equally

[18]E. C. Lindeman, "Integration," in Hopkins, *Integration Its Meaning and Application,* p. 29.
[19]Charles H. Cook, Jr., "Memorization Revisited," *College English,* XVI, 4 (January, 1955), 180.
[20]A. Meiklejohn, *The Liberal College,* p. 75.
[21]"A Basis for Integration in General Education," *The Educational Record,* XXXV, 3 (July, 1954), 221.

important characteristic of relatedness, deduced from such criticisms as "Student does not see relationships," "suspicion of relational thinking," "specialization cannot give insight into general relationships."

Positive demands currently made upon the curricula in higher education also enable one to deduce a further and most vital characteristic of *wholeness* and *design*. This may be concluded from phrases and statements like the following: "a synthesis," "a synoptic view," "unified whole," "seeing design," "unifying conception," "an organic whole whose parts join in expounding a ruling idea and in serving a common aim," "plan of correlating internally and adhering to the lines along which item was originally presented." In short, it will be necessary, as Raymond Wheeler says, that the educator, if he is to understand the problem of integration, first "inspect the logical pattern of his thinking. It is only by starting with insight into the nature of the problem as a whole that he can make any progress with the specific and special problems which confront him."[22]

However ambiguous in formulation and difficult in practice integration appears to be, however rare explicit studies of the problem are, the crucial character of this issue is repeatedly emphasized in twentieth-century discussion of higher education. The present volume is an attempt to correlate scattered thought and practice, to think through the issue itself, and to present positive practical ways of meeting the need.

In this study the approach to a clarification of this perplexing and important question of integration in higher education is threefold: Part One, educational integration in Western education, an historical over-view; Part Two, concepts of integration and the objectives of a Christian liberal arts college, a constructive, systematic formulation of the idea of integration and the idea of the college as a whole; and Part Three, exposition of some contemporary practices contributing to educational integration, together with specific curricular proposals practicable for a small Christian liberal arts college existing in mid-twentieth-century America and seeking to improve its central work as a teaching-learning community.

---

[22]"The Problem of Integration," in Hopkins, *Integration Its Meaning and Application*, p. 48.

5

Chapter Two

Integration
in Ancient
and Medieval Education

THE main integrating factor in early Greek education was undoubtedly the aim of producing "the good citizen." Education was treated as a branch of statecraft, and the city-states themselves were the highest educational institutions. They have frequently been referred to as university states; but as the various states had special problems to deal with and developed their own peculiar traditions, differing interpretations of the term "good citizen" naturally arose.

In Sparta, where a small caste of conquerors had to be continually on the alert against a suppressed population and foreign enemies, "the good citizen" became synonymous with "the good fighter." The so-called laws of Lycurgus read more like the rules for a primitive military academy than the constitution of a civilized state. They were designed to produce a class of ascetic warriors. Physical strength, endurance, courage, and implicit obedience were regarded as the supreme virtues. Athletics, gymnastics, and military drill constituted most of the young man's curriculum. Intellectual training was limited to some reading, writing, and finger-arithmetic. Anything beyond this was banned for the general citizen. Education became narrowly and severely vocational. As might be expected, the cultural life of Sparta stagnated and decayed. "Today, among the scanty ruins of that ancient capital, hardly a torso or fallen pillar survives to declare that there once lived Greeks."[1]

But it must be borne in mind that the Spartan educational system was not designed to produce the higher cultural values. From its own specific point of view it was probably one of the most successful educational systems ever devised. For several centuries it maintained the social supremacy of the Spartiates in Laconia and the military hegemony of Sparta in Greece. Furthermore, Sparta formed a center of strength around which the otherwise feuding Hellenes could rally to turn back the Persian onslaught. Thus Sparta helped preserve that culture which other Greek states produced.

In Athens, too, at least during the period of the "Old Education," the aim was to produce the ideal citizen, fit for war and peace. A youth was to be formed into an integrated personality by cultivating all aspects of his nature. In order that he might develop a sound mind and spirit in a sound body, the educational plan was based on gymnastics, music, and literature.[2] "In treating Athenian . . . education it is of the utmost importance to realize that the intellectual and moral part of it has music and poetry for its starting-point. This is the core round which everything else gathers; this is what determines its character, influence, and ideal."[3] A modern observer will undoubtedly be surprised to find that the highly intelligent Athenians apparently placed less emphasis on intellectual training than we do. "When we compare the ancient Greek education with our own . . . as a training of the whole man, we are surprised to find ourselves put on the defensive. We suffer from an *embarras de richesses* in the intellectual world; and we can hardly see the wood for the trees. We teach one thing after

---

[1]Will Durant, *The Life of Greece* (New York: Simon and Schuster, 1939), p. 87.

[2]It should be borne in mind that "music" did not mean the same to the Greeks as it does to the moderns. "Instead of being a distinct art, as with us, and taught by itself, music with the Greeks was always subsidiary to the expression of the spirit of literature, and in aim it was for moral-training ends." E. P. Cubberley, *The History of Education* (New York: Houghton Mifflin Company, 1920), p. 30. "Greek music . . . was never as purely sensory as ours. Tied to words, its significance was always apparent. As mere melodious sounds, it had no meaning, and, therefore, no interest for them. The Greek mind felt the need for a thought content: for to his consciousness, sense and thought, emotion and reaction, were more closely integrated than they are with any modern people." Frederick Eby and Charles Arrowood, *The History and Philosophy of Education Ancient and Medieval* (New York: Prentice Hall, 1940), p. 259.

[3]Thomas Davidson, *Aristotle and the Ancient Educational Ideals* (New York: Charles Scribner's Sons, 1910), p. 73.

7

another, or a number of things at the same time, rather as the most convenient way of making room for all that seems necessary to be learned, than with the aim of bringing before the growing mind as much and no more of the best experiences as it is able to appropriate with advantage to its growth. We think of education, on the whole, as an intellectual process, as a process of learning a number of things, each of which on separate grounds is necessary to be known. The Greek thought of it on the whole as a moral process; or rather he would not have understood you, if you had asked him which of the two he supposed it to be. He would have said that the best experience, if due time and opportunity is given for assimilating it, necessarily enters into the tissue of the mind, and determines its feelings and desires no less than its views and ideas."[4]

As life developed in complexity, however, following the Persian Wars when Athenian commercial and diplomatic interests spread throughout the Mediterranean world, intellectual training demanded a more important role than formerly. The "Old Education," which had satisfied rather well the needs of an isolated and simple community, was deemed inadequate to wrestle with the problems of a growing cosmopolitan state. Furthermore, the individual, who in the past had been subordinated under the state and the gods, now began to flex his muscles and declare that "man is the measure of all things." The state and very likely the gods themselves are manmade, created for the benefit and the convenience of humanity and therefore subject to change whenever the interests of humanity should so demand, thus the reasoning ran. "With the old civic ideal of devotion to the public good dying out, with the old religious and moral ideas being rejected on every side, and with the desire for fame, fortune, and personal gratification becoming dominant, new demands were made upon education. The goal of education for this new age was preparation for personal advancement. The aim of the young men of Athens now was individual excellence for individual success. The older objective of social service and public usefulness was changed to one of selfish and rugged individualism. The youth of Athens wanted a training that would

[4]Bernard Bosanquet, *The Education of the Young in the Republic of Plato* (Cambridge: Cambridge University Press, 1908), p. 11.

free them from the hampering restrictions of the old standards of life and develop within them the skills most useful for personal advancement and political preferment."[5]

The foremost teachers of this "New Education" were the Sophists, far-traveled, versatile men who came to Athens with a cosmopolitan and questioning attitude toward life. They did not form a well-defined school, but in general they held that all knowledge is acquired through the senses, that truth is relative, not absolute and universal. Gorgias stated that each individual has the privilege and the duty to decide what his relationship with the state, the gods, and his fellow-men should be. Most important of all, as far as the ambitious young men of Athens were concerned, the Sophists were instructors in oratory who could teach them how to rise to the top in a democratic society where so much depended on the ability to sway public opinion. A veritable craze for "adult education" seems to have swept the more well-to-do classes in the city. Distinguished Sophists opened schools where rhetoric can be said to have been a formal integrating element, but such a wide variety of supporting subjects was spread before the student that one is reminded somewhat of the "cafeteria style" offerings in many modern institutions. The Sophists were publicists rather than philosophers and emphasized variety rather than depth of learning.

Naturally the "New Education" raised a storm of protest from the conservatives, who ascribed all evils to the Sophists and others who forsook the old order of things. Most famous of these were Aristophanes, who lampooned the innovators in his comedies, and Xenophon, who wanted to save Athens by inducing her to imitate Sparta. But there were others who realized that the disintegrating forces in Athenian life could not be checked by a return to the past. A naturalistic outlook on life had undermined faith in the old gods and the restrictive statism of former generations. "The old ethical and social sanctions, divine and human, having, under the influence of individualism and rationalism, lost their power, where and how shall we find other sanctions to take their place? To answer this one question was the aim of Socrates' whole life."[6]

---

[5]E. H. Wilds, *The Foundations of Modern Education* (New York: Farrar and Rinehart, 1936), p. 98.
[6]Thomas Davidson, *Aristotle and the Ancient Educational Ideals*, p. 707.

In reply to the Sophistic contention that "there is no truth, and if there were, it could not be known," Socrates maintained that truth lies hidden in the depths of man's mind and that it was the object of education to educe, draw it out, from this recess. He had no curriculum to suggest, but he had a method, that of eternal self-examination: "the unexamined life is no life for man," he declared, and he adopted as his own the behest of the Delphic oracle, *Know Thyself*. If men learned to know themselves they would also fathom the universal concepts and truths such as *justice, goodness, patriotism,* and *piety,* since they lie hidden in every man's soul. "Virtue consists of knowing these concepts and making them operative in the lives of men—and the search for virtue is the highest aim of education," so he seemed to reason. Clearly, Socrates' whole life and theory of learning were integrated about this noble quest.

In the mind of Plato this search for virtue expanded into an all-embracing philosophy. Plato believed with the "Old Educationists" that education should be training for citizenship, and in *The Republic* he described a utopia in which education and statecraft become virtually synonymous. But the philosopher-statesmen, who are to rule in his ideal republic, after years of study and contemplation transcend the narrow confines of an earthly state and attain a vision of the divine in their contemplation of the supreme idea, the idea of the *Good* which comprehends and unifies all existence. Thus Plato arrives at a grand integration of all temporal and spiritual life. Those few who can rise through the studies of myths, poetry, music, gymnastics, sciences, dialectics, and higher philosophy to a vision of the divine will be given to understand that truth is one and indivisible. He quotes Socrates as saying that "the detailed sciences . . . must be brought into the compass of a single survey to show the connection between them and the nature of real existence";[7] or as he puts it in another passage: " . . . when all these studies reach the point of intercommunication and connection with one another, and come to be considered in their mutual affinities, then, I think, but not till then, will the pursuit of them have a value for our objects; otherwise there is no profit in them."[8]

---

[7]M. Cary and T. J. Haarhoff, *Life and Thought in the Greek and Roman World* (London: Methuen and Company, 1951), p. 292.
[8]Plato, *The Republic* (New York: Charles Scribner's Sons, 1928), pp. 298-299.

Aristotle, like Plato, held strongly that the state should educate its citizens in the ways of virtue. "And, since the state, as a whole, has but one aim, it is evident that the political education of all the citizens ought to be the same, and that this is a matter for the state to attend to, and not one to be left to individual caprice, as is now almost universally done, when every parent attends to the education of his own children and gives them whatever schooling suits his fancy."[9] In other words, the state should work out a well integrated curriculum and see to it that all prospective citizens followed it for the good of the whole society and consequently, according to Aristotle, for the good of the individual himself. Then he proceeds: "It remains to inquire what shall be the nature of the education, and the method of imparting it. . . . The present state of education leaves this question in a perfect muddle, no one seeming to know whether we ought to teach those subjects which enable people to make a living, or those which foster worth, or, finally, accomplishments. All have had their advocates. In regard to those studies which have worth for their aim, there is no general agreement, owing to the fact that different people have different views as to what kinds of worth are admirable, and consequently differ in regard to the means to be employed for the cultivation of them. One point, however, is perfectly clear, viz., that those useful things which are necessary ought to be taught. But it is equally clear that a distinction ought to be made between liberal and illiberal studies, and that only those useful subjects ought to be taught which do not turn those learning them into craftsmen. We ought to look upon every employment, art, or study which contributes to render the bodies, souls or intellects of free men unfit for the uses and practices of virtue, as a craft. For this reason it is that we call all those arts which lower the condition of the body crafts, and extend the term to the money-making trades, because they pre-occupy and degrade the intelligence. As to the liberal arts, to cultivate an acquaintance with them up to a certain point is not illiberal; but any over-devotion to them, with a view to attaining professional skill, is liable to the objections mentioned. It does also make a great difference for what purpose we do or learn

[9]Quoted by Thomas Davidson, *Aristotle and the Ancient Educational Ideals*, p. 179.

11

a thing. If a man does a thing for his own, for his friends', or for worth's sake, it is not illiberal, whereas if he does it often for the sake of anybody else, he will be held to be doing something mercenary or slavish."[10]

While Aristotle shared Plato's love of philosophy, he took a far keener interest in the natural sciences than his master had done. Like Plato he asserted the interrelatedness of all knowledge, but he refused to recognize the sharp dividing line between the world of sense and the world of reason which had played such a central part in the philosophy of Plato. "He exemplified better than any other the Greek capacity to 'see life steadily and see it whole.' In the words of Roger Bacon, 'he set in order all parts of philosophy.' "[11] He was a firm believer in the theory of *teleology*, that nature is purposeful in all its operations, that every structure and function are related to a final purpose.

In the centuries following Plato and Aristotle the disintegrating forces which they had attempted to check, rolled on with increasing force. The teachings of the two great philosophers had little direct influence on educational practices in the generations immediately following. Philosophy and the natural sciences tended to go their separate ways, the former becoming more and more mystical and divorced from existence until it culminated in Neoplatonism. In the natural sciences the Greek mind made discoveries during the Hellenistic period which were unsurpassed until the age of Copernicus, Kepler, and Newton. But somehow the discoveries seemed to remain isolated and no great systematizers appeared to carry on the work of Aristotle. Was there too much specialization and too little vision? The schools of rhetoric flourished long after the conquests of Alexander the Great. But as democracy and local patriotism gave way to autocracy and cosmopolitanism, rhetoric lost its cause for being. The vitality and passion which had characterized Greek oratory gave way to hollow bombast, which found its main joy in florid, pretentious language.

Unlike as Athens and Rome were in most respects, there is a marked parallelism between the histories of their educational ex-

---

[10]Quoted in *ibid.*, p. 190.
[11]M. Cary and T. J. Haarhoff, *Life and Thought in the Greek and Roman World*, p. 204.

12

periences. While Rome was a small agrarian-military state, she too had her "Old Education" which aimed at "the development of the *vir bonus*—the good citizen, the good soldier, the good worker. The *vir bonus* was the man possessed of all the virtues essential for the exercise of his rights and the discharge of his duties and obligations. The virtues chiefly prized and inculcated were piety, obedience, manliness, courage, bravery, industry, honesty, prudence, earnestness, sobriety, dignity, fortitude and gravity."[12] But as conquest and commerce brought her in touch with the entire Mediterranean area, her intellectual horizon widened and demands arose for a "New Education" which should better satisfy the requirements of a complex civilization.

In Rome emphasis was laid primarily on the utilitarian and practical phases of life. There was little reflection about the ultimate aims of education, and no great philosophers arose as in Athens to correlate it with all other human aspirations. This does not mean, however, that the Roman commentators were champions of a narrow vocational training. The contrary was usually the case. As an evidence of this can be mentioned Marcus Vitruvius Pollio who, about the beginning of the Christian era, wrote a famous work on architecture *(De Architectura)* in which he maintains that architects should be broadly and liberally educated. "To avoid scattering, studies should be interrelated, so that the body of one's knowledge can be one, just as a body with many members is one. . . . No other writer of antiquity has pointed out more clearly than has Vitruvius the continuity of things, action, and knowledge. He understands perfectly how closely allied are the practical arts, fine arts, and systematic knowledge; that manipulation and thought are interdependent—as are practical and scientific thinking. Greek theorists did not regard the training of the hand as worthy of being called real education; but Vitruvius, though he recognized the supremacy of reason in human action, recognized also that ideas grow from craftsmanship, so that thought and workmanship together have 'equipped with delights the refinements of life, increased as it were by their several crafts.' "[13]

[12]E. H. Wilds, *The Foundations of Modern Education*, p. 122.
[13]F. Eby and C. Arrowood, *History and Philosophy of Education, Ancient and Medieval* (New York: Prentice-Hall, 1940), p. 551.

In the Roman Republic as in democratic Athens, men became "inflamed with an incredible passion for eloquence," as Cicero put it. Numerous schools of rhetoric sprang up where young men could obtain training preparatory to entering the legal profession or public life. Like the schools of the Sophists in Athens, the Roman schools of rhetoric covered a wide variety of subjects since an aspiring politician should be prepared to discourse convincingly about practically any matter. Emphasis was, however, placed on law, history, and philosophy. All the writers on oratory, such as Cicero, Tacitus, and Quintillian also stressed that an orator must be a man of high moral principles. "We are to form then, the perfect orator, who cannot exist unless as a good man; and we require in him, therefore, not only consummate ability in speaking, but every excellence of mind. . . . For I cannot admit that the principles of moral and honorable conduct are, as some have thought, to be left to the philosophers; since the man who can duly sustain his character as a citizen, who is qualified for the management of public and private affairs, and who can govern communities by his counsels, settle them by means of laws, and improve them by means of judicial enactments can certainly be nothing else than an orator."[14]

While the Roman Republic endured, rhetorical training undoubtedly helped to elevate cultural life. But when absolutism replaced republicanism, rhetoric ceased to be a preparation for actual life, and as in Greece after Alexander the Great it soon degenerated into florid linguistic exercises. "This power of using words for mere pleasurable effect on the most trivial or the most extravagantly absurd themes, was for many ages, in both West and East, esteemed the highest proof of talent and education."[15] It was not only this type of education, however, which went into decay during the last centuries of the Roman Empire. Stagnation and corruption apparently seized all phases of life despite the efforts of moral philosophers and dictatorial law-givers. A general feeling of pessimism sapped the powers of the ancient world.

---

[14]From Quintillian's *Institutes of Oratory*. Selection found in E. P. Cubberley, *Readings in the History of Education* (New York: Houghton Mifflin Company, 1920), p. 38.

[15]Samuel Dill, *Roman Society in the Last Century of the Western Empire* (London: Macmillan and Company Limited, 1910), p. 425.

Into this despondent, decaying world Christianity entered, giving new meaning to life and new objectives to education. During the early centuries when the Christian view of life was struggling desperately for acceptance, many apologists were prone to deride "the wisdom of the wise" as the complete antithesis of their own interpretation of truth. "What is there in common between Athens and Jerusalem? What between the Academy and the Church? . . . away with all projects for a 'Stoic', a 'Platonic' or a 'Dialectic' Christianity," exclaimed Tertullian; or even more explicitly: "The Son of God was born, I am not ashamed of it because it is shameful; the Son of God died, it is credible for the very reason that it is silly; and, having been buried, He rose again, it is certain because it is impossible."[16] But such Greek Fathers as Clement of Alexandria and Origen championed Christianity as the end product of philosophy and reasoned that an intellectual comprehension of the mysteries of their religion could be gained only through liberal culture. Thus it came about that the early Christian educators took over from the Romans the Seven Liberal Arts (Trivium and Quadrivium) and made them the basis for all later medieval higher education. Through these seven liberal arts the medieval educators hoped to give their students a synthesis or an integration of the essential learning which had been salvaged from the classical world.

After the passing of the so-called "Dark Ages," Europe settled down to more peaceful conditions. By way of the Moors, Greek philosophy, especially Aristotle, was recovered and scholasticism assumed its herculean task of harmonizing classical learning with the Christian dogmas. It is probably safe to say that the human mind never tried more valiantly to integrate all knowledge than scholasticism did during its best period. The many *Summas* which were produced at that time, especially the two *Summas* of Thomas Aquinas, prove eloquently how seriously scholasticism took its task. The numerous universities which sprang up at that time and the thousands of students from all parts of Western Europe who crowded the lecture halls or disputed heatedly about all conceivable problems show what an intellectual ferment scholasticism had stirred up. Practically no attempt was made to enlarge the realm

---

[16]Quoted in J. V. Langmead Casserley, *The Christian in Philosophy* (London: Faber and Faber Limited, 1949), pp. 21-22.

15

of knowledge; the aim was to pass on a body of acquired learning regarded as embracing all that was possible of human attainment. Synthesis, order, integration was the goal rather than exploration and expansion. As long as this was a challenging task, scholasticism was a vital force. But scholasticism bore within itself the seeds of its own destruction. In order to achieve its grand integration of all knowledge it appealed to reason and to the learning of the ancients. The time came when these two forces would not tamely submit to being subordinated under the dogmas of the Church. With the coming of the "New Learning" and the revival of the scientific spirit, the great intellectual structure of scholasticism was threatened with disintegration. Humanists like Erasmus heaped scorn upon the schoolmen's "array of magistral definitions, conclusions, corollaries, and propositions" and charged that they were attempting "to discover in thick darkness what in reality has no existence whatever." This was, of course, a very biased attitude, but it is undoubtedly true that when scholasticism had achieved the unification of medieval knowledge and the systematization of theology its main role in intellectual history had been played.

As floods of new interests washed over Europe toward the end of the Middle Ages, the old educational system lost touch with the dominant intellectual currents of the day and the disputations in the universities tended to degenerate into hairsplitting dialectics as ancient rhetoric had degenerated into pomposity when the conditions which fostered it ceased to be.

Chapter Three

Integration
in Modern Education

I N EACH period of modern history a larger social goal or cultural ideal has determined both the aim of education and the
shaping tradition through which that aim was to be realized. The
medieval period aimed quite deliberately at synthesis in terms of
authoritatively given goals and methods, and in the twentieth century integration about a common center has once again become
a matter of concern and experimentation. But it is doubtful
whether integration and synthesis as such were counted as desirable goals during the intervening centuries. The trend was rather
one of dispersal, as men sought to occupy in piecemeal fashion the
whole planet and the entire range of facts. From the standpoint of
their peculiar and, in many respects, similar historical situations,
medieval man and many alarmed twentieth century men would
regard the social and educational history of the four intervening
centuries as a steady process of disintegration and fragmentation. They would argue that whatever coherence and relatedness
the modern period possessed should be attributed not to the
deliberate aims of school and society, but rather to the continuing
power of traditional values and institutions strong enough to
withstand the disruptive consequences of the movement toward
dispersal.

The modern world was born out of the struggle of the new
bourgeois society to establish itself over the remnants of a disintegrating feudal order. Through a series of great political,

economic, and cultural revolutions, the bourgeois way of life became the determining, though not the only influential, factor in Western civilization. Despite the notorious tendency of historical "periods" to slide into one another, it may not be entirely misleading to suggest that the struggle of the new society for survival falls into two phases.

1

UTOPIAN REASON IN THE EARLY MODERN PERIOD

The early modern period, extending from the Renaissance to the Industrial Revolution, saw the rise of the bourgeois society through the creation of the requisite intellectual, technical, political, social, and economic instruments for the conquest of the physical environment. The later modern period, extending from the Industrial Revolution to the First World War saw the triumph of bourgeois society through the creation of a world-wide mechanism of production and exchange.

In the first phase of the modern period, the over-arching social goal was conceived in "this-worldly" rather than "other-worldly" terms. The vertical dimension of life was recognized, but the Church's hold upon the masses of men had been loosened. It was the horizontal dimension of life which captured the imagination and enlisted the efforts of the new middle class, which was bent upon the reconstruction of society

This reconstruction was to be accomplished through the use of reason, rather than through following the prescriptions of religious authority and social tradition. Reason was understood during this revolutionary era not merely as the technique of drawing valid inferences, but as the power of apprehending that which was true and just. Man *as man* possessed an organ of truth. The development of reason as the quest for truth was identified with the development of humanity. If every individual surrendered himself to the search for knowledge, truth would be discovered and a "natural system" of thought and action would be established.

Reason was conceived in revolutionary or utopian terms. It was not interested in describing the contents of the world simply because the world was there to be described. Reason was interested

18

in examining the range of actual fact because such examination supplied materials for the reconstruction of society in conformity with what was considered to be "natural" and "reasonable." Utopian reason was concerned with ends beyond the existing order.

In his splendid essay, "The World Situation," Paul Tillich gives a most valuable clue to an inclusive and profound understanding of the unity within the variety of modern history. He holds that in the struggle out of which the modern West was born, one basic presupposition was always present. It was the belief that reason in each individual would be found to be in harmony with reason in every other individual. Thus, the liberation of reason in every person would lead to the realization of a perfect humanity and to a system of harmonious relations between individuals and society. Tillich calls this basic presupposition the "principle of automatic harmony." In an illuminating paragraph he describes the way in which this cultural principle found expression in every realm of life. (It should be noted that this description applies to the whole of modern history and proceeds in a topical rather than a chronological fashion.)

This principle of automatic harmony found expression in every realm of life. In the *economic* realm, it was believed that the welfare of all would be best served by the unrestrained pursuit by each individual of his own economic interest; the common good would be safeguarded by the "laws of the market" and their automatic functioning; this was the root-principle of the economy of *laissez faire*. In the *political* realm, it was supposed that the political judgment of each citizen would lead automatically to the right political decisions by a majority of citizens; community of interest would assure sound democratic procedures. In the *international* realm, the play of interest among the nations would result in a comparatively stable balance of power between the sovereign states. In the sphere of *education,* the essential rationality of human nature would produce, through free self-expression by each individual, a harmonious community. In *religion,* personal interpretation of the Bible and individual religious experience would follow a sufficiently uniform course among all believers to assure moral and spiritual conformity and to create and maintain a religious community of individual worshippers, the Church. Finally, this all-controlling idea found *philosophic* expression in various doctrines of preestablished harmony, those of Leibnitz, Descartes, and their schools. The individual monad is a microcosm of the world. Ripening according to its own inner laws of logic, it develops in preestablished harmony with the whole of being.[1]

---

[1]"The World Situation," in H. P. Van Dusen, *The Christian Answer* (New York: Charles Scribner's Sons, 1945), p. 3.

19

Belief in reason and in "the principle of automatic harmony" was the creed of the new society and of virtually all its intellectual and political leaders. And experience seemed to confirm it. The liberation of individual reason in economics and religion, in politics and education, did not bring on the disruptive consequences forecast by traditionalists and reactionaries. On the contrary, tremendous creativity was set free without the destruction of sufficient conformity to maintain national and religious communities.[2] In the power of this belief the new society overcame all reactionary opposition and by the nineteenth century had achieved the victory it sought.

The aim of education was perfectly consistent with the social goal, the guiding principle, and the basic presupposition of the new bourgeois society. Reason as the principle of truth demands education for and through reason for everyone, and the massive achievements in educational theory and practice in Western civilization are due largely to this creative impulse. Education during the early modern period aimed to actualize humanity in every individual, assuming that if the individual were to be placed in the presence of excellent things or were to follow his natural interests, he could be depended upon to discover truth and to use it constructively.

Classical humanism furnished the shaping tradition. In the schools which followed the older traditions, it was combined with an intensive religious instruction, which gave to life and learning a theological perspective, either Roman Catholic, Lutheran, Calvinistic, or Anabaptist. In the schools which struck out on the newer paths, classical humanism existed in combination with mathematics, modern languages, and the earlier forms of our present natural and social sciences. Classical humanism was the common factor in most educational schemes. Generally religion was recognized as one element in the development of the humanistic personality, but not its ground or center.

Deliberate attention to the problem of integration and fragmentation could scarcely be expected of an age in which belief in autonomous reason and "the principle of automatic harmony" had

---

[2]*Ibid.*, p. 4.

declared and justified itself to the mind of man. Integration or coherence could be left to take care of itself. No ecclesiastically, politically, or philosophically authorized curriculum or perspective was explicitly and universally used. No fears of fragmentation were generally expressed, but narrowness and traditionalism were widely denounced. Yet, because of the widespread belief in the law of harmony, the character of the age did possess a certain coherence. Mathematics furnished a pattern of method and all realms of being and meaning were to be included in the construction of the "natural system of thought and life." This "principle of automatic harmony," which supplanted the explicit and bestowed theological pattern of integration followed in former centuries, was accepted as a working hypothesis or unexamined assumption, and it did succeed in lending a measure of uniformity and direction to the intellectual and social efforts of the new society. Yet its success as an agent of coherence was due to the presence within it of three traditional and unannounced ingredients: belief in the unity of truth, in the contingency of nature, and in the rationality of man.

Belief in the unity of truth, expressed in terms of an alliance between faith and reason, was the characteristic note of scholasticism in its prime. The assumption of St. Thomas Aquinas was that religion is rational and reason is religious since both spring from the same source—the Creator God, who alone is perfectly rational. Faith and reason, theology and divine revelation, are organically continuous with each other. Between a natural theology soundly reasoned and a divine revelation properly apprehended there can be no opposition. Reason leads up to revelation, and at that point yields to a faith which is above, but not contrary to reason. The contemplation of the universe can convince us of the existence of God, and reason confirms the probability and the authenticity of what is offered to it from above as revelation. The whole creation moves around God as its center.

Despite the dichotomy between faith and reason introduced in the late Middle Ages by the notion of "Two Orders of Truth" (according to which faith is founded upon the arbitrary will of God and can not therefore be proved or validated by reason) and in the Reformation period by the divorce between religion and

21

philosophy, the conception of God as perfect intelligence endured in the form of the rooted modern belief in the presence of intelligible order and system throughout nature. The fundamental thought of modern natural science, at any rate until recently, has been that there is a "universal reign of law" throughout nature. Nature is rational in the sense that it has everywhere a coherent pattern which we can progressively detect by the steady application of our own intelligence to the scrutiny of natural processes. The reason why Galileo, Newton, and the other founders of modern natural science so confidently assumed the thorough-going coherency of the pattern of natural events lay in their acceptance of the "dogma" that nature has its origin in a God who is Himself perfect intelligence and must therefore reflect the character of its source. Whitehead affirms that the confidence of European science in the intelligibility of the world derives from the medieval insistence upon the rationality of God.

Similarly, belief in the contingency of nature is an explicit product of medieval theologizing, and it survives today in the form of convictions which provide the basic preconditions of the scientific method, namely, that nature is a fit object for scientific interpretation and man is the proper agent of scientific inquiry. The medieval Christian thinkers held that God is able to create whatever kind of world He chooses. Thus creation is a free act of the divine will and physical existence in its very nature is finite and contingent. "It does not have to be as it is, for we can easily imagine that it could be otherwise. It does not even have to be at all, for we can quite easily imagine its non-existence. It simply happens to be. It has always an accidental character. This is what philosophers mean when they say that nature is contingent."[3] Any reality is a contingent reality which might conceivably, that is, without logical self-contradiction, have been otherwise or not have been at all.

The doctrine that nature is contingent means that nature is not self-explanatory. There is no possible way of establishing by rational thought what nature must or ought to be like, for it does not possess within itself the ground and reason for its own existence. If nature is not self-explanatory, it follows that nature can only

[3] J. V. L. Casserley, *Graceful Reason* (Greenwich, Connecticut: Seabury Press, 1954), p. 63.

be known empirically. Since nature might have been other than it is, had God so chosen, the only way of finding out what kind of world He has in fact chosen to create is to examine it with all possible care. A contingent natural order can only be known by careful empirical observation and experiment.[4] Although the medieval theologians did not try to build any new kind of scientific structure upon this doctrine, the doctrine itself is the indispensable metaphysical foundation of modern science.

The third ingredient, belief in the rationality of man, has been discussed in preceding pages. It is only necessary here to point out that Western civilization has always rested upon a humanism: a classical humanism which saw man intellectually as the "rational animal," or a Christian humanism which interpreted him spiritually as the "child of God," or since the close of the Middle Ages, a more confused humanism which has oscillated between the two. "That man may validly be distinguished from nature is a presupposition which lies almost as deeply around the roots of the development of modern science as our traditional belief that God must be absolutely distinguished from nature. The possibility of science presupposes not only that nature is a distinct order of reality about which it is possible to be objectively scientific, but also that man is a kind of being who is capable of being objectively scientific about nature."[5]

These basic preconditions of the scientific method were impressed upon and have since been kept alive in the Western mind by the theological beliefs that God Who is Perfect Intelligence created nature by an act of His own will and made man in His own image. The vestigial hold of these unifying perspectives supplied "the principle of automatic harmony" with its integrative capacity.

2

TECHNICAL REASON IN THE LATER MODERN PERIOD

In the second phase of modern history, the new bourgeois society came to triumphant power mainly through the creation of a world mechanism of production and exchange. The Industrial

[4]J. V. L. Casserley, *Morals and Man in the Social Sciences* (London: Longmans, Green and Company, 1951), p. 65.
[5]*Ibid.*, pp. 140-141.

Revolution began in Western Europe in the middle of the eighteenth century and was fully established by the middle of the nineteenth century. Together with the triumph of political democracy, this great movement brought about a profound transformation in social conditions and in education.

The over-all social goal was the perfection of a technical society which had been created by the victorious bourgeoisie. The guiding principle of the development was still belief in reason. But a most significant change took place in the character of reason. As the new middle class society gained success in its struggle for survival, its revolutionary impetus disappeared, and reason was no longer regarded as the principle of truth and justice, but rather as a tool in the service of the gigantic industrial civilization.

Paul Tillich draws an illuminating series of contrasts between the "utopian reason" of the first period, and the "technical reason" of the second period of modern society. He writes:

> Revolutionary reason had been concerned with ends beyond the existing order. Technical reason became concerned with means to stabilize the existing order. Revolutionary reason had been conservative with respect to means but utopian with respect to ends. Technical reason is conservative with respect to ends and utopian with respect to means. In fact, technical reason provides means for ends, but offers no guidance in the determination of ends. It can be used for any purposes dictated by the will, including those which deny reason in the sense of truth and justice.[6]

Through the use of the tools placed in his hands by technical reason, man became increasingly able to control physical nature and to create a world-wide mechanism of production and competitive economy. The possibly disastrous consequences of the transformation of reason into a technical instrument, dominated by instinct and will, and unrelated to ultimate ends or realities, went unnoticed as men continued to rely on "the principle of automatic harmony." This "law of harmony" with its implicit cohesive ingredients served as a retarding factor within the fissiparous tendencies of the age. As such, it furnished the only sort of integration desired by the leaders of what came to be the dominant pattern of education. Classical and theological patterns of integration were still utilized by some of the private and church-sponsored colleges.

---

[6]Tillich, "The World Situation," p. 4.

24

In subservience to the demands of technical reason, so-called "realistic" education based on the natural and technical sciences step by step supplanted education through the humanities. As education became subjected to the basic pattern and drive of industrial society, occupational education for particular purposes increasingly replaced humanistic education for a perfect humanity. The natural sciences, which became markedly positivistic, tended to provide the shaping tradition for all knowledge and education.

Within this general perspective, we can see the detailed educational history of the nineteenth century as the development of democratic education, founded upon positivistic natural sciences and purely anthropological social sciences, and integrated in terms of the dominant nationalistic political and economic ideals. This pattern included accompanying voices of protest, which, in the name of older ideals of intellectual and religious integration, criticized the prevailing trend as a movement toward fateful disintegration.

At the beginning of the nineteenth century, the universities of Germany were unique among European schools with respect to the aims and organization of education. German scholars proudly ascribed their superiority in research and production of a steady stream of brilliant investigators to two conditions: freedom of investigation *(Lernfreiheit)*, and freedom of teaching *(Lehrfreiheit)*. German professors were accorded opportunity for free and unbiased research such as scholars of no other country enjoyed. They were far less responsive to tradition than others. Not only were they free to search for truth and to impart it without hindrance, but they evolved a form of university organization which actually necessitated scholarly industry and progressive thinking, within the scientific framework of thought.

Oxford and Cambridge, on the other hand, were slow to sponsor research, and Parliament, at the request of the bishops, refused to endow research activities. As a consequence, many of the greatest scholars in England have done their work outside the universities. Cardinal Newman thought this was quite proper and said: "The object of the university is the diffusion and extension of knowledge rather than the advancement. If its objects were scientific and philosophic discovery, I do not see why a university should have students." But Thomas H. Huxley took the opposite view. After an extended visit to German universities, he wrote:

> The German universities, from being beneath notice a century ago, have now become the most intensely cultivated and the most productive intellectual corporations the world has ever seen. The student who repairs to them sees in the list of classes and of professors a fair picture of the world of knowledge. Whatever he needs to know there is someone ready to teach him; whatever his special bent, let him but be able and diligent, and in due time he shall find distinction and a career. . . . They are not "boarding schools for youth," nor clerical seminaries; but institutions for the higher culture of men, in which the theological faculty is of no more importance or prominence than the rest; and which are truly "universities" since they strive to represent and embody the totality of human knowledge, and to find room for all forms of intellectual activity.[7]

The universities of both England and Germany grew out of the original university organization of the Middle Ages, with the four faculties—arts, theology, law, and medicine. However, the English preferred to pursue the study of law and medicine by the apprenticeship system, and these professional studies dwindled into insignificance so far as the universities were concerned. Oxford and Cambridge became aggregations of colleges rather than learned professional schools; they exalted "liberal" culture and the B.A. degree. The German institutions, on the other hand, exalted the professional faculties and emphasized the doctorate degrees in medicine, law, philosophy, and theology. The divergence of the two types was further increased by their experiences during the Reformation. The German universities suffered much more acutely than the English, and in the subsequent reconstruction they departed more radically in curricula and methods from the medieval type.

Partly because of the influence of the provincial universities, which were deeply interested in the modern natural sciences, and partly because of influences from Germany, Oxford and Cambridge were examined in 1850 by royal commissions, and a certain amount of reform was accomplished in administration, curricula, and teaching methods. They rapidly became efficient in the scien-

---

[7]F. Eby and C. Arrowood, *The Development of Modern Education* (New York: Prentice-Hall, 1934), pp. 730-731.

tific and specialized studies. In commenting on this development, Dampier writes:

During the second half of the 19th century, the intellectual isolation of the nations of Europe, which had lasted through the first half, was again broken down. Facilities of transport increased personal intercourse, scientific periodicals and the proceedings of learned societies brought new results to the cognizance of all those interested, and science became once more international, as it had been prior to the 17th century. On the other hand, the different departments of knowledge became more specialized, and, as national barriers were overthrown, departmental isolation increased. . . . The experimental method provided for the more thorough study of each subject but left less time for general surveys, and men of science tended not to see their wood for its trees. . . . Save for a few broad generalizations, the fissiparous tendencies lasted till the end of the 19th century.[8]

Despite the growing conformity of the English universities to the German model, there were strong voices of protest making themselves heard. Newman, Jowett, Whewell, and Mill supported the traditional aims of the older universities and looked with alarm upon the tendency described above by Dampier. Whewell wrote that the

. . . chief duty of the university is to produce good citizens. It should train an elite who are to be the future leaders in affairs and in the learned professions. Thus it differs from a seminary, a technical college, or a research institute. For neither training in the technique of particular callings, whether ecclesiastical or secular, nor the advancement of knowledge is its primary function, though it may contribute to each. The training it gives is an initiation of select young people into their cultural inheritance. In Matthew Arnold's words it seeks to familiarize them with "the best that has been thought and said in the world" and so to bind together the generations through their sharing in a common intellectual estate.[9]

The supporters of the traditional ideals argued that education should aim at mental development for its own sake and not for any ulterior end. Exposing young men to the acknowledged masterpieces of human thought and knowledge would evoke a culture valuable for what it is rather than for what it does. Yet those who had cultivated the essentially human endowments would also be the most effective in terms of practical judgment. Newman wrote:

[8]W. C. Dampier, *A History of Science* (New York: The Macmillan Company, 1943), p. 312.
[9]*On the Principles of English University Education,* quoted in Walter Moberly, *The Crisis in the University* (London: SCM Press Limited, 1951), p. 31.

"'A cultivated intellect, because it is good in itself, brings with it a power and a grace to every work and occupation which it undertakes.'"[10]

According to Newman, the generations can be bound together in a common intellectual estate only if education is general rather than specialized. The student needs to gain a synoptic view which will enable him to see any particular subject in its relation to the whole scheme of knowledge and experience. This sense of coherence or proportion does not necessarily arise through the study of an extremely wide curriculum. Provincialism rather than catholicity flows from a smattering in many fields of study. True enlargement is gained through the proper teaching and study of the classics and mathematics. This sort of study enables the student to apprehend "'the great outlines of knowledge, the principles on which it rests, the scale of its parts.'"[11] This is, Newman continues,

. . . the education which gives a man a clear, conscious view of his own opinions and judgments, a truth in developing them, and a force in urging them. It teaches him to see things as they are, to go right to the point, to disentangle a skein of thought, to detect what is sophistical, and to discard what is irrelevant. It prepares him to fill any post with credit and to master any subject with facility. It shows him how to accommodate himself to others, how to throw himself into their state of mind, how to bring before them his own, how to come to an understanding with them, how to bear with them.[12]

Between 1825 and 1875, a heated struggle raged on the American scene in regard to the ideal for higher education in this country. A number of causes were slowly at work transforming the character and purposes of the colleges. Among the chief of these were: the increased number of students preparing for secular occupations; the demand for instruction in modern languages, natural and applied sciences, and social sciences; the development of professional training; and, above all, the introduction of the German ideals of scholarship or research. German ideals influenced our schools most profoundly through a number of brilliant college and university presidents. With but a few exceptions, all the men who determined educational policy during the nineteenth century

[10]*Ibid.*, pp. 31-32.
[11]*Ibid.*, p. 32.
[12]*Ibid.*, pp. 35-36.

had received the impetus for their reforms from contact with German universities.

Of these, the earliest and most enthusiastic admirer of the German system was Henry Tappan, president of the University of Michigan from 1852 to 1863. Rivaling his efforts were those of Charles Eliot, president of Harvard from 1869 to 1909. The central issue of the struggle in which these men and others were engaged was whether the university ideal or the ideal of the traditional college should dominate. The institutions which blazed the new trail were Harvard in the East and Michigan in the Middle West. Upon entering office, Tappan added a "scientific course," equal in standard and parallel to the classical course but leading to the degree of Bachelor of Science. Up to this time, courses in the natural sciences had not been included in the college of arts curriculum. Courses of lectures for graduate students were offered. The lecture system gradually superseded the textbook and recitation method of instruction. By these measures, specialization was made possible. History, English, literature, political science, and natural sciences enriched the curriculum. Professional schools of law, medicine, and engineering were organized, coordinate with the college. President Tappan admitted that he had produced a school which was in part a university and had university ways; however, the vast majority of the students remained of secondary school grade and needed secondary methods of instruction and discipline.[13]

The controversy over the organization of higher education flamed to its climax at the time of the inauguration of Eliot as president of Harvard. This date indicates the final dominance of German ideals. Ecclesiastical control was revoked. The fair proportion of students preparing for the ministry practically disappeared. The elective system was adopted and the curriculum was broadened.

The leaders of the university party looked upon the existing American college as little better than a high-grade secondary school. They saw in the scholarly activity of the German universities the ideal of higher learning, and they expected to infuse this

---

[13]F. Eby and C. Arrowood, *The Development of Modern Education*, p. 741.

new spirit into the old collegiate organism. They believed that a complete change of aims and methods, as well as the raising of standards of work, was imperative. The supposedly easy-going pursuit of prescribed courses must give way to the enthusiastic pursuit of knowledge determined by the student's interests.

The college party looked upon these new ideals and innovations in practice as a radical departure from the methods of training which the light of experience had shown to be best. A thoroughgoing preliminary training, such as the American college offered, was deemed absolutely essential before students could profit by the freedom and specialization of the German university system. The college leaders were not opposed to research and specialization as such, but they held that it was not appropriate for the American scene at that time, since our students were not prepared for such training and needed somewhere along the way the strict regimen of unified intellectual discipline.

One of those who emphatically defended the traditional curriculum was Dr. Noah Porter of Yale. Immediately after Eliot's inaugural address in 1869, Porter proceeded to attack every innovation that had been adopted during the first half of the century. He supported the fixed curriculum rather than the policy of free electives, the study of Latin, Greek, and mathematics, rather than modern languages, English, natural and social sciences. Yale had long played a prominent role in stressing discipline as the basis of higher education. A report of a committee in 1827 affirmed that the college curriculum was a definite thing, and the required subjects were able to furnish the best discipline of minds. This report denied that Yale was not progressive and insisted that the institution had properly found "what was and what was to be the best college course possible for American youth. Any change from the existing order was to be resisted as one resisted a dire calamity to students, college, and commonwealth. For the safety of all, the present excellent, adequate and comprehensive system of collegiate education must and should be preserved."[14] The influence of these ideas on other colleges appears to have been strong; for graduates of Yale were then moving into the Western and South-

---

[14]*Ibid.*, p. 293.

ern states as educational workers and were carrying with them the idea of discipline and the thoroughness of the Yale program.

Although the elective system began at the University of Virginia in 1825, it did not make general headway until Harvard and Michigan took the lead in its adoption. At Harvard in 1825, the course of study was the same for all students. By 1886, the only required course in the arts faculty was freshman English composition. In 1855, the elective system was granted to the seniors at Michigan, and by 1880 the fixed curriculum had been abandoned entirely.

Yale, Harvard, and Michigan launched graduate studies after the middle of the century. The real credit for launching this type of study must, however, go to Johns Hopkins University, which under Gilman in 1876 became the first real university in this country. At the other schools the graduate departments were closely related to powerful undergraduate colleges with settled traditions. But Johns Hopkins was a new type of institution, with no college to dominate it.

It is plain that new schools and some of the old ones were being organized on the German model and were operating on the basis of the principles of public service, occupational training, research, and an enormously expanded curriculum. Yet there was general agreement among the educational leaders of the time that the colleges failed to become universities in the German sense of the term. Dr. Tappan of Michigan admitted that there was a tendency to attempt to add the higher work rather than to improve the quality of the work they were capable of doing. In taking on university functions and methods before it was able to do so efficiently, the college laid itself open to the charge that it had become a hybrid institution, part college and part a weak imitation of a university.[15]

At the inauguration of Eliot in 1869, James Bryce is said to have told him that Harvard was "no real university, but only a struggling college, with uncertain relations to learning and research, loosely tied to a congeries of professional schools."[16] And in 1888, Bryce wrote in his *American Commonwealth*:

[15]F. Eby and C. Arrowood, *The Development of Modern Education*, p. 745.
[16]*Ibid.*, p. 747.

If we define a university as a place where teaching of a high order, teaching which puts a man abreast of the fullest and most exact knowledge of the time, is given in a range of subjects covering all the great departments of intellectual life, not more than twelve and possibly only eight or nine of the American institutions fall within the definition. . . . Most of the Western State universities . . . have an ambitious program, but neither the state of preparation of their students nor the strength of the teaching staff enables them to do justice to the promise which the program holds out. They are true universities rather in aspiration than in fact.[17]

When Eliot was furiously reorganizing Harvard, Henry Cabot Lodge remarked that under the old plan "a certain amount of knowledge, no more useless than any other, and a still larger amount of discipline in learning were forced on all alike. Under the new system it was possible to escape without learning anything at all by a judicious selection of unrelated subjects."[18]

During the next few decades the criticism of the widened elective curriculum increased. A writer in the *Atlantic Monthly* in 1883 deplored the multiplicity of college studies and the elective system and proposed in place of the chaotic curriculum of the time the principle of general courses in the social and biological sciences not unlike the orientation courses that have been developed in recent years.[19] A writer in the *Atlantic Monthly* for August of 1885 insisted that among the fallacies then present in the educational thought of the country were the elective system, preoccupation with practical considerations, and the insistence upon education for the "struggle of life."[20]

Education conducted in June of 1900 a symposium on "The Problems which Confront Our Colleges at the Opening of the Twentieth Century," in which a number of distinguished university presidents participated. Among the pressing problems listed were the elective system, personal freedom of students, the controversy over the classics, the interest of students in merely securing degrees, the tendency toward specialization, the lack of interest of students in politics and government, the failure of the colleges to imbue students with public spirit, the need for the integration of the cultural and the disciplinary values in the college curricu-

---

[17]E. W. Knight, *Twenty Centuries of Education* (Boston and New York: Ginn, 1940), p. 139.
[18]*Ibid.*, p. 287.
[19]*Ibid.*, p. 298.
[20]*Ibid.*, p. 299.

lum, the loss of simplicity in college education, the growing complexity of administration, the predominance of athletics, the apparent failure of the college to integrate their programs with actual life, and the danger that the colleges would unwittingly blunder into or be led to by placing emphasis upon crass materialism.[21]

By the turn of the century the subject of higher education had a more prominent place in magazines and newspapers than it had ever before held in such publications, and between 1900 and the close of the World War of 1914-1918 there was a wider discussion of higher education in the United States than this country had ever witnessed. While the increased number of students attending colleges and universities was regarded as a good sign in 1900, a slight uneasiness was felt here and there about either the "other-worldliness" of the traditional schools or the disintegration of the newer schools. An editorial in a prominent magazine in June, 1900, praised the general trend of education but criticized some of its practices, such as the elective system, the growing demand for Ph.D.'s in the colleges, and the lack of contact between teacher and student.[22] Scribner's deplored the tendency toward "Teutonizing in Education," whereas a writer in Education urged the colleges to train their students for business, to foster business, and to give specialized courses leading to all kinds of business.[23]

An editorial in Scribner's warned against our acquiring the faults of the German system through the tendency to let learning swamp common sense, tact, the sense of proportion, and the sense of humor. The Forum deplored the standards of the market place and countinghouse in education. Woodrow Wilson, in his inaugural as president of Princeton, declared that the colleges should deal with the spirits and not the fortunes of men. The Nation editorialized on "Education as a Public Peril," and warned against the relaxation of discipline. Professor George Trumbull Ladd, in "Disintegration and Reconstruction of the Curriculum" in the Forum, urged that the curriculum be made over, that certain courses be required, and that the liberal arts course be reduced to three years.

[21]Ibid., p. 300.
[22]Ibid., p. 301.
[23]Ibid.

33

He frowned upon the excessive and injudicious use of the elective system.[24]

During the early years of the present century protests were being made widely against emphasis upon the business preparation of college students, against the increasing departmentalism, and also against those professors who knew little outside their own specialties. Preserved Smith, writing in the *Educational Review* in 1913, charged that lack of co-ordination in instruction in the colleges and the disconnected way in which fragmentary information was imparted accounted for the unreality, unpracticality, and lack of inspiration in higher education. The professors should correlate their work instead of side-stepping for fear of treading upon one another's subjects. The *Nation* compared the university to a department store, saying that it was ceasing to be the home of idealism and perhaps of ideas, and bemoaned the tendency toward early specialization in college, which was due to the influence of the business world.

In describing the way in which Harvard, the original classical Puritan college, had evolved into a multiplicity of cultural and professional institutions, more or less loosely related, but under the management of the university corporation, Eby and Arrowood comment bitterly on the victory of fragmentation over coherence:

> Practically all our larger American universities have developed this same character, though the number of professional schools varies greatly in each institution. Around the college of arts and sciences have usually been grouped between fifteen and twenty-five professional schools. New degrees have been originated to satisfy the demand for recognition of distinctive curricula. Some of these adjunctive schools admit students from the high schools, on the same basis as does the college of arts and sciences. Some require one year of college work; some two years; some three years; and a few now require a complete college course. The resultant institution, the outgrowth of all these innovations, exhibits a patchwork representing mainly the compromises of divergent interests and not the unity of master minds. . . . The college of arts and sciences remains as a poor correlation of the secondary school and the university. It still clings to the tradition of general culture; but its methods, curriculum, and spirit are controlled by the interests of the professional schools about it and the graduate school above it.[25]

Since the World War of 1914-1918 hundreds of books and thou-

---

[24]*Ibid.*
[25]*The Development of Modern Education*, p. 747.

sands of magazine and newspaper articles have dealt with the college curriculum. Higher education has become a subject for serious concern and the role of the curriculum has been seen as a central part of that concern. The last three decades have seen a strong swing away from freedom of election to a measure of prescription by the faculty, a change that seems to have come about as a result of several influences. Before the First World War, chaos was threatening to reign under the rampant elective system, many of whose romantic promises were unfulfilled. Meantime there was a growing belief among many educators that the college students of this country needed acquaintance with "a common intellectual world." This belief concerning the collegiate curriculum took the form of experiments with required or elective orientation, of general or synoptic courses in the natural and social sciences, and of the establishment of group requirements, major and minor sequences, and fields of concentration.

In his inaugural in 1909 President Lowell of Harvard said:

American college students ought . . . to study a little of everything; for if not, there is no certainty that they will be broadly cultivated, especially in view of the omnipresent impulse in the community driving them to devote their chief attention to the subjects bearing upon their future career. The wise policy for them would appear to be that of devoting a considerable portion of their time to some one subject, and taking in addition a number of general courses in wholly unrelated fields. But instruction that implies a little knowledge of everything is more difficult to provide well than any other. To furnish it there ought to be in every considerable field a general course designed to give men who do not intend to pursue the subject further a comprehension of its underlying principles or methods of thought.[26]

Three years later President Meiklejohn said in his inaugural at Amherst:

Now I do not object to a man's minding his own intellectual business if he chooses to do so, but when a man minds his own business because he does not know any other business, because he has no knowledge whatever of the relationships which justify his business and make it worthwhile, then I think one may say that though such a man minds his own affairs, he does not know them, he does not understand them. . . . He is making no intellectual attempt to understand his experience in its unity.[27]

---

[26]E. W. Knight, *Twenty Centuries of Education*, p. 310.
[27]*Ibid.*

35

Just after the World War, whose aftermath stimulated colleges to provide orientation or general courses, Columbia, Indiana, Williams, and several other institutions began to pay serious attention to the problem of general as opposed to specialized undergraduate instruction. By 1922 forty-one colleges were making provision of this kind for their students, as compared with only eleven institutions before the World War; and by 1926 seventy-nine institutions were offering orientation or general courses for standard college credit. Such courses are numerous now and are annually introduced throughout the country by institutions that see the need for basic courses which promise to bring some order out of the chaos which followed the unchecked elective system.

In retrospect, it seems quite clear that the concern over remedying educational fragmentation was but one aspect of the general uneasiness which twentieth century society felt when it faced up to the fact that reason had lost control over man's historical existence. This situation became manifest in two world wars and their psychological and sociological consequences. It was seen that the foundation of bourgeois society had broken down: namely, the conviction of automatic harmony between individual interest and general interest. In the name of this basic presupposition individuals and communities had been set free from organic ties for the sake of almost unlimited lateral expansion in every area of cultural life.

In our century it has become apparent that this principle was true only to a limited degree and under especially favorable circumstances. Its validity was dependent upon the continuing power of traditional values and institutions. When these retarding and disguising factors disappeared, "the principle of automatic harmony" was revealed in all its patent insufficiency.[28]

---

[28]Paul Tillich, "The World Situation," p. 6.

Chapter Four

Integration
in Contemporary Education

T HE contemporary age, which Tillich calls the third stage of Western civilization, is often characterized as a period of fear, uncertainty, loneliness, and meaninglessness.[1] It is nevertheless also an age which is seeking antidotes to these depressing symptoms of cultural disintegration. Movements toward security and synthesis and a search for the meaning of life are going on. This striving for a path out of chaos may be seen in many forms—Fascism, Communism, the "New Deal," youth movements, ecumenical movements, the United Nations. For better and for worse the experiments continue in an effort to produce a more satisfying, a more unified world. Education in the United States has not escaped the effect of this ferment.

The trends in political, economic, and social change have been visible in educational changes, particularly in our institutions of higher education. The elective system in our colleges, expressive of the "laissez faire" and "rugged individualism" period of our history, was a revolt against a static, standardized curriculum. In the contemporary period this frontier brand of unrestricted freedom has given way. On the economic and social front a more controlled economy, provisions for social security, a greater awareness of the inescapable relatedness of each individual to other individuals and of our nation to other nations reflect the spirit of

---

[1] Paul Tillich, *The Protestant Era* (Chicago: The University of Chicago Press, 1948), p. 245.

the present age. The Marshall Plan for aiding Europe and the Supreme Court decision on segregation are illustrations of the mood. In education the adoption of prescribed curricula for teaching the important truths of man's nature and his relation to his universe has gradually been modifying the elective system. There has been a definite movement toward a more planned, more integrated, and more meaningful education. One must recognize, however, that this trend is only beginning, for ours is still a technical, materialistic, and secular age. Education beyond the elementary and secondary levels, with some significant exceptions, is still predominantly occupational and technical and often narrow and limited.

Some of the educational changes in the United States may be attributed to the explosive influx of students into the secondary schools and the colleges. "While the total population of the United States was roughly doubling between 1890 and the present [1939], the number of high school students was increasing more than eight times."[2] It is only natural that under this rise of student enrollments, education should reflect more accurately than before the wishes of the population as a whole. The wants and felt needs of new classes of students pouring into our schools brought the elective system to its zenith. That these needs, basically economic, found their first expression in a host of technical course offerings was perhaps quite natural. The importance of other goals has been felt by most students, but the trend away from a predominantly occupational drive has not been rapid.

Of the attempts at integration in the contemporary period in America none has been more successful in terms of unification around a single goal than training in the schools of technology. A science-conscious civilization has held up the lure of employment and honor to those who with single purpose strive to satisfy some of man's specific physical desires. The technical role of the engineer, the physician, or the physicist is one which satisfies to some extent the search of the individual for purpose and unity in life. But the inadequacy of the single goal of technical competence has

---

[2]R. Freeman Butts, *The College Charts Its Course* (New York: McGraw-Hill, 1939), p. 265.

recently been recognized by scientists and the schools which train scientists. Man's life is more than building a molecule or a bridge, more than discovery of the secrets of the atom or a cell. The awareness of the need for breadth in education has resulted in the adoption, even by schools of technology, of prescribed courses in the humanities and the social sciences. President J. R. Killian, Jr., of Massachusetts Institute of Technology maintains:

> It is M.I.T.'s duty to prepare its students for social responsibility and for a rich and complete life. But, important though these objectives may be, technological and sociological problems are now so inextricably interwoven that the humanities and social sciences are also essential components of a man's professional education. Without an adequate cultural background, a technical specialist is no longer qualified for leadership in his own field.[3]

Unfortunately many students and their parents still ask the question with only dollar signs in their eyes: How am I going to *use* this college program? And many of our colleges and universities answer this demand with a program narrowly integrated by a constant and dominating occupational emphasis.

Other attempts at synthesis in the college program have a broader goal. Survey courses were among the first expressions of these movements. Early examples of such courses were "Social and Economic Institutions" offered at Amherst in 1914 and the Erskine course in "Contemporary Civilization" started at Columbia in 1919. An extension of courses of this type to all areas of the college became widespread after the first World War. The Chicago Plan and the Columbia Plan are particularly well-known examples of university-wide efforts at integration. They were attempts to avoid either a fragmented curriculum or a completely specialized curriculum. Most colleges in the United States have made some attempt to "eradicate the fatal disconnection of subjects that kills the vitality of our modern curriculum."[4] There is a growing conviction that education should "search for unity, for synthesis, a recognition of common needs and opportunities."[5]

[3]B. Lamar Johnson, *General Education in Action* (Washington, D. C.: American Council On Education, 1952), p. 14.

[4]Alfred North Whitehead, *The Aims of Education* (London: Williams and Norgate Limited, 1932), p. 10.

[5]B. Lamar Johnson, *General Education in Action*, p. 19.

1

GENERAL EDUCATION

This current movement in higher education has come to be known as general education. The term is by no means well defined, but it does in two words state the basic direction in which education is moving. Paul Dressel once humorously wrote the following limerick:

> General Education's defined
> In phrases both trite and refined
> But no matter how stated
> It always is fated
> To describe the speaker's mind.[6]

Despite the vagueness of the phrase, there is considerable agreement on many of the things for which it stands. There is a growing awareness that every student must have an intelligent insight into many areas of knowledge and into the interrelatedness of those areas. There is further agreement on some of the attributes which should characterize the man or woman who graduates from college. Many educators would say with Theodore Greene that

the goal of education is to prepare each individual, so far as his native endowment permits, to live well in his society and in the universe in which he finds himself; that that educational process is best which advances us most efficiently towards this goal; and that that academic community is best which best initiates and sustains this educational process.[7]

A more extended definition is given by McGrath:

General education, as we conceive it, is that which prepares the young for the common life of their time and their kind. It includes the fund of knowledge and belief and the habits of language and thought which characterize and give stability to a particular social group. It is the unifying element of a culture. It prepares the student for a full and satisfying life as a member of a family, as a worker, as a citizen—an integrated and purposeful human being. It does not overlook differences in talent, interest, and purpose; nor does it attempt to form everyone in a single mental and spiritual mold. Seeking to make possible the

---

[6]Paul L. Dressel, "Trends in General Education," *College and University Bulletin*, V, 2 (March, 1953), 1.
[7]Theodore Greene, *Liberal Education Reconsidered* (Cambridge: Harvard University Press, 1954), p. 24.

maximum development of the individual consistent with the general good, it encourages respect for inventive genius and tolerance for variations in opinion, while at the same time it rests on the principle that deviations in thought or in act must be based upon understanding rather than ignorance of the purposes, standards, and values of society.[8]

With this concept of a common, necessary education and the resulting picture of a broadly intelligent graduate there is general agreement except by some schools of technology. Beyond these generalizations there is considerable disagreement as to the nature of the common body of training and knowledge which all men should possess, as to the exact role the college should play in developing the student, and as to the educational methods which should be used.[9] These three areas of disagreement have resolved themselves into a number of fundamental issues which have been widely debated.

2

SOME SPECIFIC CONTEMPORARY ISSUES RELEVANT TO INTEGRATION

A few of these issues of contemporary education will be examined, for it is interwoven within their pattern that we find the problem of integration in our own day. The approach to integration will, therefore, be oblique; yet this problem, Dressel and Mayhew point out, is the most important single task of higher education today.

a. *Intellect vs. Total Personality*

What shall be the central integrating goal of a college? Shall we be basically concerned with the intellect, or shall we be basically concerned with other aspects of the student's life?

There are many from Newman to Hutchins who believe "if education is rightly understood, it will be understood as the culti-

---

[8]Earl J. McGrath *et al., Toward General Education* (New York: The Macmillan Co., 1948), pp. 8-9.
[9]P. L. Dressel and L. B. Mayhew, "Basis for Integration in General Education," *The Educational Record,* XXXV (June, 1954), 221. "Those who . . . attempt it [to solve the problem of integration] find themselves bewildered by lack of any generally accepted set of principles, concepts, or processes around which integration can be developed. This lack is the major present weakness of general education. Unless it is remedied shortly, general education will itself become the victim of just such a reaction as gave rise to its inception."

vation of the intellect."[10] An extreme expression of this view is stated by Hutchins: "We have excluded body building and character building. We have excluded the social graces and the tricks of trade."[11] This view does not deny the importance of the many aspects of living other than the mental but assigns the development of these to other agencies and not to the college curriculum. The college years are regarded as too short to do anything but develop the center of man's educational capacities, his mind. Hutchins expounds this philosophy as follows:

It hardly helps us here to say, as many anti-intellectuals do, that education must educate the whole man. Of all the meaningless phrases in educational discussion this is the prize. Does it mean that education must do the whole job of translating the whole infant into a whole adult? Must it do what the church, the family, the state, the YMCA, and the Boy Scouts allege they are trying to do? If so, what is the place of these important or interesting organizations, and what becomes of that intellectual training which educational institutions might be able to give if they could get around to it? Are we compelled to assume that our students can learn nothing from life or that they have led no life before coming to us and lead none after they come? Moreover, what we are seeking is a guide to the emphasis that higher education must receive. Talk of the whole man seems to imply that there should be no emphasis at all. All "parts" of the man are of equal importance: his dress, his food, his health, his family, his business. Is education to emphasize them all? . . . Is it too much to say that if we can teach our students to lead the life of reason we shall do all that can be expected of us and do at the same time the best thing that can be done for the whole man?[12]

For many this is unrealistic and narrow. The view point of dissenters who believe in education of the "whole man" is stated by W. M. Cowley:

. . . the purpose of the college is the training of the whole student, not of his mind alone. I take this stand because it is my deep conviction that in education and in living intelligence is not enough. Intelligence is not enough because thinking is only part of living; because students come to college not only for the training of their minds but also for the enrichment of their lives as people; because college students need the advice and direction of mature and experienced adults who understand their problems; because as expressed in the motto of Hamilton College they seek to know themselves; because such self-knowledge is emotional and social and spiritual as well as intellectual; because not only the student's mind comes to college but also his body; because, as most

[10]Robert M. Hutchins, *The Higher Learning in America*, p. 67.
[11]*Ibid.*, p. 77.
[12]Robert M. Hutchins, *Education for Freedom*, pp. 36-37.

42

alumni will testify, the lessons in human relations learned from one's fellow students complement the lessons learned from books and professors; because college is not only an intellectual enterprise but also a social and spiritual environment; because society expects from college graduates not only intelligence but also civilized attitudes, matured emotions, and cultivated character.[13]

It would seem comparatively easy to integrate a college toward a single goal of intellectual growth. Extra-curricular programs can be curtailed, except those which develop the mind. Guidance and assistance to students can deal primarily with course work and intellectual activities. All the energies of the college are thereby focused in one direction.

Integration of the "total personality" program is, on the other hand, far more complex and more hazardous. Extra-curricular activities can be accepted as part of the educational process and be incorporated into the college program. Guidance is extended to the student's emotional, social, moral, and health needs. Even the class work does not have to be solely intellectual. The danger of such a program lies in the possibility that outside activities will completely submerge the intellectual challenge of an institution.

There are few colleges which have consciously narrowed the whole institutional program to the training of the intellect. As an example of other objectives, one can cite that for a Christian college a focus around religion is inevitable both in and outside of the curriculum. Writers such as Moberly, Brown, Lowry, and Maritain have a common thesis that Christian faith need not stifle the intellect but may unify and integrate intellectual life. The question each Christian college must answer is: How far shall the total personality concept steer us away from the single aim of intellectual development? Most leaders in Christian higher education would at least answer that training of the intellect is the only aim which justifies the existence of a college, even if it does not remain the sole aim of a Christian college. Most would go further to propose that the curriculum should not be diluted with non-intellectual pursuits but rather be maintained as four years of vigorous, intellectual search for truth and understanding. The danger to the multiple-purpose church college is that in recogni-

---

[13]W. M. Cowley, "Intelligence Is Not Enough," *Journal of Higher Education,* IX (1938), 476.

tion of goals other than that of intellectual growth, the prime goal of mental development through the curriculum may be diminished or forgotten. In a pungent passage Kenneth Brown has pointed to one temptation toward lopsidedness:

> And the college calling itself Christian in seeking to sell itself to the parent-church as a worthy offspring, worthy of more generous support, has often been tempted to present in its show-window not the intellectual strengths of the institution—strong, exciting teaching and strong, exciting learning—but rather the array of pre-ministerial students, the figures on student church attendance, the denominational affiliations of the faculty, the number of church suppers eaten by the president—interesting data, but not basic to Christian education.[14]

The Roman Catholic colleges have often been cited as having one of the well integrated liberal arts programs in contemporary higher education. Roman Catholic educators have emphasized and developed integration in their curricula and have worked constantly to shape patterns of integration. In practice, their colleges may not achieve their desired goals, but they are always aware of what in their judgment the goals should be. Roman Catholic institutions are aided by a common acceptance of theology as the most important integrating factor in the curriculum.

Theology is construed by the Roman Catholic as a study of God on an intellectual basis. He takes care not to use the terms *religion* or *religious education,* because these terms are broader and may have emotional, moral, and aesthetic implications which do not have a place in an educational institution as does theology, which is rational and intellectual. Nor is theology confused with other subjects which have a place in the curriculum, such as church history or philosophy. Theology is conceived of as a discipline worthy of study in its own right and also as the intellectual foundation for the integration of all other courses in the curriculum.

The emphasis on the term *theology* rather than *religion* is consistent with the concept that the prime function of a college is the training of the intellect. From Newman's time to the present, with only occasional dissent, the job of the college has been clearly perceived by Catholics as being "the making of minds."[15] A dis-

---

[14]Kenneth I. Brown, "The Classroom of the Burning Bush," *Christian Scholar,* XXXVII (1954), 179.
[15]P. L. Dressel and L. B. Mayhew, "Basis for Integration in General Education," p. 222.

tinction is made between ultimate and proximate aims of a college.

> The ultimate purpose of the Catholic college of liberal arts . . . is to bring souls closer to God with the aid of grace, and to assist them in fulfilling the purpose of their creation. . . . The Catholic college . . . is to prepare its students to become contributing citizens in a democracy. . . . The Catholic college . . . must be concerned not merely with the spiritual but primarily with the intellectual purpose of its existence, and if adequate efforts to achieve both ends are made, a satisfactory degree of attainment in both may be expected.[16]

The integrative role of theology is brought about by an awareness in all teachers of the relationship of theology to every special field of study. This does not imply a lack of autonomy of the various disciplines nor an artificial introduction of theology into the classroom. It does mean that students will learn to recognize theology as an intellectual foundation for the structure of all parts of the curriculum.

Primary concern with the ends of education does not preclude a remarkable agreement among Roman Catholic writers on what should be taught in a liberal arts college. Cunningham has presented a "wheel" analogy which sums up his concept of an integrated curriculum.[17] The hub or core structure should be language, theology, philosophy, and history. Language is chosen because in it lies our expression of all our thought. The role of theology has already been explained. Philosophy, often grouped with theology in importance, is valued because through it we view all reality. It is the instrument of theology. History is valued as vicarious experience and as a guide from the past to the present. The spokes of the wheel give breadth to the curriculum and cover areas not part of the core, such as literature, fine arts, mathematics, natural sciences, and social sciences. The rim of the wheel is made up of the peripheral studies in an area of concentration which gives depth and intensity to a student's education.

An illustration of Catholic thinking concerning integration and general education may be found in the new liberal arts curriculum at Notre Dame:[18]

---

[16]Wm. F. Cunningham, *General Education and the Liberal College* (St. Louis: B. Herder Book Co., 1953), p. 51.

[17]*Ibid.*, p. 100.

[18]*The New Plan of Studies* (College of Arts and Letters, University of Notre Dame, 1954).

First Year

Philosophy
    Introduction to Liberal Arts
    Logic
    Philosophy of Nature
Rhetoric—written and oral expression
Mathematics
European History (6 hours per week)
Foreign Language
Physical Education and/or ROTC

Second Year

    (followed by a comprehensive examination)
Theology—one semester—Ethics
Philosophy—one semester—contains introduction to Psychology
Literature
Natural Science—choice of one, e.g., Physics, Biology, etc.
American History
Social Science—unified course combining Sociology, Political Science
    and Economics

Third Year

Theology (Dogmatic Theology)
Collegiate Seminar—This is an extensive reading course in master-
              works of world literature covering all disciplines.
              There are group discussions.
Major Sequence—two courses
Elective or ROTC

Fourth Year

Philosophy—one semester
Theology—one semester
Major Sequence—two courses
Departmental Seminar—senior essay
Elective or ROTC

The Roman Catholic college of liberal arts ideally does not prepare a student for a particular career, although it may give him the background for a career. Concentration but not professional training in one of the arts or sciences is desirable. This is ideal, but in practice there are many compromises and variations.

Economic circumstances and the meager resources of our Catholic colleges for student aid will only too often compel a student to elect a professional program during the last two years of college. This is particularly true in the women's colleges where expenses are high and opportunities for student employment low.[19]

If students must be prepared not only for living but also for earning a living, let the proportion of professional courses to those in the purely liberal arts be as small as the purpose of taking professional courses at all will permit.[20]

The training of the intellect is not the exclusive objective of the Roman Catholic college although it is its *most important* concern. "The human intellect can not be isolated from the human person and other parts of man must be developed to complete the education of the whole man."[21] On the campus many activities, including participation in the sacraments, are construed as essential to his whole education. Selected extracurricular activities, if considered to be "the immediate putting into effect of the principles studied in class," are to be integrated with the classroom. "They would become part of the educational process, rather than something thought of as apart from that process."[22] Nevertheless, in spite of this awareness of other goals, Catholic educators are consistent in their emphasis that "the school must never become so engaged in health or social education and character formation that it turns out superficially enlightened intellects."[23]

b. *Functional Organization vs. Broad Transfer of Learning*

Developments in the field of psychology have had a significant influence on education in the United States. Until the latter part of the nineteenth century, it was accepted that formal discipline was necessary and satisfactory as an educational principle. It was assumed that learning in one set of circumstances is automatically transferred to other situations. The classical languages and mathe-

[19]Wm. F. Cunningham, *General Education and the Liberal College*, p. 149.
[20]*Ibid.*, p. 25.
[21]*Ibid.*, p. 51.
[22]John Julian Ryan, "On the Meaning of Integration," *Integration in Catholic Colleges and Universities*, edited by Roy J. Deferrari (Washington, D. C.: The Catholic University of America Press, 1950), p. 21.
[23]Wm. F. Cunningham, *General Education and the Liberal College*, p. 53.

matics are examples of disciplines which were thought to be particularly beneficial in developing a general improvement of all mental processes.

Early in the twentieth century, experiments in psychology by Thorndike and Woodworth resulted in a formulation of the theory of identical elements which held that transfer of learning would take place from one activity to another only to the extent that the two activities contained identical elements. Thus the training of certain muscles in playing the piano would aid in operating a typewriter.

More recently it has been proposed that transfer of learning can take place without identical elements. Ralph W. Tyler and others have shown that while detailed information from a course is soon forgotten, generalizations or laws are retained and may be applied by the student to solve problems with which he had no previous experience.[24] This newer concept of transfer of learning has been the psychological justification for the view that general courses can be taken by all students for a common necessary background.

A sharp controversy has nevertheless arisen as to the proper method of teaching a general education program. Despite the same accepted goal, there are two radically different approaches to teaching general truths. One has been called functional organization and the other broad transfer of learning.[25]

The present day functionalist believes that a general education can be achieved through developing the curriculum in relation to the student's needs and areas of living. Ruth Eckert says that the courses in the General College at Minnesota

begin with the known and proceed to the unknown, they start with the geographically and temporally near and progress to the remote. The underlying assumption in several of these programs seems to be that a study of contemporary situations better prepares the student for life and that, properly taught, such courses are as stimulating and productive of intellectual values as the more traditional curriculums.[26]

The antifunctionalist aims at transferring a more enduring cultural heritage which is not apparently as closely related to the

---

[24]*Cooperation in General Education*, p. 20.
[25]*Ibid.*, p. 38.
[26]*Outlines of General Education* (Minneapolis: University of Minnesota Press, 1943), p. 9.

student's everyday life. By selecting the best of the reading, writing, and thinking of Western culture he hopes the student will gain a basis for intelligent daily living which is not limited to the myopic vision of the day's newspaper. This is the traditional viewpoint of the liberal arts college as well as of other general education programs such as the "great books" and the "survey" courses.

Tyler has summed up the usual "weighted" arguments which each side has presented:

> A functionalist might argue: "General education is education for the common life of today—and tomorrow. Let us, therefore, study that life and base our courses upon it—upon the problems our students will face and the activities they will perform. We mustn't depend on transfer of training from traditional liberal arts subjects to take care of the major contemporary problems of students and society." An antifunctionalist might reply: "You will end by teaching trivia. Let's give a thorough education in the fields which the human race has found worth studying over the centuries. Then, if there is any time left, we can add any other things that seem to have been omitted. How to live—today or tomorrow or any other time—depends principally upon insight into the central values of living; for these we must turn to the cultural heritage of the Western World."[27]

Both of these viewpoints represent current attempts at integration. They differ in the method selected. The colleges which are usually cited as extremes of the two positions are the General College at Minnesota, representing a functional organization, and St. John's of Annapolis, the broad transfer of learning.

c. *Election vs. Prescription*

About the time of World War I the concept of complete freedom in course selection came into disrepute. It has been widely condemned by many educators since that time, and today there are few colleges which permit complete election. Sir Walter Moberly has clearly stated the objection:

> But the "elective system" assumes that there are no such things as vitamins of the intellect, no objective principles of mental diet, an assumption with small intrinsic plausibility and much discredited by experience. Under this system the graduate is apt to have acquired nothing but a smattering of unrelated subjects.[28]

---

[27] R. W. Tyler, *Cooperation in General Education*, p. 45.
[28] *The Crisis in the University*, p. 175.

The "progressive colleges," Bard, Bennington, and Sarah Lawrence, do have an individualized and student-centered program, but even of these Benezet reports: "The choice by the student of a course program is nowhere treated as a 'free election.' The adviser system functions in varying degrees to help him pick those courses which seem best fitted to his nature and purposes."[29] In practice this results in a diet of courses remarkably similar to that found in most liberal arts colleges. Here the adviser serves to integrate the program rather than having it done by a "core curriculum" or other curricular devices.

There are a few colleges like St. John's with a completely prescribed curriculum and many with a partially prescribed curriculum. There are obvious integrative values in having every student take the same course for four years or even for two years. There is a unity of purpose and a common methodology which binds together the efforts of the college. The prescribed curriculum does not leave the choice of "vitamins" to the whims and often immature judgment of the student, nor does it leave a loophole for poor or prejudiced advising.

Most colleges do not choose a completely prescribed curriculum for several reasons. There is a danger that the individuality of the student will be ignored and, further, that his natural drives and interests will not be used to motivate the learning process. These dangers assume much less significance when only a portion of the four-year program is mandatory. There probably will always be some rebellion on the part of an uninformed undergraduate against a course or a program which he is obliged to take. The degree of rebellion need not be permanent if some effort is made to "sell" the proper educational outlook and if the teaching is adequate.

Is there a set of studies which every student ought to share? The concept of prescription assumes that there is a hierarchy of studies and that those prescribed are the most important. To be sure, there is no general agreement on the order of importance of the fields of learning, but there is a remarkable unanimity of emphasis on certain areas. A few examples will illustrate this point. Ortega lists as the five great cultural disciplines: Physics, Biology,

---

[29]L. T. Benezet, *General Education in the Progressive College* (New York: Bureau of Publications, Teachers College, Columbia University, 1943), p. 138.

History, Sociology and Philosophy.[30] Barzun describes the importance at Columbia College of the threefold areas of Natural Science, Social Science, and the Humanities.[31] Lowry lists Literature, History, Philosophy, Fine Arts, Science, and Religion.[32] Greene cites English, Foreign Languages, Mathematics, Fine Arts, Natural and Social Sciences, Humanities, History, Philosophy, and Religion.[33] Mark Van Doren stresses Poetry, Fine Arts, Mathematics, Literature, Language, Science, Philosophy, History, and Religion.[34]

One should not assume that all proponents of prescription would agree with the above lists of "classical" courses. The "functionalists" would list their own courses. The General College of the University of Florida requires "Reading, Speaking and Writing" and Pasadena Junior College prescribes Homemaking and Guidance.

Of particular importance are those subjects with special capacities and responsibilities for educational integration. As Theodore Greene states, "without the skills of synoptic interpretation, man is doomed to cultural and sectarian myopia, to provincialism and prejudice."[35] To overcome this narrowness we need, according to Greene, History, Philosophy, and Religion. These are the disciplines which are most frequently regarded as especially integrative, although the Natural and Social Sciences and the Fine Arts (including Literature) are also often put in this class.

There is a difference of opinion concerning the necessity of putting prescribed courses at a particular point in the four-year program. Many believe that introductory courses, particularly all general education courses, should be offered only in the first two years without any specialization during this period. Only thus can a student gain some concept of the scope and unity of knowledge without the distraction of specialization. The student by avoiding early specialization can also escape a false start in a special area for which he may not be suited. In addition there is concern over the sometimes disrupting effect of seniors taking freshman courses.

---

[30]Ortega y Gasset, *Mission of the University* (London: Kegan Paul, Trench, Trubner & Co., 1946).
[31]Jacques Barzun, *Teacher in America* (Boston: Little, Brown & Co. Inc., 1944).
[32]Howard Lowry, *The Mind's Adventure.*
[33]Theodore M. Greene, *Liberal Education Reconsidered.*
[34]Mark Van Doren, *Liberal Education* (New York: Henry Holt and Co., 1943).
[35]T. M. Greene, *Liberal Education Reconsidered*, p. 38.

51

Arthur Bestor has little sympathy for the frequently recommended exclusion of upperclassmen from "lower division" courses. He contends:

. . . they are apt to forbid a graduate student or even an upperclassman from taking for full credit a course whose number indicates that it is on the introductory level. This is absurd. Where, may one ask, should a student be introduced to a new subject if not in an introductory course? . . . If the introductory course is a really rigorous one, there is no reason why it should not be elected for full credit by upperclassmen and graduate students. Only in this way can advanced courses become and remain truly advanced ones, and a rational system of prerequisites be maintained. The difference between an introductory course and an advanced one has almost nothing to do with the chronological age of the student or his academic status.[36]

Perhaps the most common handling of the timing of prescription is described by McGrath:

The patterns of general, special, and elective studies in terms of the four years of college and in terms of the interests and abilities of students must inevitably be determined by individual institutions. We believe, however, that two principles should govern such arrangements. The interest which the student has in a particular subject or field should be capitalized from the very beginning of his college work, and the general and special studies should not, therefore, be separated by being offered only in certain years either early or late. The latter arrangement in our opinion leads to an artificial splitting up of knowledge and increases a natural inclination on the student's part to favor special or vocational studies at the expense of his general, cultural development. Hence we think that the student should begin his study of general and specialized subjects at the outset of his college career and continue to study both until graduation or until he leaves the institution. The exact proportion of either to be pursued in a particular year should be determined by a number of factors which cannot be predicted. We believe it to be a sound principle of curriculum building, however, that the proportion of general studies should be considerably larger in the early years and the proportion of specialized study should increase as the student progresses toward graduation. Under this plan the high degree of motivation which the student customarily brings to specialized study would be used to advantage from the very beginning. Each student would, therefore, be able to pursue his own special interests throughout his college years but like all his contemporaries he would be required to complete a program of general studies before graduation.[37]

The real issue in most colleges today is not whether or not to

---

[36]Arthur Bestor, *Educational Wastelands* (Urbana: The University of Illinois Press, 1953), p. 165.
[37]*Toward General Education*, p. 20.

52

achieve integration through prescription; that is usually accepted. Rather it is concerned with the extent and nature of the basic prescription.

d. *Specialization*

From the German educational system of the nineteenth century higher education inherited a devotion to professional training. To-day some schools of technology are still narrow, exclusive, and limited to an area of utility or interest. This is not the rule in the liberal arts colleges. Most of these strive for the dual aim of breadth and specialization. The problem is the proper blending of the two, particularly the avoidance of the domination of general education by specialization. Whitehead, who is so often quoted for his positive stand on integrated studies, states the dilemma in his *Aims of Education:*

> I know it seems contradictory to allow for specialism in a curriculum designed for a broad culture. Without contradictions the world would be simpler, and perhaps duller. But I am certain that in education wherever you exclude specialization you destroy life.[38]

Few schools have attempted a real integration of specialization and general education perhaps because this is a "contradiction." There exists the possibility of using the drive of specialization to give motivation for general education. Professor Aydelotte of MIT has demonstrated the series of successive steps by which an engineer can be led from a natural desire to write a clear business letter to the study of English literature and perhaps to industrial and social history. Area studies and integrated courses may also point out the relatedness of a specialty to the larger range of man's knowledge. These attempts are as close as modern education has come to satisfying the elusive integration of specialization and general education.

3

PROGRAMS OF GENERAL EDUCATION

General education is not synonymous with integration, but the latter is one of the important aims of the former. Most of the

---

[38]Pp. 15-16.

experimentation in integration can be found within the framework of the basic types of general education programs developed in the past thirty-five years. Since these patterns are well known and have been widely described, only a brief summary of a few of them is necessary here.

a. *The St. John's Program (great books)*

The curriculum at St. John's College at Annapolis, Maryland, was reorganized in 1937 so that the four-year program of each student is devoted to reading and discussing one hundred great books of Western civilization. During the first two years the student studies fifty books covering two thousand years of culture, and in the last two years the other fifty books covering the more recent three hundred years up to 1900. Mathematics and language are taught under a tutorial system in which students are drilled five times a week in each of the two areas. Greek is taught the first year, Latin the second, French the third, and German the fourth year. The great books are studied in small seminars twice a week. Each week all the students attend one formal lecture which may be on any subject of interest to the faculty. Laboratory work once a week is limited to the instruments and experiments described in the classics read. The curriculum was meant to be designed for students of any and every type of ability.

The program was organized by advocates of the "Great Tradition," such as Hutchins, Adler, Barr, and Buchanan. It was set up to counteract three tendencies in higher education: (1) the elective system, (2) the lack of intellectual discipline and creative thinking, and (3) the dissipation of a student's energies in nonintellectual activities on the campus. Proponents of the plan maintain that by making a student familiar with the best in the thinking of the past he will be able to cope with current and future problems of everyday living.

Critics of the plan, such as Harry Gideonse, Sidney Hook, and Howard Mumford Jones, have emphasized the unnatural pre-occupation of the St. John's program with the past. Only two books published in the twentieth century are on the list and both of these are in mathematics. According to its opponents, St. John's ignores the tremendous additions to knowledge in the last fifty years in the physical sciences, in psychology, political science, economics, sociology, and history. These dissenters maintain the program is weighted on the linguistic and mathematical side. There have been other objections such as the ignoring of any individual tastes (the curriculum being completely prescribed), the absence of music and the visual arts, the emphasis on dialectical training, and the limitation of the reading to Western culture. Although it is one of the best integrated curricula in this country, many feel the intellectual harmony is too dearly bought.

Yet even critics of the St. John's plan have attested to its merit as an experiment. The reading of the great classics after being publicized through the St. John's venture has been reproduced formally and informally on many campuses in our land. There has been a hesitation, nevertheless, to adopt this type of curriculum except in a limited fashion. Perhaps the principal objection is voiced by B. Lamar Johnson: "There is widespread agreement among most educators that this approach is most nearly successful with students of superior scholastic, abstract, and verbal abilities." Only a few of these students are found on most campuses.

b. *Course Distribution*

The most common reform of the elective system has been the one whereby some courses are prescribed while others are electives. This program started with the efforts of President Lowell who at Harvard in 1909 held that the student should know "a little of everything, and something well." This is the present plan at St. Olaf College.

There are many variations of this program, but in principle they are the same. A major and perhaps a minor are required of each student with a certain number of credit hours specified in each field. There are often divisional requirements with the student being permitted to select a certain number of courses within a group. Usually a few courses are specifically prescribed, such as those in English or Religion.

This program has the advantage that it allows for some freedom of choice in courses to suit the individual needs of a student while still making him aware of the major areas of learning. It is often criticized for the ease with which students restrict their efforts and take a bare minumum of courses outside their major areas of study. It is also thought that despite area requirements there is often no overall plan for tying together the course program to give a coherent view of knowledge.

c. *Individual Program*

Progressive colleges such as Bennington, Sarah Lawrence, and Bard start with the student's own interests and plan a college program around these interests with the help and advice of a college instructor. These course programs are designed to include a broad educational background but make no attempt to avoid techniques that may be required for an occupation. Thus President Leigh of Bennington has stated:

> For example, stenography and typewriting can be pursued as incidental parts of undergraduate work in the case of those young women who plan definitely to enter the secretarial field after graduation. The type of intellectual asceticism which fears that contact with practice or reality will destroy the field for culture will be studiously avoided at Bennington. Breadth and thoroughness of work requiring sustained intellectual effort, whether directed toward a vocation or as preparation for leisure, will be the test of success rather than a program distinguished by its isolation from practical usefulness.[39]

In practice, as Benezet has pointed out (p. 50), the pattern in these schools is basically the same as that in which course distribution is followed. The program still centers around natural science, social science, literature, and fine arts.

d. *Survey or Integration Courses*

Under this plan students usually take a combination of survey courses plus electives of their own choice. The survey course is designed to give a broad introduction to an area of knowledge, a field of interest or a manner of thinking. This one might study Unified Physical Science, Contemporary Civilization, or Great Issues. These courses may be given to introduce a first-year student to the college curriculum or they are often given as senior

---

[39]Robert D. Leigh, *The Educational Plan for Bennington College* (New York: 1931), p. 11.

capstone courses to help tie together basic elements in the fourth year.

Survey courses have been offered in an infinite variety from an encyclopedic skimming of a field to an emphasis on problem solving or the intelligent study of a few great themes. At their worst they have been a diluted, watered-down union of a few traditional courses. At their best they have challenged students and teachers in the best possible introduction to the world of the intellect. Some colleges such as Reed, Colgate, and Columbia have been extraordinarily successful in achieving integration through these courses. It has required, however, strong administrative support and an excellent staff with time and equipment to do a good job.

The survey courses have found proponents among both the functionalists and the antifunctionalists. The course titles illustrate the differences. Communication Skills may be offered instead of Rhetoric or Literature, Personal and Community Health rather than Biological Sciences, and Consumer Problems and Psychology of Personal Adjustment rather than Social Sciences.

4

This brief survey of integration has indicated that unlike most of the previous periods of educational history, our own age is undergoing a conscious, critical questioning as to the wholeness and the coherence of our teaching. There are many answers and many proposals for achieving what seems to be a universally recognized goal. It is only natural that a busy college administrator or professor may be dismayed at the variety of plans and methods. One response is to recognize the merits of different answers to the problems of education and then to forget all of them. Still another simple and virtuous way of ignoring the larger problems of education is to concentrate on one's own field or current activities. In any case we can easily choose to drift because of the difficulty of making a conscious decision as to our direction. We need the reminder of Arnold Nash that "true objectivity and impartiality in the sphere of scholarship does not consist in saying that there is much to be said on both sides but that it lies in a resolute attempt to discover the truth between contending theo-

57

ries."[40] Nash further holds that for a college or university "the real question becomes therefore not, 'Shall we or shall we not have a planned university?'—that is not a live option—but rather, 'On what basis shall it be planned, and to what purpose?' "[41]

With regard to the vital problem of integration we must examine carefully the history of education and in rethinking our task against this background try to formulate solutions that best fit the purpose of our own college. About this and every other important quality of a college it should be possible at least to say as does the Harvard Report, "What we possess exists by intention and design, not by accident or default."[42]

---

[40]Arnold S. Nash, *The University and The Modern World* (New York: The Macmillan Company, 1944), p. 26.
[41]*Ibid.*, p. 232.
[42]*General Education in a Free Society*, p. 185.

PART TWO

Christian
Higher Education
and Integration

Chapter Five

The Christian Church
and Liberal Education

A FEW years age, Dr. Conrad Bergendoff, President of Augustana College (Rock Island), asserted that there are many Lutheran colleges in the country and yet there is no Lutheran or Protestant philosophy of education. Apparently he meant that such an important enterprise ought to involve a clear and conscious understanding of the nature and purpose of the undertaking. Apparently he wanted to raise the questions: Why is the Church engaged in higher education? What is the essential relationship between the faith and this educational venture?

1

CHRISTIANITY AND HUMAN CULTURE

Education, formal and informal, is the central conservational and developmental activity within a culture. Therefore the question of the place of the Church in education has a broader form: What should be the relationship of a faithful Church to the culture in which it exists? This broader form of the question may not be raised and answered consciously any more frequently than the narrower form. Yet individuals have been deeply concerned with such root problems, as were Tertullian and Augustine. Those who do not ask the question nevertheless answer it (though ambiguously) in ways of thinking and of acting individually and institutionally. We can discern at least four ways in which Christians have thought out or acted out the relationship between the faith and human culture and similarly between the faith and education.

a. *Rejection*. Finding themselves in a culture either hostile or distracting, those who have come to know the reality of God and the resulting radical change in scale of values may quite understandably devote themselves to a life of prayer, praise, and meditation. This could mean the rejection of common cultural values and ordinary pursuits. What else is worth a man's life but to be with Him who is Truth and Life? What are the activities of daily life but a diversion which binds a man's thoughts and desires to things of earth and time? What is man's seeking after knowledge but "an immoderate, hydroptic lust," as Donne put it, which displaces divine Wisdom? Is it not in this seeking that ignorant and sinful men imagine themselves to be on the way to wisdom and goodness? This is the view of a desert religion, a religion of withdrawal, a religion of rejection, which aims at letting first things be first— and which finds that first things are quite enough to require a man's entire life.

The essential rejection of human culture in a religion of withdrawal is not altered by the fact that monastic orders had more than a little to do with regenerating European cultural life, halting social disintegration, helping to re-establish education, and preserving the given fund of literature, arts, and thought, even contributing to horticultural science. In spite of deserved praise bestowed upon monastic orders because of their cultural benefits, their explicit purpose was not cultural regeneration but the regeneration of their members' own souls.

The position of rejection, stated with vigor and incisiveness by Tertullian, is not calculated to encourage the establishment of colleges concerned with transmitting the heritage of Western life and thought or with serving the claims of present-day needs. This position is anti-cultural, at best a-cultural. There are, to be sure, the universals of language and subsistence which cannot be escaped; nor can one erase his birth. Nevertheless these inescapable elemental links to human culture can be drastically reduced by withdrawal into the religious life of world-transcending devotion.

62

b. *Immersion.* Another possible relationship could be called *immersion,* the polar opposite to rejection. In closely identifying itself with human cultural life in order to alter or enhance it, immersion religion may become dominated by that very culture. This tends to make the Church and the faith more and more conditioned by the culture and essentially indistinguishable from other institutions and ideals aimed at the common good. The Church in education becomes part of the public education process, and Christianity, identified with the culture, becomes tribal religion.

c. *Split Adaptation.* A third possible position, split adaptation, shares with the religion of withdrawal and rejection the criticism of human culture as being relative and transient: at its best a heroic human striving doomed to failure and at its worst a snare and a delusion. Men's highest accomplishments and the lowest are equalized under divine judgment. Every man before God is stripped of all his presumptions and pretended merits. There is no genuine cultural progress, at least never to the point of delivering men from relativities and their own evil. The faith is not to be confused with human arts, sciences, and philosophy— nor with theology. The "split" is this: the realm of faithful inwardness in devotion to the transcendent and eternal contrasted to the realm of evanescent human creativity, knowledge, and action.

If the split results from regarding human culture as proud, forgetful creatureliness arrogating to itself the prerogatives of God, the "adaptation" results from a readiness to conform to this very world which has already been denied. One is in the world, not translated out of it. A citizen of two worlds and at home in both of them, the split adaptationist is moderately cynical of the immersionist, who seems to reduce religion to high social morality. Rather than this, the adaptationist without anguish conforms to the morality and practices commonly accepted by his time and place. In a culture such as ours, this view produces the anomalous pious materialist preoccupied quite normally with creature comforts and the acquisition of money and property against the evil day. Moderately sceptical and positivistic, he will not be the first by whom the new is tried in the realms of thought and value, but without much scrutiny of the relationship of his faith and established ways of thinking and valuing, he will follow the drift of majority public opinion and practice.

Sometimes there may be an uneasiness over this unreflective adaptation in one's "majority life" and the cloistered irrelevancy of one's faith. This may result in a selective legalism touching some fragments of ideas and a few specific kinds of activity—what one Methodist theologian called "Methodist sins."

Split adaptation may very well include education under Church auspices. Instead of being a replica of secular education under private direction, this educational program would be "education plus." This is the educational motto appropriate to the double view of cultural conformity and cultural transcendence. In practice this means the adoption of current educational thinking, value criteria, and programs, with the addition of "religion courses and chapel." The relevance of the faith to the curriculum and teaching is not a matter of concern, for there are two realms, faith and human culture. The presuppositions and implications of teaching and courses are left unscrutinized and the inner relationships within the curriculum left unexplored. The aims of education in this view are the aims of society at the time, plus religion courses and a religious atmosphere which have little bearing on the secular aims and content provided by autonomous culture.

From the standpoint of a cultural analysis, Tillich concludes:

> Because Protestantism has no definite ideal of culture, education in its sphere of influence can result only in a dualism of religious faith and humanistic idealism in which the former is ultimately forced aside. The situation in our whole higher educational system speaks eloquently of this fact.[1]

From the standpoint of a Christian university professor, George Anderson of the University of Kansas describes the position of the split adaptationist and points toward critical participation (d):

> A few months ago a Lutheran faculty man remarked that there are no problems confronting college teachers save those that are the products of our imaginations. Relating the Christian view of man to particular subjects and disciplines, he said, is simple and easy. One is just. One is honest. One is devoted to duty. One is rigorous in upholding standards of excellence, of right and wrong. One treats his

---

[1]*The Religious Situation* (New York: Henry Holt & Company, 1932), p. 164.

colleagues with kindness and Christian forbearance. In short, one witnesses to his Christian faith in these observable ways and one exudes a kind of "Christian aroma" . . . .

For some the problem is not so simple since expressing Christian convictions on the campus is partly if not chiefly a matter of one's philosophy of education. Some feel that to witness on the campus only in the realm of observable conduct is to live as if John Dewey with his unchristian view of man had never lived and, incalculably more important, it is to teach as if the Master Teacher had never taught. These folks will wonder if a teacher can be an economic determinist six days a week and on Sunday profess to follow the Lord of history who taught that man does not live by bread alone. They will wonder if they can teach as if knowing the truth more and more in the fields of science will automatically free mankind, and only on the Sabbath remember the premise and the promise, "If you continue in my word . . . you will know the truth and the truth will make you free." Some will wonder if a Christian teacher can on Sunday express his belief that an individual human soul is of infinite worth and on Monday teach as if the individual is just another piece of protoplasm to be molded and manipulated for some group purpose.

. . . Maybe there isn't any problem at all. Maybe we can all sit back and relax in the full knowledge that the relevance of the Christian faith to higher education is so simple that we should forget it and devote all of our energies to obtaining promotions in rank and raises in salaries. But before we decide to yield the whole area of higher education to the materialists and secularists, or shift our obligations to our bretiren in other denominations, should we not . . . ?[2]

In education as in other areas of human concern, split adaptation tends toward a (1) Christian absolutizing of some relativities of social morality and current thought (e.g. adapting the Christian view of "vocation" to bourgeois occupationalism) and towards (2) selective legalism (unstudied "dangerous ideas" and proscribed activities). This selective legalism is an ineffective remnant of the Christian critique of human life. The main effect, however, of split adaptation is to shed an aura of religious sanctity over contemporary cultural aims and substance without incisive penetration, coherent criticism, and relevant re-ordering and re-newal.

d. *Critical Participation.* This suggests a fourth possible relationship between the faithful Church and its cultural context. This view finds (1) fatal omissions in the rejectionist withdrawal from culture in order to come closer to a pure life of devotion. It finds

---

[2]"Real or Imaginary," *Lutheran Faculty,* November, 1954 (Division of Student Service, 327 S. LaSalle St., Chicago, Ill.).

(2) fatal weaknesses in the immersionist absorption by culture. It finds (3) tragedy without consciousness and anguish in the complacent, faithless dualism of world-denying and world-accommodating split adaptation.

In this view of critical participation there is properly a tension between Christian faith and human culture. This tension arises out of the Christian proclamation which, addressed to existing men in time and human culture, calls them to a life of faith within a new dimension transcending time and human culture. Grounded neither in time nor in human culture, the faith is urgently relevant to men existing in time and culture: hence the polar tension.

Even if Christianity intended and if the Christian Church sought to eliminate all relationships with human culture, this would be impossible short of the death of the Church and the vanishing of faith among existing men. The Church and the faith are in culture because they are in time where men are. For the Gospel to deal with temporal men it must involve some relationship to the human, to men and their culture. Furthermore, whatever judgment rests upon men and time processes, this world is nevertheless God's world and He reveals Himself to men through the mediation of His world (Luther's *larvae Dei*) and through His dealings with men in time. Creation and Incarnation mark Christianity as a religion of eternity concerned with time, of the divine seeking man in suffering love and involving him and his life where he is.

Critical participation holds that the easy optimism of immersion, the pessimism of rejection, and the acquiescent compote of the two in split adaptation do not recognize the inclusive concern and critical distinctions implicit in the Christian faith and outlook. Critical participation is rather a tragic optimism. One with this view knows that the best of human efforts is far short of adequacy, and yet the Christian is to live out his life in time among men. Although not seduced by promises of heaven on earth, he knows that even in time relative ethical decisions must be made and that the bases and ends of cultural activity do make a difference to men and to the witness of the faith. He knows that one's life in his culture ought to be both an expression of grateful obedience to God as well as a loving concern for men and a loving criticism of the structures of thought and society.

The critical participator sees the Christian life as a dual citizenship in the City of God and in the City of Man. The two are not the same, and yet ultimately the God of creation and of time is the God of salvation who enters into daily life where nothing is finished. This does not surprise him, for he knows that even a saint, Christianly understood, is one who is becoming that which he already is. With the peace which passes comprehension, the Christian and the Christian community live out the Christian ethic in a world which knows little peace even of its own kind. This means a continuity-discontinuity, a tension, which must remain unless the faith becomes removed from human culture in the detachment of rejection, becomes irrelevant in the faithless obscurantism and selective legalism of split adaptation, or loses itself by immersion in the cultural context.

Maintenance of this tension of critical participation means that two perils will be avoided, though not with ease. There is the peril of seeking only sanctity by retreat from the cultural context, the danger of dissolving obedience and witness in contrition, confession, and hymn-singing. There is also the peril of losing elevation and the Christian critique of human existence and culture, the danger of abandoning the life of faithful thought and action to the winds of doctrine and socially given norms. Critical participation has the special perils of both rejection and immersion and has the special task which split adaptation neglects. Only by maintaining this tension of critical transcendence and concerned cultural participation can the Christian Church be true to its calling. Only when this tension is maintained can there be faithful and beneficial participation in cultural life.

A consequence of this view is a critical and appreciative concern for education. A corollary of the doctrine of creation is the givenness of the world and the unity of truth; a corollary of man's finitude and fallen state is the incompleteness and twistedness of his knowledge of the truth. Therefore, earnest studies of man's world, of man's creations, of man's actions, of man's thought, and of man's valuing have their characteristic structures and methodological principles which give them relative autonomy, but only as parts and levels of the whole world of discovery, thought, creativity, exploit, and valuing. For the Christian this world of man's knowing and aspiring is subject to the critique of faith, faith seeking to understand itself (theology) and faith in critical-appreciative conversation with man's attempts to order and understand his experiences, judgments, presuppositions, and actions (Christian philosophy).

In a world in which neither events nor knowledge and understanding are finished, the total unity of truth can never be attained even as a conceptual view. Critical-appreciative participation would mean polemics as well as a patience growing out of the conviction that beneath contradictions and contingencies there is a wholeness and relatedness of being and a wholeness and relatedness of knowledge and wisdom, however unattainable this is for finite, temporal men.

Man's intellectual creative world, therefore, is of central concern for the Church, because this is the heart of the cultural context in which it is and in which men think and act. The orientation of Christian thought and life is not to be removed from the educational work of the culture; instead, this central conservational and formative activity of the culture is worthy of being undertaken, understood, criticized, re-orientated, and renewed in love to God and to self and to neighbor with all our heart and all our mind.

This concern for human culture and for education (especially, liberal education) is a familiar story in the life of the Christian Church. At its best the relationship has not been accidental.

The thesis of this chapter is that the Church has a definite stake and a special interest in liberal education. Since the liberal studies deal with the central powers and the core studies of human knowing, they constitute the unique and decisive area of education where the Christian viewpoint can and must make its impact. Furthermore, since the liberal studies are the prerequisites of all human learnings, they should also be the first concern of the Church in its program of higher education. Only when the liberal education program has been "secured," and that not in a half-hearted way, should the Church feel able to turn its attention to

68

the subsidiary and, incidentally, far more costly specialized occupational and technological studies.

Let us turn our attention, therefore, to an investigation of the meaning of liberal education, after which we shall evaluate its role in Christian higher education.

2

HISTORY OF LIBERAL EDUCATION AND THE CHRISTIAN CHURCH

a. *The Greeks and Romans.* The liberal arts originated with the Greeks, and chiefly with the Sophists. Werner Jaeger has written of the Sophists:

> Before them we never hear of grammar, rhetoric, and dialectic . . . clearly the systematic expression of the principle of shaping the intellect, because it begins by instruction in the form of language, the form of oratory, and the form of thought. This educational technique is one of the greatest discoveries which the mind of man has ever made: it was not until it explored these three of its activities that the mind apprehended the hidden law of its own structure.[3]

Man had followed the laws of grammar or reason by custom, but with the Sophists these laws were consciously studied. The Sophists blunted their own influence, however, by a relativizing theory of knowledge which regarded logic as merely rhetorical tricks whereby one might win an argument and "make the worse appear the better cause." In this respect their views were a threat to a serious philosophy of education, and Socrates and Plato especially combatted their relativism by an affirmation of the absolute value of truth and logical principles. Plato's Academy and Aristotle's Lyceum were major forces in the history of Western education. One might speculate what would have happened if the ancients had turned toward Plato's mathematical emphasis, "measuring," rather than towards the "classifying" emphasis of Aristotle (a more biological approach), or to rhetoric as such. C. N. Cochrane has pointed out that the historical importance of the victory of rhetoric cannot be exaggerated:

---

[3] *Paideia,* trans. Gilbert Highet (New York: Oxford University Press, 1954), I, 314.

For, by imparting to Classicism precisely that "literary and aesthetic bias" which Plato had so earnestly deprecated, it modified the whole complexion of Western culture, giving to it a rhetorical cast from which it was hardly to free itself under the most powerful stimulus of modern mathematical and physical science.[4]

Thus grammar, rhetoric, and logic became the chief educational instruments of formal education in Europe (not until the seventeenth century did mathematics come into its own again). In late antiquity these studies were called the *trivium,* and with the *quadrivium* (arithmetic, geometry, music, and astronomy) made up the seven liberal arts.

Cicero and Quintillian made the chief Roman contributions in the history of the liberal arts. Cicero's emphasis was the relation of law, philosophy, and history to the liberal arts, whereas Quintillian made a special treatment of rhetoric. In general the Romans propagated the Greek ideal of liberal education, but with major emphasis upon rhetoric.

b. *The early Church and Augustine.* The early Church was so occupied with its missionary task that its educational task was exhausted in its instruction of the catechumens. By the time of Augustine, however, as the Church became more and more a part of the historical scene, it began to interest itself in the total task of education. In *De Ordine* (Concerning Order), Augustine remarked:

> And those who are content with authority alone, and expend their efforts on good morals and holy desires, condemning the liberal arts or not being up to them, I do not see how they can be really happy among mortal men, though I believe with unshakable faith that they will be free and happy to the greatest extent in the next life, who have lived best here.[5]

Augustine saw in liberal education a way whereby the Church might combat heathen philosophies by requiring such an education of its own leaders. "This is the order of learning, or there is none," he remarked of liberal education.[6] Augustine planned to write treatises on the various liberal disciplines, but succeeded in writing only one, *De Musica.* According to his intentions philos-

---

[4] *Christianity and Classical Culture* (New York: Oxford University Press, 1944), p. 146.
[5] *De Ordine*, II, 9, 26.
[6] *Ibid.*, II, 17, 46.

ophy was to be substituted for astronomy in the quadrivium. Augustine recognized that the earliest disciples were not educated men, that God had chosen the weak things of the world to confound the wise. But he saw also that the utmost effort of intellect was necessary to understand the ways of God to man, and along with Jerome and Ambrose he desired to consecrate human learning to the uses of the Christian life. The liberal arts would be indispensable aids to the study of the Bible. In Greece the liberal arts had paved the way for philosophy; in Rome, for oratory; in the Church, for the good life and the study of scripture and theology. *Credo ut intelligam*—I believe that I may know—faith aids reason, and understanding is the reward of faith—so Augustine believed.

c. *The Middle Ages.* In this period the Church carried on the wider educational task, and the seven liberal arts (trivium plus quadrivium) were the basic studies. In the Carolingian age logic began to assume more importance, and the study of the trivium easily eclipsed that of the quadrivium. Theology was the central study, of course, with the seven free arts and a rudimentary sort of medical study as the handmaids of the queen of the sciences.[7] Philosophical and theological problems dominated the intellectual scene from the eleventh to the thirteenth centuries. The medium of expression was Latin, its rhetoric being the chief emphasis of South Europe, whereas its dialectical (i.e., logical) use was stressed in Northern Europe. The realm of knowledge moved up a ladder from grammar, rhetoric, and logic to metaphysics, with theology at the top ruling and encompassing all.

The founding of universities in the late Middle Ages bore witness to the central importance of the liberal arts for the Church. The universities of Naples, Paris, Oxford, Prague, and the like, were all centers of liberal learning as well as being famed for certain professional schools, as Paris for theology, or Bologna for law. In them all the classical heritage was enriched with the treasures of the Fathers of the Church, not least the writings of

---

[7]H. O. Taylor, *The Medieval Mind* (New York: The Macmillan Company, 1919), I, 302, argues that the indifference of Augustine and Ambrose to natural knowledge was the most palpable intellectual defect of these men, leading to the result that there was no incentive in the Middle Ages to study the natural world.

Augustine, all of which had been until then preserved in monas-
teries. The tremendous intellectual achievement of a Thomas
Aquinas in his *Summas* was possible only by means of this tradition. Aquinas did not give an explicit treatment of the liberal arts,
but he saw that they freed man's highest powers, his intellect and
his will, for their proper activity. The liberal arts studied man,
and the study of man trained man's highest powers.

d. *The Reformation.* Luther once remarked, "When schools
flourish, then things go well, and the Church is secure. Let us have
more learned men and teachers."[8] Like Aquinas, Luther did not
treat the liberal arts in any specific way, but it is clear from his
writings that he valued liberal education highly. He himself was
a university professor, after all, and often spoke disparagingly of
"the same old blockheads, unable to converse on any subject or to
be of assistance to anyone."[9] He thought that children should
receive instruction from learned schoolmasters in languages, history, and the other arts especially, in order that they might see
as in a mirror the character, life, success, and failure of the whole
world.

As a result of this knowledge, they could form their own opinions and
adapt themselves to the course of this outward life in the fear of God,
draw from history the knowledge and understanding of what should be
sought and what avoided in this outward life, and become able also by
this standard to assist and direct others.[10]

Luther disparaged philosophy because he identified scholastic
philosophy with Roman Catholicism, and condemned both in the
same breath. This had unfortunate consequences for the relations
of faith to reason in the centuries that followed, for Protestant
thinkers felt they had to be nominalists rather than realists in
philosophy, although Protestant theology was always realistic.
The result was an ever-widening breach between natural science
and theology in the modern period.[11] Melancthon hoped to save
the day for philosophy, but his Aristotelian predilections were not

---

[8]*Conversations With Luther,* trans. Preserved Smith and H. P. Gallinger (Boston:
The Pilgrim Press, 1915), p. 96.
[9]*Works of Martin Luther* (Philadelphia: A. J. Holman Company, 1915-1932),
IV, 122.
[10]*Ibid.*
[11]Cf. Otto Piper, *God in History* (New York: Macmillan Company, 1939),
p. 54.

calculated to provide a permanent basis. In their general estimate of education Melancthon and Luther were quite agreed: "the school must be the next thing to the Church."[12] Since their time the Lutheran Church has been characterized by its strong interest in education.[13]

On the Reformed side of the Reformation the same emphasis on liberal education obtained. John Calvin was himself a great humanist who became a great reformer, never regretting or denying his education. The great Swiss educator, Pestalozzi, comes from this tradition. In the United States the public school is very largely an outcome of the establishment of schools by the early Calvinist Puritans in New England. Harvard, Yale, and Princeton, great bulwarks of liberal education to this day, were established by Calvinists.

The Counter-Reformation movement in the Roman Catholic Church was no denial of the importance of liberal education either, as can be seen in the Jesuits. Under Ignatius Loyola the Jesuits established a system of studies that was a particularly effective method of developing certain aspects of man's intellect. In the nineteenth century a significant reaffirmation of the liberal arts viewpoint came from Cardinal Newman's *The Idea of a University*, which argued that a Christian university must be centered around the liberal arts.

Thus, down through its long history the Christian Church, whether Protestant or Catholic, recognizing the liberal arts as the core learnings of the human mind, has seen their peculiar closeness to the concern of the Church in education.

3

A CHRISTIAN PHILOSOPHY OF LIBERAL EDUCATION

The Lutheran Church throughout its history has always upheld and supported the arts and sciences of the human mind, the world and culture, as a God-given realm of creation. Man did not create this realm. God gave it to man as both a gift and a task.

---

[12]*Works*, V, 298.
[13]Cf. the folk-school of Grundtvig, the Danish Lutheran, notable for the fact that liberal studies are the chief studies of the curriculum, especially theology, philosophy, literature, and history.

God gave to man his reason, whereby he might create the arts and investigate the sciences within this realm of culture. The Christian, therefore, enters the realm of culture, not because he ought to, but because he wants to. The God-given gift of reason impels him to cultural activity. The believer's commitment to Christ not only gives him a faith but also an outlook, a new outlook within which he sees all the spheres of life.

Fundamentally this is an ethico-religious outlook, wherein the personal meaning of life is affirmed as central. Using Pascal's terminology, the order of charity (i.e., *agape*, love) is higher than mind, and mind is higher than body. While this order was always present in the creation from the beginning, it was not unambiguously revealed until the coming of Christ. The fact of creation indicates both the reality of the object (it is created, and one can love only what is other than oneself), and the reality of the subject (it is not a by-product of nature, but a unique person), as well as the relation of God to nature. The doctrine of creation, moreover, rules as inadequate all secular attempts to explain the world (mechanism, materialism, pantheism, deism, and the like) as well as the assertion that the world is wholly inscrutable. The world is intelligible—this is the grand assumption of all knowledge —but such a belief is justified only if one realizes that things are intelligible because the divine light shines on them. The world is uniform—this is the grand assumption of natural science—but such a belief is justified because the world is the creation of the one true God. The grand assumptions of knowledge, therefore, are justified only by faith in the God and Father of our Lord Jesus Christ, in whom it is revealed that higher than intelligent understanding is love.

Next to the ethico-religious center of man, then, there is nothing more human than the arts and sciences, the products of the human mind as ends, not as the application of the mind to other purposes. The order of mind, one might say, is next to that of love, and the inner core of the uses of mind (arts and sciences) is presupposed in all applications of intelligence (such as the useful arts, applied sciences, and technologies). There is no implication here that mind is excluded from the order of love, for each order

74

takes up into itself the order below it, and consequently we can understand why everything in the order of the mind must serve human life as a whole. Nevertheless, each sphere has relative autonomy, such that a scientist "who does not carry on his researches simply and solely for the sake of truth is no true scientist, and the artist who does not work simply in order to create a work of art is no true artist."[14] Through the order of love we shall not learn how to think, but love should impel us to learn how to think better in order that we might thereby better serve God and fellow men in love. Moreover, we do not come to faith without our minds. The old Lutheran dogmaticians used to speak of faith as consisting of knowledge, assent, and trust (*notitia, assensus,* and *fiducia*). In the last analysis faith is primarily trust, but knowledge and assent are likewise involved.

We grant, then, that life is more important than knowledge; nevertheless knowledge is of great importance, both in life and as knowledge in itself. In culture the mind is exercised upon elements that are ends in themselves, relatively speaking, but also in the state, in marriage, or in one's job, one must exercise his mental abilities. Experience teaches man nothing unless he reflects on his experience. And he must learn by a sort of trial and error method, for he is not God. Therefore, he must pause and reflect before he acts; his life is a constant "withdrawal and return," to use Toynbee's phrase. What the believer's action ought to be in the local community, or the church, or the state—all call for his reflection on the ends of man in these communities. But then he must act, even though he does not have full knowledge or understanding. He must act from confidence in Christ, that is, by faith and hope. All of the orders in which man lives—political, economic, cultural— are provisional, awaiting the final redemption of the coming of our Lord. Then these orders will be fulfilled, for Christ is the fulfillment of the law, not its destroyer. The earth will not be destroyed, but renewed. No work of culture will endure, but culture itself will be fulfilled in that new heaven and new earth.

It is the duty, therefore, of the student who finds himself at a liberal arts college to become acquainted with all the areas of

[14]E. Brunner, *The Divine Imperative,* tr. Olive Wyon (Philadelphia: The Westminster Press, 1947), p. 485.

culture, as well as eventually to concentrate upon one. For the time being the life of learning is his calling. At the same time he lives also in the other spheres of life—as a child of parents, as a citizen of his country, as a member of the Church, and the like. His major task in college is preparation for adult life through learning. The college can equip him in his intelligence primarily; all the other orders help him, along with college, to grow in moral and spiritual stature as he lives in fellowship with God. The aims of a college (to help him learn how to think and to evaluate) are invaluable for the student no matter what his future "job" will be, inasmuch as intelligence is required in any job he may have. But no occupation is an end in itself, and with the interests he has gained in college, he may put his leisure time to more rewarding use. This should not be thought of selfishly, but in terms of service to others. The more educated a man is, the more service he can render. Not only love of man and God will characterize his life, but love of truth, beauty, and goodness as well, and actually this is to love the values that God has placed in His creation. Culture is a symbol of the future truth, beauty, and goodness we shall enjoy in God's new creation.

Therefore, while we would indeed insist that the ethico-religious is essential to man, culture (or the intellectual) follows close behind. It is the *fides quaerens intellectum* ("faith seeking understanding") of Anselm. The personal meaning of life is first, and culture does not enable us to be more personal than the most uncultured of men who know Christ. Even so, the order of mind, the gift of reason, fallible, limited, and obscured though it be, is certainly to be regarded as one of man's most treasured endowments, to be used for the glory of God. Its cultivation is the task of man, not merely in school and college, but also in his leisure hours no matter what the nature of his occupation may be.

4

THE SERVICE OF THE CHRISTIAN LIBERAL ARTS COLLEGE TO THE CHURCH

a. *It provides educated churchmen.* Although many of our colleges were founded to give a basic education for men going into the ministry, the contemporary purpose of education in the Church is considerably broader. That is to say, we believe in liberal education as the indispensable background for community leaders in any occupation, including the ministry. If the sphere of culture is a God-created order, then the Church stands for the best kind of culture, just as it stands for the best kind of economic, political, and marital life. It stands for the best, and although it cannot determine the inner technics of any sphere, the Church knows the ends for which these orders exist and to which the means must be subordinated. Perhaps the best analogy one can use here is that of "conscience." The Church in Norway during the last war spoke of the Church as the "conscience of the state." The Church as the communion of true believers cannot be identified with the secular order, for the Church is a new creation. But as organized, the Church is an institution of this creation, subject to its laws. Although the purpose of the organized Church is to serve the true Church, the organized Church nevertheless stands in an indirect relation to the other created orders, namely, as the "conscience" of them all. In relation to politics or economics, for example, the Church ought to champion and encourage justice, and protest against injustice wherever it occurs. In relation to culture the Church as such does not exist to create culture, but since the Incarnation did not abolish the Creation, the Church defends the ideals of truth and beauty, and protests against untruth and ugliness wherever it appears. Many would insist that the Church ought to be the conscience of these spheres in an official manner; others would say it should be indirect, ethically through the individuals who make up the Church. Either way it is the individual who in particular must work out the implications of the voice of the Church, working for justice here and supporting cultural projects there. The Christian liberal arts college exists to provide the men and women who as members of the Church are also these responsible individuals in the community. Churchmanship and citizenship are all-embracing terms for this aim.

Even the Church itself ought to be an example to others as well as to her own people right within her walls. That is to say, the Church must set a high standard of culture in its own worship,

77

witness, and work. The Church does not witness to God's implanting of beauty in His creation when it constructs ugly church buildings or provides furnishings for them that are contrary to an educated aesthetic judgment. Nor does it witness to this order when a preacher betrays illogical thinking in his sermon. The Church must stand for the best everywhere, whether in building or in thinking. Anything less would be an insult to God's created order. This does not mean that God cannot work His will without a beautiful church or logical thinking, but it does mean that the Church can raise unnecessary obstacles to others if it offends taste and understanding. Here an educated laity can be of invaluable service to a local congregation, and can take the lead, for example, in seeing to it that only the best goes into a Church building. It can also be expected that a pastor's education in liberal arts will be an aid, not a hindrance, to his work. If we believe otherwise, we have no right to continue our belief in the highest possible education of our ministry. The Lutheran Church has never considered ignorance or lack of culture a virtue in its ministry. The minister should be one of the most highly cultured men of his locality, not that he may glory in his cultivated intellect or lord it over others, for this would be a sad misunderstanding of the aim of a liberal education. The really cultured man is not a high-brow snob; he is the kindliest, most considerate of men. He can adapt himself to all people. He knows that intelligence is not an end in itself; only the snobbish intelligentsia believe this. The Church has no place for the latter. Culture is not the end for the minister, but it is a good means. The vices of culture, intellectualism and estheticism, occur when culture is regarded as an end in itself. But the minister should read widely, not merely in theology, lest he become out of touch with his people and with the significant issues of the times.

The Church must likewise have concern for its members' mental culture as well as their moral culture. If the Church does not feel it ought to speak officially, let the members of the Church (and here we think of the Christian college graduate particularly) urge upon the community that it is robbing man of his due if it does not provide certain instruments of culture for them. Libraries, museums, picture galleries, parks—all are as much a need of any community as better sewers and street lamps. The Church must be the conscience of the community not only in respect to politics, then, but also in respect to culture. In both, the education of the Christian liberal arts college ought to be giving its holders a sense of responsibility in the community. All men live by nature in the created orders, but not all men understand the true meaning of these orders. Here is the mission of the Christian college graduate: to let this understanding become known by his thought and actions.

In this way the Christian liberal arts college can help the Church itself to overcome a tragic obscurantism which sometimes appears in opposing faith to knowledge or faith to art—as if somehow knowledge and art were outside the orbit of God's will. The Church dare not make any particular culture its end, or the sphere of culture as such an end, but as long as this creation lasts, the Church does have a responsibility to uphold the order as a God-created order. Even its first task of evangelization and teaching is hindered if people cannot read or understand. Are we in danger of realizing William Temple's warning that our modern mechanical education is producing a generation adept in dealing with things, indifferently qualified to deal with people, and incapable of dealing with ideas? Hence the contention of the British Bishop of Carlisle that "for a revival of religion there is needed a great rebirth of poetry and of the highest literature."[15] Our Church colleges can produce men and women who will never let such things atrophy, and, no more than we make the state an end in itself when we defend good citizenship, no more do we make culture an end in itself when we encourage the cultivation of intelligence and cultural responsibility on the part of believers.

We must not fall into a notion of religious life as separate from secular life. All life is sacred, under God's rule—the Kingdom of God on the left hand (Law, the old creation) and the Kingdom of God on the right hand (Gospel, the new creation). We must not commit the "angelic fallacy" of thinking that faith takes us away from the world. On the contrary we are not to be of the world, but we are to remain in it. We are to use the world, not

---

[15]*Towards the Conversion of England* (Toronto: 1946), p. 13.

abuse it. Therefore, Paul tells people to get back to their jobs. As a Christian a man is not going to read nothing. C. S. Lewis puts it this way:

> If you don't read good books you will read bad ones. If you don't go on thinking rationally you will think irrationally. If you reject aesthetic satisfactions you will fall into sensual satisfactions.[16]

Under the Church's influence, learning and the arts have flourished. The spiritual life is not a renunciation of God's creation; it is rather critical participation in the world out of the love of God and in service to men.

b. *It stands for a Christian philosophy of life.* The theological seminary of the Church is a professional institution, preparing men for the ministry and the teaching of theology. The college has a special place. It is the educational arm of the Church which is engaged in the study of all areas of culture. The universe of knowledge, then (not on the level of the graduate school, however), is the concern of the liberal arts college. But why should the Church be interested in having such institutions?

As C. S. Lewis has said: "If all the world were Christian, it might not matter if all the world were uneducated. But, as it is, a cultural life will exist outside the Church whether it exists inside or not."[17] Therefore, as he argues, for Christians to be uneducated and simple would be to throw down our weapons

> and to betray our uneducated brethren who have, under God, no defence but us against the intellectual attacks of the heathen. Good philosophy must exist, if for no other reason, because bad philosophy needs to be answered. The cool intellect must work not only against cool intellect on the other side, but against the muddy heathen mysticisms which deny intellect altogether.[18]

Bad philosophy needs to be answered, and this means not only in a philosophy department, but in the philosophy that molds the Christian attitude to any particular area of study—in the natural and social sciences and in the humanities. Do our colleges teach sociology and psychology in the same way as a secular university? Or does the essentially Christian philosophy of society, thus the

---

[16]*The Weight of Glory* (New York: Macmillan Company, 1949), p. 46.
[17]*Ibid.*, p. 50.
[18]*Ibid.*

80

Christian notion of man and God as applied to society, affect the teaching? This is only one example, and it could be multiplied throughout the curriculum. Are we giving all students a consciousness of the unity of learning and the organization of truth within a Christian outlook? This is a problem of curriculum and teaching. We know that in secular universities either a naturalistic or a pragmatic theory of education, or at least an indifference to religion in education, is frequently apparent. What does it mean for us to make religion central? Unless the Christian college is providing a leadership that can see life steadily and see it whole within a philosophy of education that makes Christ and His truth central, we are yielding by default to pagan philosophies.

It should be apparent now why the Church has such a stake in liberal education. It is here where the battle of ideas is joined—not in the engineering school, or the business college, or in the occupational training programs. It is in the humanities, the social sciences, and the natural sciences that a Christian philosophy can make a tremendous difference, and where the Christian Church must scrutinize pagan philosophies of culture. In these areas ideas are the important things, and anyone who doubts that ideas make a difference has only to look at the world in our day, split in two by an idea broached by a Karl Marx. In the battle against secularization the Christian liberal arts college can be a mighty arm of the Church. It is no time for weakening the liberal arts program—now is the time for its strengthening up to the limit of our resources and men.

c. *It promotes culture and research.* Lastly, the Christian college also aims to make a contribution to the world at large through the research work of its faculty in particular. It will be unable to command the manifold research facilities of the large university, but it can succeed in doing research on a smaller scale. In some areas it can easily compete with and even excel the larger universities. In the realm of the fine arts, for example, especially music, the Lutheran Church college has made a real contribution to American culture. In some of our colleges truly creative work in the literary and visual arts is being done. But there can also be fundamental research into the basic and general aspects of knowl-

81

edge. In developing and unfolding the implications of Christianity for knowledge the Church college can make a significant contribution to education. The Church college ought to be making some exciting experiments in curricular inter-relationships that might affect all education. Essentially, however, when all is said and done, the Christian college's aim at heart is to be the best college it knows how to be. To give its students the finest possible education is its real task, and the Christian college must always be on guard against what Hoyt Hudson has called the two biggest threats to the small college: vocationalism and the "university ambition."[19] Let the Christian liberal arts college have the courage of its convictions—to be a college of liberal education with a Christian philosophy radiating from its center.

5

CONCLUSION

Today the Christian liberal arts college is a very necessary arm of the Church in the Church's never-ending battle against the secularization of life. The Christian liberal arts colleges of our Church are a standing testimony to the Church's concern for the best culture of its members, a learning that is to be gained within a true community of scholars with a common mission, and a learning that is integrated within the context of the world-view which as Christians we believe to be the only true and valid framework of knowledge. Because cultural expressions are the weapons in the battle of ideas, the Church's stake in liberal education is most crucial. The Church must see in its liberal arts colleges the essential sphere of its mission in higher education, the place where it can make a contribution impossible in any other kind of higher education.

---

[19]*Educating Liberally* (Stanford University, California: Stanford University Press, 1945), p. 108.

Chapter Six

Liberal Education:
Its Character
and Structure

HAVING surveyed the history of liberal education in brief, with special attention to its honored place in the educational thinking of the Church, we may now turn to a systematic approach. What is liberal education? What are the relationships among the liberal studies? Answers to questions like these will help indicate their significance for Christian higher education.

1

NATURE AND CONTENT

In general it may be said that while human learnings are almost infinite in number, the liberal studies[1] constitute the core studies

---

[1] In view of the current use of the phrase "general education," distinctions might helpfully be made between general education, liberal arts, and liberal education.

General education designates a portion of an entire education, namely, that portion which is aimed at an introduction to subject matter which should be every educated man's cultural inheritance short of rigorous scholarly understanding; it should provide an elemental competence in the basic areas of human knowledge and in the use of the intellectual instruments of thinking and expression.

The liberal arts are likewise a part of education. If one follows the earlier established use of the term, it would designate the indispensable arts of inquiry, thought, and communication (languages, logic, mathematics, and methodologies in various areas). The liberal arts in this sense are primarily instrumental and are presupposed (and included if necessary) in general education.

A liberal education includes the liberal arts and general education: that is, competence in the intellectual arts and an introduction to our cultural heritage of the arts and sciences. Liberal education goes further toward a comprehensive understanding of the arts and sciences in depth and inclusiveness, and toward a higher degree of mastery in a selected area.

The two-fold distinction of *disciplines* and *sciences* employed here seeks to avoid the present confusion in the use of the three terms discussed above. At the same time the discussion of liberal education as concerned with disciplines and sciences includes the aims and substance signified by all three of the above definitions.

of these learnings—namely, those learnings that are specifically intellectual in nature. All human learnings presuppose and require the human intellect. Those learnings which focus their attention on the skills and contents of intelligence as such would be more basic than those which, using them as a basis, apply these core studies to other aims. These core studies can be examined, from two viewpoints: (a) as *disciplines* of the human mind, whereby the mind is sharpened and taught how to think and make judgments, and (b) as *sciences* of the human mind, whereby the mind is brought into relationship with knowledge.

a. *As disciplines.* Theodore M. Greene has suggested that we could define the curriculum as the arranging of tasks or disciplines which guide the learner. He lists the following aims of these disciplines:

to communicate clearly	—language, mathematics, artistic idiom
to inquire accurately	—natural and social sciences, historical, philosophical, and literary methodologies
to evaluate wisely	—the humanities
to understand synoptically	—history, philosophy, theology

Logic, the most basic liberal art of all, ought to be specifically included. Its aim as a discipline might be said to be:

to reason validly—logic (and mathematics).

(1) *To reason validly.* No matter what one studies in the liberal curriculum, one must "use" his intellect, and the art that governs this use is *logic.* "If the purpose of liberal education is to form our judgment, then the theory of judgment, which is logic, makes it aware of its own principle."[2] Logic is the common structure of all knowing—whether theoretical or practical. It is the structural coherence of all knowledge, and the formal unity of all scientific learning. It is the basic liberal art, because it aims to put *order* in that which is presupposed by all knowledge—reasoning. As we shall see, it is the basic theoretical science also.

(2) *To communicate clearly.* This is the function of language

---

[2]Gustav E. Mueller, *Education Limited* (Norman, Oklahoma: University of Oklahoma Press, 1949), p. 63.

study, and occurs in both English and foreign language study. Grammar is the study which investigates how a language is put together, how one should read; rhetoric is the study of the way whereby human beings express themselves, whether by writing or speaking. Besides word "symbols," there are other symbols of communication in more specialized media—such as mathematical, musical, and technical notation and artistic idiom, which might be called the "grammars" of these fields.

(3) *To inquire accurately.* The mind is disciplined to make accurate inquiry by the aid of the natural sciences, the social sciences, and also the various methodologies. The natural and social sciences are not viewed here in terms of content, but in terms of ways of knowing. The natural sciences, for example, train the mind in the exacting methods of experimental inquiry. The social sciences train the mind in the methods whereby social phenomena may be described more accurately, such as the case method, sampling, and the like. The various methodologies of other areas—such as in literature, or history, or philosophy—reveal that method is not of a single piece but depends on what is being examined. Literary method, for example, is very often a desperate need of students who find that they do not really know how to analyze a piece of writing.

(4) *To evaluate wisely.* Literature and the other fine arts, ethics, philosophical and theological, and aesthetics help the mind to make more adequate judgments of beauty and ugliness, right and wrong. To study and to become acquainted with the fine arts is both to cultivate one's ability to make aesthetic judgments and to increase one's capacity for aesthetic delight, and thus enhance one's perception of everyday human experience. The arts also illumine human experience through drama, novel, poetry, painting, sculpture, etc., and by so doing strengthen and discipline the imagination, which conditions moral insight. All works of art pass judgment, directly or indirectly, on the world as it is. Ethics is a direct cultivation of the mind to make distinctions between right and wrong, good and evil, by studying the criteria whereby such judgments may be made. Axiology (philosophy of value) is the critical study of the nature, criteria, and status of all values.

85

(5) *To understand synoptically.* The study of history, philosophy, and theology enables the student to get an outlook of the whole, to integrate his study. The integrative, synoptic aspect proper is inculcated by history and philosophy, whereas the integrative center is provided by Christian theology, for the Christian college has been defined as the kind of college that finds its integrating faith and philosophy in the Christian religion. History trains the mind in making synoptic judgments in terms of *time;* whereas philosophy does this in terms of *system.* All things are related in both a temporal and a systematic way. The historian weaves artificially separated strands of life together in the relationship of time. The philosopher seeks to understand human existence and experience in terms of value (axiology and ethics), in terms of knowledge (logic and epistemology, theory of knowledge), in terms of beauty and creativity (aesthetics), and to understand reality as a whole by means of metaphysics (the study of being as being, or the meaning of reality as a whole, not its aspects, which are the provinces of the special sciences). Theology deals with the philosophical questions of the origin and destiny of man and the universe, and answers them in terms of divine revelation. In this manner it trains the mind to see all things and all knowledge from a theological perspective.

In this way the liberal arts curriculum, then, *disciplines* the mind, making it flexible and ready for the problems of life and knowledge.

b. *As sciences.* Secondly, the liberal arts may be regarded from the aspect of content, rather than discipline. In this sense they are "sciences,"[3] or as knowledge as such.

(1) *Logic.* As already indicated, logic is the basic discipline, since reasoning is a prerequisite of all spheres of knowledge. Persons who have never studied logic nevertheless use (or should use) logic in orderly thinking and in making the simplest judgments. But logic is also the most formal of all the sciences in terms of its content, for the formal structure of inference, whether deductive

---

[3]It should be clear to the reader that we use "science" in its original sense, as "knowledge," equivalent to the German word for "science": *Wissenschaft.* Thus there are *Naturwissenschaft* and *Geisteswissenschaft,* "nature" and "mind" sciences. American usage often restricts "science" to the former, but this is quite arbitrary.

or inductive, is a theoretical science. Since it is a normative science, providing norms or criteria for evaluating inferences, it is also a practical science. The very structure of the liberal arts rests upon logical distinctions and methodical thinking: e.g., the descriptive sciences rest upon class concepts abstracted from individual cases; mathematics rests upon quantitative classes abstracted from sense particulars; history rests upon individual concepts and singular propositions. Because it is the basic discipline and the basic science, one may say that logic is the chief liberal art, the prerequisite for all branches of learning.

(2) *Language.* Grammar and rhetoric are the sciences which deal with language, whether English or foreign languages. Grammar comes first—the study of language in its components, learning how to read and understand any given language. The study of rhetoric is concerned with communication through language, written or spoken. Both grammar and rhetoric, then, are necessary for logic, since ideas are symbolized by language. However, logic is not about words, but about ideas, and thus it is as necessary for language study as language is for logic. Both are indispensable for a liberal education. The purpose of a foreign language study is a kind of self-alienation, in a breaking and expanding of one's ordinary habits of perceiving and being.[4] Through it one also becomes acquainted with a culture not his own, and thereby gains perspective about his own culture, not to speak of his own language.

(3) *Mathematics.* This is the science of number, and therefore seeks to trace the relationships between abstract quantities, as in arithmetic, geometry, trigonometry, calculus, and the like. It is the most formal of all the sciences next to logic, being in itself an application of logic to quantitative classes.

(4) *Natural Sciences.* The basic sciences of nature are physics, chemistry, and biology (botany and zoology), which aim at an experimental and systematic understanding of nature by the use of descriptive methods based on logic and observation. Some refer to the physical sciences as "deductive," and the biological sciences

---

[4] *Ibid.*, p. 54.

87

as "correlational."[5] Others use a term like "empiriometric" to refer to the method used by the physical sciences, reserving "empiriological" for the methods of biological science.[6] However we analyze the methods, these sciences are empirical (descriptive) and rational (hypothetical and constructive) in their approach to nature. Besides these descriptive studies of nature, one could also mention at this point both the philosophy of nature and the theology of nature as other approaches to nature, having different aims, of course.

(5) *Social Sciences.* These descriptive sciences—sociology, anthropology, psychology, economics, political science—aim at a systematic understanding of human behavior, subjected to empirical verification, to be sure, but not amenable to the experimental method in all instances. That is why the case method, sampling procedures, questionnaires, etc., are used in the social sciences. These studies are observational and descriptive in nature like the natural sciences. Besides these descriptive studies of human behavior, one could also mention the philosophy and theology of man, which deal normatively with *what man is* essentially, rather than *how he behaves* actually. The evaluational study of human behavior, ethics in particular, would be based upon conclusions as to what man is. The conclusions as to how man behaves suggest means whereby ethical choices can be implemented, but they are not a basis for ethical choice.

(6) *History.* Sometimes history is considered a social science, but at other times it is regarded as belonging among the humanities. Perhaps one may think of it as a bridge between the two areas. It has already been referred to as one of the two synoptic studies of the liberal arts. As the study of recorded events history aims to tie together the complicated strands of life and culture in both a record and interpretation of the past. Some see this connecting link primarily in terms of individuals, and others more particularly in terms of political movements. However this may be, man's past is the object of historical study, enabling a person to gain temporal perspective as well as understanding.

[5]Henry Margenau.
[6]Jacques Maritain.

88

(7) *Literature.* The study of literature also deals with the past, though in a way different from that of the historical approach. Through imaginative re-creation and analysis of the literary creations of the past and present, one finds in artistic form a portrayal of man's greatness and his misery. Poetry, Aristotle said, is truer than history, for it reveals universal truths about persons in their concrete actions and relations with one another. Poetry is the very center of the humanities, as humanities are the center of the liberal arts. Through literature man comes to know himself. Through its study one also comes to know excellence in human writing, felicity of style, and created beauty—but for a liberal education it is the knowledge of man which literature imparts that is most significant.

(8) *The Fine Arts.* The other fine arts (music and the visual arts) also speak the language of beauty, the free creation of form. Man is naturally an artist, but the practical necessities of life tend to overlay his artistic nature to such an extent that one aim of aesthetic education must be to release his artistic nature and let him experience that artistic joy and self-expression are not less important than the performance of routine duties. The work of art humanizes nature, and reveals the fact that nature has values as well as processes. Beauty is one of these values, and the arts impart this heightening of existence in their free creations of the human spirit. All works of art have their aesthetic aspect, but all works of art also pass judgment upon the world as it is and communicate through significant form what the artist has to say. One can hardly be considered educated unless he can see in architecture, painting, and sculpture sensible expression of eternal truths. Music combines the abstractions of mathematics with the most direct appeal to sensible emotion. It is desirable that men be trained to perceive through media other than language or formulae.

(9) *Philosophy.* "All education is philosophical education"[7]— so writes a philosopher, but Cardinal Newman also expressed the same notion. For the aim of liberal education is to help a man realize who he is. This cannot be done without understanding

---
[7]*Ibid.,* p. 116.

what philosophy is, and vice versa. Man is understandable if you know his purpose, what he believes in. Philosophers disagree, it is true, but to live philosophically is to live in reflective dialogue—to examine, criticize, defend, and act out what one believes in. At the heart of philosophy is the quest for what is ultimately real— metaphysics. Man is human because he is metaphysical. Some find ultimate reality in knowledge of nature, others in aesthetic experience, some in matter, others in mind, and still others in numerous other values—but the quest goes on. Philosophy aims to reflect on the meaning of human existence: on the presuppositions of human knowledge in epistemology; on the art of thinking in logic; on values in axiology; on human conduct in ethics; on human self-expression in aesthetics; on reality as a whole in metaphysics. Philosophy is not wisdom, but the love of wisdom, and thus it always has a window open on theology, at the same time that it has its own tasks. Theology cannot dictate metaphysical conclusions any more than it can conclusions in chemistry.

(10) *Theology*. This field of college study is quite commonly called "religion." However the term used here is more accurate. Philosophy and theology have much in common with each other— especially metaphysics and systematic theology. Where the former deals with reality as a whole from the viewpoint of natural reason, the latter deals with the same from the aspect of revelation and this is developed especially by showing the relation of God to reality as a whole. The two also have differences in content. Philosophy deals with natural being in its interrelations (man, nature, and cosmos); whereas theology is interested in the relations of natural being to divine being in the history of salvation and in the victory of God over death and evil.[8] But theology includes more than systematic theology with its corollary study of Christian ethics. It includes study of the Bible, the basis of systematic theology, and Church history as well.

So much, then, for the various liberal arts in terms of their content. However, it might be helpful to point out the distinction between the theoretical (c, 1) and practical (c, 2) sciences. The

---

[8]Paul Tillich, *Systematic Theology* (Chicago: University of Chicago Press, 1951), I, 18-28.

practical sciences include logic and language, but the chief practical sciences are the arts (including literature) and ethics. Thus the other fields, aside from the arts and ethics, would be theoretical sciences. What does this distinction suggest to the Christian college?

c. *Theoretical and Practical Sciences*

(1) *Theoretical sciences.* In teaching the theoretical sciences it is freely admitted in a Christian college that absolute academic neutrality is a myth. A Christian teacher is not under the delusion that he escapes making value judgments or synoptic interpretations. These inescapably enter into a teacher's statements even when he is not aware of them. It is the duty of the Christian teacher, there-fore, to become aware not merely of Christian ethics but also of philosophy and theology as well. It would not be impertinent to suggest that every Christian teacher should become both a lay philosopher and a lay theologian. He should be aware of the epistemological and metaphysical presuppositions of his own subject matter; he should seek to understand the Christian philosophy of his subject matter. Many teachers, even in Christian colleges, are unwitting positivists, making no attempt to relate their field to philosophical and theological contexts, but hoping that their private faith along with chapel exercises plus religion classes will overcome this deficiency. The result is the unfortunate one of secular education in the classroom "plus"—the plus being the teacher's faith (private), and the public profession of the college—which to the student can only appear as irrelevant to the subject matter he studies.[9] Certainly the aim of the Christian college is contrary to this pathetic bifurcation of faith and knowledge. Teachers whose knowledge in their field is expert and mature often combine this with theology so naive as to be a positive danger. Value judgments and synoptic interpretations are perhaps more apparent in the social sciences and humanities, but they are not avoidable in the other academic studies. To eliminate "education plus," Christian educators must become more aware of philosophical and theological presuppositions in their thought and teaching.

---

[9]Martin Hegland, *Christianity in Education* (Minneapolis: Augsburg Publishing House, 1954), p. 2.

(2) *Practical sciences.* What has been said above about the teaching of the theoretical sciences would apply here too, but we wish to call attention to some other problems in connection with the practical sciences (ethics and fine arts). The practical order was divided by Aristotle into two spheres, the sphere of action and the sphere of making. Action is the use to which we put our freedom, which depends upon our will. According to Christian teaching, however, the unregenerate will is bound in slavery to sin. This does not mean that man has no good left in him,[10] nor that he can make no choices, but rather that his choices are all made within the sphere of law, or morality. Thus he can never satisfy God, for no man can keep the law perfectly. According to Christian thought human action is good only when it is freed from the law and free for the "spontaneity of the good." We attain an approximation of this in the "first fruits" of the indwelling of the Holy Spirit, although we are at the same time the natural man. Therefore, goodness must be evaluated religiously, not merely morally. The Christian still must observe the law, but he is no longer "under" it, no longer under its curse. Christian ethics cannot by its very nature be something merely "learned" in the classroom—it must be learned more adequately in the everyday discipleship of the believer. One cannot conclude that this means the denial of criteria or standards, on the one hand, or that it means a self-regarding ethic on the other. Freed from concern over one's own salvation, the believer, under the constraint of gratitude, is free to turn toward his neighbor in love, as Luther argued in his *Treatise on Christian Liberty.* For the believer, then, religion and ethics are inseparable, although for purposes of study and reflection one may study dogmatics and ethics separately.

In measuring action from a purely human viewpoint, however, we do judge on the basis of law, for everything human is under the reign of law. The Church calls its own people as well as the pagan to obedience to the laws of creation. The Christian's ethical behavior ought to exceed that of the law's requirements, but he

---

[10]This is the labored charge made so often by Roman Catholic thinkers against Luther and Calvin, e.g., John Wise, *The Nature of the Liberal Arts* (Milwaukee: The Bruce Publishing Company, 1947), p. 193. If man had no good left in him, he would be the devil, or even worse, non-existent.

can do no less than the law. Christianity did not introduce the ethical consciousness into human life. Natural ethics or philosophical ethics exists in men's spontaneous or reflective value judgments and can profitably be studied by itself or in preparation for study of Christian ethics with its unique answer. Natural ethics may be taught indirectly by reference to its embodiment in literature, social studies, and philosophy as well as directly in philosophical ethics.

As to the fine arts ("finished" arts, not used primarily for other purposes), we find ourselves in the province of human making or productive action, not primarily in the sense in which we use our freedom (ethics), but in relation to the *thing produced*. This kind of action may be regarded as good if the work produced conforms to the end peculiar to it. Aesthetics, then, is the normative science of making. Art is intellectual because in its method of working one perceives the pondering, the brooding, and the maturing of the creative imagination. The artist desires to impress his idea upon a given matter, whether this matter be metal, sounds, building materials, pigments, people, or even concepts. Thus the arts are wider than the fine arts, although the latter are usually the arts included among the liberal arts because of their intrinsic value and their more intellectual character—that is, the products are ends in themselves and have intelligible substance. Plato would have used the word "artisan" rather than "artist" in connection with the applied arts. The work of beauty, then, is an end in itself—it is the work of an artist; works dedicated to utilitarian purposes are the work of the artisan. Architecture is on the borderline here, for it is the most functional of the fine arts, and the most artistic of things utilitarian. Because the work of beauty is intellectual, the fine arts, including literature, are subsumed under the liberal arts.

Education as a subject matter is really a practical science, and thus an art. It aims at the "making" of men and women, or as one sometimes hears the word, "molding" them. Such an art must respect the nature of its materials, however, for the personalities of the men and women it seeks to mold transcend the usual kind of material at the disposal of an art.

Knowing, then, concerns what is; action and making are governed by what ought to be. The fact that there are such normative sciences of these realms, viz., logic, ethics, and aesthetics, reveals that man does not, as a matter of fact, reason correctly, act rightly, or create beautifully. Let both scientist and artist then, realize they are first men before they are scientist or artist. That is why ethics is the most important of the normative sciences, and for the Christian, this means Christian ethics.

Why is there no Christian logic nor Christian aesthetics? The answer, we believe, lies in the fact that our thinking and making are structured by the laws of creation, and the ends of these studies (aside from theology) lie either in understanding creation or in creating within the bonds laid down by creation. Our moral action, on the other hand, is under the imperative of the Gospel. The believer is a new creation, and must endeavor to express the motivations and qualities of the new creation. The Gospel does not abolish natural knowledge or natural art, but sets them within a new context, rooted in "the underlying teleologic structure of the universe."[11] Thus they are no longer independent realms of the human mind, for the Incarnation has shown us in an unambiguous way what God's purpose is with this world. Thereby a Christian philosophy is made possible, whereby there can be a Christian criticism of art and literature and a Christian interpretation of the natural and social sciences.

2

PURPOSE

The liberal arts are called arts, although they include both theoretical and practical sciences, because they aim to "make" or to "produce" a certain kind of mind. The purpose of liberal education is to form the intellect—and by so doing, to set it free, which is what is meant by "liberal" in the phrase "liberal education."

The liberal artist, then, is a person who is making his mind, and the liberal educator is the educator who is interested in providing the opportunity for persons to become liberal artists. To reiterate, the aim of liberal education is the formation of the mind so that the

---

[11]Otto Piper, *God in History*, p. 31.

student may gain an intellectual grasp on human experience. This should have a decisive effect on both his being and his action. Liberal education is both an education in the practical (or artistic) rules of good thinking (discipline, means) and an education in the acquisition of knowledge, by a real grasping of truth and beauty and goodness (the ends of intellectual effort). Christian liberal education aims not only to develop a free mind by forming the intellect, but also to produce a person who is devoted with his free mind to the furtherance of Christian values. Nevertheless, its primary aim is intellectual, or it could not be called "education." By inculcating precision of thinking and the understanding of truth, beauty, and goodness, the liberal arts, Christian or secular, aim at the liberated mind, freed from shoddy thinking and undiscerning judgment and in Christian education freed *for* service to God and mankind.

3

THE LIMITATION OF AREAS OF STUDY IN LIBERAL EDUCATION

By restricting its attention to the core learnings, liberal education is in a position to accomplish its end. It makes no attempt to study everything, for such an attempt would be doomed to failure so far as education is concerned. The result would be a formless, not a formed, mind. Thus there is a narrowness about liberal education, a narrowness that is so wide in its implications, however, that it is a liberating narrowness. In order to form the mind, liberal education rules out certain areas, not as being inferior to the liberal arts, but as being exterior to them. Training of every kind is not the same as education. Training deals with *man as a special function* within society. Education concerns the *essential man* by developing and informing his elemental human powers. To say this implies nothing against training, but it does suggest that we do not confuse essential education with functional training. Liberal education is sometimes impugned as "useless," an epithet which identifies the useful with the utilitarian. There are, however, activities that are not utilitarian but are far from useless or valueless![12]

---

[12]Cf. quotations from Robert D. Leigh, Chapter IV, p. 56.

That a formed mind is useful to society and to the individual himself should hardly be questioned. Liberal education is the study of those activities of man for the sake of which everything else is done—activities concerning man as man, namely, his intellectual, moral, and spiritual interests. We need to learn how to do well what we are called upon to do as moral agents, or to do well what we must for the cultivation of our minds. This is not only preparation for an educated citizenry, but for enlightened churchmanship as well. Both essential education and training for a specific function are needed, but education is both prior to and indispensable to any training at its best.

There is also a limitation in liberal education due to its intellectual nature. It does not propose to encompass the whole of a man's life. Man is more than an intellectual being. He is also a moral and spiritual being. Although liberal education helpfully includes the formal study of ethics and religion, such education is not indispensable to moral goodness and religious devotion. There are many people of both virtue and sainthood who have not gone to college. Liberal education is concerned with man as an intellectual, moral, and spiritual being, and as "education" it must perforce deal with all of these aspects of man from an *intellectual* approach, the approach of intelligible teaching, learning, and understanding. By an intellectual approach not everything about man's moral and spiritual nature is grasped. Ethics and theology can be taught and can be very helpful in a student's moral and religious life, but the student as a moral, religious person is not thereby automatically improved. An educated person ought to be aware of the more extensive implications and profounder aspects of ethics and theology, and this can be done through classroom instruction; in addition, however, he needs, as does any person, moral experience and religious living to discipline the will and bring knowledge and action into effective harmony. Christian ethics would point out that the power of the Holy Spirit is indispensable to the Christian life—which means not only that the study of ethics is necessary, but also that hearing the Word of God, partaking of the Sacrament of the Altar, prayer, meditation, and active response are necessary. Thus there is a distinction between instruction and preaching. Such instruction is instruction about the Church and what the Church has recognized and confessed to be the true faith. "As such, instruction of youth has to teach, not to convert, not to 'bring to a decision,' and to that extent not to proclaim."[13] The crossing of the boundary line into proclamation will be unavoidable, but it is not normative, since the teaching of ethics and theology is science, instruction, and investigation.

The problem here is that of a distinction between knowing and being what one knows, between learning and becoming what one has supposedly learned. Liberal education modestly operates primarily in the sphere of knowledge: teaching and learning. For this reason liberal education disclaims for its central teaching task any grand purpose to shape the entire human being. The Church, the chapel, the dormitory, the playing field, the commons—all of these help to form a human being. Let the center of the college, the classroom, do what it is capable of doing—form the intelligence.

Even the campus educates, and college administrations and faculties must be concerned with what kind of education the campus is giving. It is not the function of the campus to educate the intelligence—this is the function of the classroom. But any college is a campus as well as a classroom. Therefore, in its community life, a Christian college in particular has a duty to promote a favorable atmosphere, moral and spiritual, for the growth of its members. Its campus must be conducive to study and promote the Christian spirit in college life, defined as: humility, unselfishness, helpfulness, generosity, objectivity, and freedom from envy in personal relations among both students and faculty.[14]

As a *community* of scholars, both junior (students) and senior (faculty), the college campus must be a place where there is concern for the social competence and moral character of its members. As a community of *scholars* the primary basis for unity in the college community should be the college's belief in and propagation of the "intellectual virtues." Baron von Hügel listed these virtues as: candor, courage, intellectual honesty, scrupulous ac-

[13]Karl Barth, *Church Dogmatics,* trans. G. T. Thomson (Edinburgh: T. and T. Clark, 1936), I, 1, 55.

[14]A. John Coleman, *The Task of the Christian in the University* (New York: Association Press, 1947), p. 19.

97

curacy, chivalrous fairness, endless docility to facts, disinterested collaboration, unconquerable helpfulness, perseverance, manly renunciation of popularity and easy honors, love of bracing labor and strengthening solitude.[15]

The college as a whole must accept responsibility for the moral and spiritual formation of its students, since the classroom with its intellectual investigation of morals and religion is only a part, albeit central, of the whole. Dormitory life, social functions, eating places, and the like, must strive to promote a true collegiate community life—an integration of intellectual, ethical, and religious interests. In this connection the all-too-prevalent cafeteria system in our Church colleges might be called in question for not providing that community aspect which ought to characterize the mealtime in a college community. But all of these aspects are secondary to the central aim of the college—the formation of the human mind. This is the college's *raison d'etre*, without which it would not be a college at all. Unless the central aim is being met, especially by means of a top-grade faculty and a solid curriculum, then the other features would be quite meaningless.

The self-limitation of liberal education suggests also that education does not end in college. Liberal studies prepare a man for a lifelong devotion to them. A liberal college recognizes that life cannot be composed merely of liberal studies—it only insists that for four years the student devote himself to them as if they were everything. Only in this way can mastery of these arts and sciences be assured. Furthermore, these arts and sciences are so demanding that extraneous studies should not be allowed to crowd them out. Not all parts of man are of equal importance—his dress, his food, his health, his business, important as they are, are not as important as his intellectual, moral, and spiritual nature. The studies that occupy themselves with these aspects of man are the liberal studies—therefore, let the liberal arts college be what it is supposed to be. Let it have the opportunity to concentrate all its energies on the infinitely important task of teaching the student how to think, how to communicate thought, how to make accurate inquiry, how to discriminate values, how to see relationships

---

[15]Quoted in *ibid.*, p. 58.

—how, in fact, to become an integral human being, with an intellect that is formed rather than formless.

4

THE STRUCTURE OF LIBERAL EDUCATION

We turn now to an examination of the hierarchy of structure and interrelationships existing between the various liberal studies. This might be described as the relation between the inner, central studies of man and God to the outer, less central studies. The "inner to outer" relationship is what Brunner calls "the law of closeness of relation."[16] Man's relationship to God is central; next comes his relationship to man, then to nature, and finally to the symbols whereby he expresses himself (logic, language, mathematics). The latter are *basic* studies, but not *central* studies.

According to this structure of closeness of relation, the study of religion is central in the Christian liberal arts college, for man's ultimate concern is God and His relationship to man, and central to religious study itself are systematic theology (or Church doctrine) and Christian ethics. Next comes philosophy, for "the coordination of the various spheres of life is the task, not of the theologian, but of the philosopher."[17] Also expressive of man's relationship to man are literature, history, the other arts, and the

---

[16]Emil Brunner, *Revelation and Reason*, tr. Olive Wyon (Philadelphia: The Westminster Press, 1946), p. 383. The nearer anything lies to the center of existence —man's relation to God and the being of the person—the greater is the disturbance of rational knowledge by sin. The disturbance is the greatest in theology, the least in the exact sciences, and zero in the formal (logic and mathematics). Thus we can distinguish Christian conceptions of the good, freedom, community, and God especially. In this way rational knowledge is corrected by faith. In theology it is no mere correction, of course, but a substitution. In mathematics or logic this correction disappears altogether, except when we are concerned with their foundations. In the sphere of law, the State, history, and the like, purely rational knowledge and faith are necessarily intermingled. When we are concerned with human beings as persons, therefore, rational knowledge needs correction by faith. *Passim*, pp. 383 ff. "In other words, the more we are concerned with the world, *as* the world, the more autonomous is the reason; but the more we are concerned with the world as God's Creation, the less autonomy is left to the reason." P. 384. Cf. chart at end of this chapter.

[17]*Ibid.*, p. 395. In the same connection Brunner writes of the relation of theology to philosophy in this wise: "They both stand under Christ, the one in an inner, and the other in an outer, circle; the one with the task of understanding the message of Jesus Christ in its inmost depths of meaning, and thus of purifying the proclamation of the Gospel and ever anew basing it upon the Word of revelation; the other with the task of making clear the truth of faith in order to throw light on the problems of Christian living in the world, and to help them to deal with these problems in a creative way." P. 396.

99

social sciences. In the next sphere of relationship come the natural sciences, and finally, the basic studies of mathematics, language, and logic.

No judgment is made by virtue of this hierarchic arrangement as to the dignity of one's academic specialization. The Christian concept of vocation contains the view that all vocations are on an equal level of dignity before God. Yet this does not remove the fact that some areas of knowledge are of more universal significance to all men than some other areas. For example, no matter what one's future occupation, he will be reading literature, listening to music, conversing, and constantly judging, acting, and thinking within the context of a philosophy of life and a theological understanding of the world. He will require understanding of these areas more than he will the descriptive understanding of human behavior or of nature, notwithstanding the importance of the descriptive sciences. The major problems of man are moral and spiritual. If one asks about the nature of the good state, how can one answer the question unless he first inquires into the nature of man and the ends of life in theology and philosophy, and then moves to the mastery of the political wisdom of the race in history, ending up with the more technical aspects of the question in political science and sociology? Logic, ethics, and aesthetics rank high because they are the normative sciences of the human intelligence.

If one is to secure a "formed" education, then, with some structure to it, the curriculum cannot be a mere encyclopedia of sciences, where the student, in what Nicholas Murray Butler referred to as "the rabbit theory of education," roams about nibbling here and there at whatever attracts or tempts.

5

CRITICISMS OF LIBERAL EDUCATION ANSWERED

In discussing some rather common criticisms, the criticism will be stated first and then the reply to it.

a. *Lack of Character Training.* It has been argued that the emphasis upon intelligence, upon "book larnin," neglects moral and spiritual factors. The duty of an educational institution of

100

the Church is to train character, to make disciples of Christ, not to develop the so-called "free mind."

Reply. It is not the emphasis upon intelligence, but rather a slighting of any systematic study of values (axiology, personal ethics, and social ethics) in the college that causes this aspect to be missed. Nevertheless, as mentioned before, liberal education does not presume to shape a man's character totally. The campus, the Church, the community are also instruments of this purpose. The primary aim of a college remains intellectual. President Wilson, when president of Princeton University, used to say that the job of education is not to train character directly, but indirectly, by insisting that students give devoted time and attention to their essential work in college—study and learning. Character is a by-product, not a result of self-cultivation. The Lutheran idea of calling is similar to Wilson's notion, with its belief that character is a result of devotion to one's calling. The calling of the college and of the college student is primarily intellectual.

It ought to be emphasized, however, that moral and religious values are also essential to the work of the thinker himself. Some moral qualities are essential even to intellectual understanding (the "intellectual virtues" mentioned before). The moral attitude with which one takes up his study makes a difference, especially in the humanities and social sciences. Much of the sterility of modern academic thought is due to defective moral attitude such as indolence, pride, resentment, or distrust.[18] The student must be faced with moral issues on the campus, and led to a life purpose. This means he must see that moral and religious issues are deeply important, whether in the natural sciences, social studies, fine arts, philosophy, and theology, or in campus life.

b. *Lack of Balance.* The emphasis on intelligence in liberal education is too one-sided. The Hebrew-Christian tradition does not believe that it is intelligence that makes man human, but rather the fact that man is created in the image of God. Then why should the Christian liberal arts college neglect manual training, applied sciences, and the like?

---

[18]Dietrich von Hildebrand, "Conception of a Catholic University," in *The University in a Changing World, a Symposium,* ed. W. M. Kotschnig (London: Oxford, 1932).

Reply. The Christian college agrees with the premise, but not with the conclusion of this criticism. The fact that man is created in God's image is what basically separates him from the rest of creation, for it means that the call of God comes to man, asking for response. The dignity of human personality is not grounded in an abstract element common to all men, but is grounded upon the calling of God. Not reason, but self-giving love is what is truly human. In God's sight all men are equal and all occupations ennobled. The Christian liberal educator has no doubt of this but would make this point: such a viewpoint does not rule out the fact that intelligence governs action, soul governs body, and the liberal college has never tried to be all things for all men—its emphasis has been intellectual because the mind of man needs devoted, concentrated attention.

Reason, therefore, has a function in human life that reveals its place next to the more central ethico-religious responsibilities of a human person. By reason man has provided himself with a civilization—the technical use of reason in affairs of state, economics, agricultural and industrial techniques, and the like. By creative reason man has also created what we call culture (not in the anthropological sense)—that is, the arts and sciences, institutionalized as all human things must be in education and voluntary social organizations (book club, music club, and others) rooted in man's intellectual nature. Liberal education is therefore concerned with culture in terms of the arts and sciences. The desire to create culture is implanted in man by the Creator. It is a gift, and because it is a gift, it is a task also, due to the fact that apart from culture man "has no right to exist, because otherwise he does not realize his God-given purpose in creation. Man's rational nature is given to him in order that he may use it."[19] Reason is opposed to God only when it makes itself God, an end in itself *for human life.* Liberal education is only a relative end for life, therefore, but the end for a college. The ideas and values of culture, revealed in the arts and sciences, are not absolutes. They are subordinate to the personal meaning of life revealed in Christ. Reflection is subordinate though necessary to the personal, ethico-religious sphere of life

---

[19]E. Brunner, *The Divine Imperative*, p. 484.

(not to theology or ethics as sciences, for they are reflections also). Liberal education chooses for a time to concentrate on the core of learning, thereby to prepare the mind of man for any activity through disciplined intellectual power and knowledge. The liberal arts student must always beware of becoming either an "intellectual" or an "esthete" (the two dangers in the study of science and art). That is why the college as a whole must be emphatic that the ethico-religious meaning of life is the essential aspect of human life, but at the same time, the specific calling of the student in college is learning, just as his calling as a laborer would be to do his labor well. Thus, for a time the student must be onesidedly intellectual, devoting his time and energy to learning. It is a restricted task, without question, but such a limitation of scope is necessary if the student is to be a student and not to disperse his mental capacities in every direction. If he is to develop his powers of intellect, the student must *be* a student.

c. *Liberal Education is Snobbish.* The very idea of "liberal" as opposed to servile is but a relic of contempt for people who work with their hands, which is Hellenic, not Christian, in origin and spirit. The Hebrew-Christian tradition has no such fastidiousness and does not believe that work must be interesting or a means of self-expression. Work is drudgery, toil, and man must earn his bread by the sweat of his brow. Liberal education ignores the Lutheran conception of calling or vocation by such an attitude. Everything is on the same level.[20]

Reply. Liberal education is not "snobbish," although it is aristocratic. It is aristocratic because it does presuppose good intelligence, and liberal education on the college level (not on the secondary and primary level, however) is not intended for everyone. The Gospel does not abolish natural knowledge—it confirms it, but puts it in a new framework of the purpose of God. The liberal arts student should not be snobbish if he realizes that all callings are equal in the sight of God *as far as the person is concerned.* This does not mean that there are not responsibilities that are more important in human life than others—those of the head

---

[20]This and the next two criticisms are taken from Sir Walter Moberly, *The Crisis in the University.*

103

of a state as compared with those of a clerk. The liberal college is just as valid an institution as a trade school or technological institute. The concept of calling does not do away with the fact that liberal education is the very core learning of mankind. The intelligence of man must be used in whatever area one chooses to work; therefore a liberal education is central to all learning. A liberal college student or teacher should have no delusion that there is something morally or spiritually better about him because he is at a liberal arts college. He should thank God for the gift of intelligence and the opportunity and obligation to develop this intelligence for the service of mankind in the sight of God.[21] A bootblack is just as important as a professor in the sight of God, but this does not mean it is a toss-up as to whether a man becomes a bootblack or a professor. One's talents and upbringing are usually a good index of one's occupation (although we must admit that economic injustice prevents many with good minds from entering college). Although the problem of high school education is not ours in this essay, we might comment that we deplore the increasing tendency to rob high school students of the liberal arts education they all deserve on that level.

To say that the liberal arts are Greek in origin and we are heirs of the Hebrew-Christian tradition, and therefore must give up the liberal arts ideal, is a *non sequitur*. As indicated before, Christianity does not abolish the order of natural knowledge. That the liberal arts may be Greek in origin does not mean they are Greek in nature—they are human studies, and the very order of human learning. "Christ has not abolished natural knowledge and secular philosophy, but these can no longer be regarded as independent realms of the human mind. They yield true knowledge only within the framework of Christian philosophy."[22] The Christian philosophy of liberal education sets the liberal arts within a new framework, but they remain the central human arts. We simply realize that intellectuality is not "the" end *of life,* and that culture and all orders of creation are subordinated to God and His saving purpose.

---

[21]"The really eminent person may recognize that, in one or more respects he towers above those of lesser talents, but he never forgets that a talent is a loan from heaven, not a license for pride and vain glory." Howard Vincent O'Brien, in "All Things Considered," Chicago *Daily News,* January 13, 1938.

[22]Otto Piper, *God in History,* p. 32.

d. *Liberal Education is Plutocratic.* Since liberal education requires leisure, it requires people who do not have to worry about bread and butter. Since most of our students come from lower middle class homes, what right have we to insist on a purely liberal arts curriculum in the face of this? Is not liberal education essentially a "luxury" education?

Reply. Liberal education is perhaps no more and quite likely less expensive than any other education or training. In fact, modern technology makes the technological institute a very expensive operation, indeed. The applied sciences are more expensive in terms of equipment than the laboratory and classroom of the liberal arts college.

What of the student? For one thing, pre-professional students are expected to secure an education before they enter professional training. Many technological firms and industries are now coming to prefer an educated man who can be trained on the job rather than a purely technical school graduate, inasmuch as the liberally educated man is more likely to have a disciplined and flexible mind, more capable of adjusting to new developments and situations than a technological graduate.

More important, however, one's conception of education enters into the picture on this question. Unless one believes it is important for men to learn what man is, and thereby to approximate to a fuller human life—by studying nature, man, and God, by learning how to think, how to read, how to write—unless one believes in these, then he, of course, will not support liberal education. Liberal education depends upon a philosophy of man that regards a person as more than a function for which he is to be trained—more than merely a lathe-operator, craftsman, clerk, scientist, or artist—regards him as a rational, moral, spiritual being: a man.

The term "school" comes from the Greek word *skole,* meaning leisure. It requires leisure to cultivate the intellect. The question is: Is it worth the money to secure the requisite leisure for study of the eternal problems of man—the moral, intellectual, and spiritual problems? One will never merely be a man with a job—he will be a person, a citizen, a husband, a churchman, a man with leisure also. What kind of man will he be?

e. *Liberal Education is Remote from Reality.* The Church must ever be close to her people and to their needs. But the liberal arts college in the Church is remote from reality. It ignores the production and distribution in which the majority of the population are engaged, and especially the nearly 70% rural population of the Evangelical Lutheran Church. It does not send students back to the farms, or even prepare them for farming. It does not directly prepare enough students for occupations. The liberal arts college moves too much in the sphere of intellect, divorced from reality, discussing literature, history, philosophy, theology, and other impractical subjects.

Reply. This type of evaluation reminds one of the grocer mentioned by Sir Walter Moberly. He told the university authorities: "Don't teach my boy poetry; he's going to be a grocer."[23] This assumes that man is only a worker, and that education is meant to make him only a worker. Since a complex technical civilization has need of division of labor, the argument goes, we must make the colleges great factories for the manufacture of specialists. On the contrary, education is aimed at men in their essential humanness rather than at men as social-economic functions, and specialism may be said to be a malady of civilization. We easily become like cogs in a gigantic machine in our highly developed society. This should not be taken as normative, however. Specialization is needed for a function, but man was not meant for it—he is the only non-specialized animal. Biologically speaking this is quite clear. There is scarcely a creature that does not excel man in respect of some physical characteristic. The specialized limbs and functions of animals, however, render them ill-adapted to unaccustomed circumstances. The hand of man is neither a paw nor a hoot, but precisely because of this non-specialization it is useful over a wider area. Man's body is soft and has no protecting fur. His young are helpless much longer than those of any animal. Why has man survived? Because of his creative adaptability which is the direct outcome of his non-specialization. He creates artificial limbs in cranes and elevators, trains and motors, to take the place of legs, airplanes to take the place of wings. The increasing specialization

---

[23]*Crisis in the University,* p. 58.

of functions in modern society is leading man dangerously near to an "insect society." Of course, if man is no more than a biological being, then the more specialization the better.[24]

A man's paid occupation at best has meaning and satisfaction which are set in a wider context of value. But a man's occupation is not the end of life, nor is it his whole life-work. With the growth of specialism and the functionalizing of men, fewer men find significance in their occupation than in an age of craftsmen. When men work to become free from labor, they have "spare time." More positively, they may labor because their work has larger meaning and also because they may thereby gain leisure for the "generalized" life of man. This leisure is primarily to be exercised within the sphere of the home, but also in Church, political, and cultural responsibilities in the community at large. Leisure also means having time in which to play as well as to work, but this ought to be understood as re-creation rather than as mere diversion or temporary escape. Leisure is not spare time, time to kill, nor pastime. Leisure is the time we have in which "we can discharge our obligation to acquire every human excellence which can grace a human person."[25] Liberal education has more than incidental significance in such a positive approach to a man's work and leisure time.

Why should even farmers have a liberal education? As with all men, not only that they might thereby understand their daily tasks in a wider setting of meaning of values, but also that they might gain intellectual precision and understanding and learn interests which could hold their attention in their leisure hours. Farming is their specialty, their calling so far as their occupation is concerned. But no more than any other labor is the farmer's calling merely one of farming. He too is a man, and it is in his leisure hours that the farmer like anyone else should be concerned with basic human problems. The Danish Folk Schools found that the major interests of the young farmers gathered there were such subjects as history, literature, philosophy, and theology. These are "human" matters with which all men are concerned. Those

---

[24]C. E. M. Joad, *Decadence* (London: Faber and Faber Limited, 1948), pp. 348 ff.
[25]Mortimer J. Adler, "The Use of Leisure," *The Gadfly*, March, 1952, p. 3.

churches which are heavily rural in constituency might take a hint from the Danes and support cultural activities even within the congregations themselves, by establishing Church libraries and the like. Our forefathers were not wrong in setting up liberal arts colleges despite the fact that the Church was rural. They seem to have understood what education meant.

Liberal education does not deny the place of work. But we do not need to go to school to learn how to work. Apart from an apprentice system, we need schools to train men for the learned professions, but not for the ordinary jobs of an industrial society.

We need to go to school, not in order to learn how to earn a living, but in order to learn how to use the life for which we are going to earn a living—to learn how to occupy ourselves humanly, to live our leisure hours well, and not to play them all away, or seek to amuse ourselves to the point of distraction or boredom.[26]

Nor are the liberal arts irrelevant for one's work. As Mark van Doren has pointed out, the liberal arts are the most practical possession men have, and "they proceed by method, not by knack."[27] Literature, history, philosophy, arts, and sciences—these are far from being impractical subjects. The intellect is sharpened and enlightened for any kind of work, and in a changing society this is an important consideration. It would be instructive to canvass graduates of any given college ten years after graduation to ascertain how many are in the work they started out in. Augustine's ideal ought to be ours, when he said that his education had given him the power to read anything that was written, to understand anything he heard said, and say anything he thought. Such an education is an invaluable possession, something not lost by a change of job. Liberal education equips the mind for any end. "College is not the final school. But it is the school that makes possible any end."[28] When war threatens on the horizon and rival ideologies threaten our very way of life, it is not job-training that is our first concern, but rather the kind of educated persons we are in ourselves.

Furthermore, liberal education is not interested in educating "gentleman amateurs" but rather "enlightened experts," although

---

[26]*Ibid.*
[27]*Liberal Education,* p. 75.
[28]*Ibid.,* p. 100.

108

experts in the rather limited areas that fall within the scope of liberal education. Liberal education includes both a general education and a concentration within a certain subject matter. Thus a student may choose to concentrate on physics, chemistry, biology, history, sociology, English, art, or philosophy. The reason why liberal educators protest the intrusion into liberal arts colleges of specialties like nursing, home economics, coaching, music education, and the like (as majors) is that these areas are essentially professional in nature, and with their emphasis on skills and techniques require too much of the student's time in the accomplishment of their professional objectives.

Perhaps some day we should establish on the campuses of our liberal arts colleges various institutes of one sort or another—as in home economics, nursing, social work, parish deaconess training, Fifth-year Education, but we ought never make the mistake of thinking of these as part of liberal education, nor should we permit them to displace liberal education. It is a genuine fear on the part of many educators that the constant addition of non-liberal subjects to the curriculum of our colleges is reducing the number of students, particularly women, who come to the college for an education. It is also strange that these far more costly occupational subjects are permitted to come upon the campus and make such a disproportionate demand upon the educational budgets of both time and money. Therefore this question is pertinent: Can we, without the above suggested, afford them economically and educationally?

f. *Liberal Education is Hypocritical.* In the medieval university the arts were only preliminary studies for the professional schools. Therefore, we should not make the liberal arts an end, as we are doing when we have only liberal arts colleges in the Church.

Reply. No Christian liberal arts college regards itself as an end in itself. On each of the campuses there are several pre-professional curricula, and faculty and administration do not despise the professions. It may, however, be questioned whether the pre-professional curricula are really necessary. The medical schools today are engaged in intensive self-searching on this very question, wondering whether it is not enough to ask the colleges to send them well-educated men, rather than "pre-medical students." The same holds for other professional schools.

This criticism really implies that the Church ought to establish a university, with several graduate schools. There are many educators in the Church, however, who feel it would be unwise for us to establish a university. We would lack the "universal" exchange of opposing ideas and forces that one can meet in the secular university. This is a problem requiring much thought, and not within the scope of this study.

Suffice it to say, then, that the liberal arts colleges do prepare students in an important way for any profession they may desire to enter, and/or if there is professional training on the campus, as for teaching, it is the kind of professional training that does not conflict with the liberal education program (although if the states continue to require more Education courses, a tendency deplored by many officials of the public schools but apparently succeeding with a majority of them, then a five-year program may be necessary for those who plan to teach).

g. *Liberal Education Fails to Liberate.* Liberal education pretends to "liberate," but actually it simply enables a person to become more clever, which, if he is still an unbeliever bound in his sins, only enables him to sin more skillfully. The mind is not really liberated, therefore, but is still enslaved.

Reply. The Christian college would probably argue that it is true that the secular liberal arts college cannot hope to liberate because it fails to set knowledge within a Christian philosophy. Knowing that she often fails to do it herself, the Christian college intends to set knowledge within the context of a Christian philosophy. Even if a successful curriculum were set embodying such an ideal, this would not guarantee success, of course. The student may fail to catch the vision raised before him, or the teachers themselves may fail to grasp it or communicate it. The learning process is not infallible in itself. Of course, liberation refers to the mind in this context. But the Christian would argue that any "liberation" short of the whole person's liberation is not real freedom. Only "justification by faith" truly liberates the person. A careful education can give a man precision of thought and an enlightened understanding, but it may have failed to bring him and his thoughts into subjection to Christ. Certainly such a person would still be caught in his own sins, and be made a more clever person, but not necessarily a better one. Thus no education really liberates except within a Christian philosophy. A liberal education can free the mind from muddle-headedness and laziness of thought, and from mistaken judgments and prejudices generally, but in its concern for the student as a person, the Christian college will not neglect the true liberation of the person through faith in Christ.

THE ORDER OF CULTURE

The Order of Culture is that order in which man's intellect is a relative end in itself—in the main, the arts, sciences, education. Technical training and the free forms of social life are at the circumference of this order. The formation of the intellect is pri-

I. IF PURPOSE IS FORMATION OF THE INTELLECT . . . THE LIBERAL ARTS

Basic studies	Theoretical Sciences	Practical Sciences
Logic	Theology, Philosophy,	The Arts
Mathematics	History	Literature
Language	The Social Sciences	Music
—Grammar	—Sociology, Political	Painting
—Rhetoric	Science, Economics,	Sculpture
—Speech	Psychology	Architecture
—Writing	The Natural Sciences	The Dance
(English and	—Biological: Botany,	Dramatic arts
Foreign)	Zoology	Ethics
	—Physical: Chemistry,	—Individual
	Physics	—Social

(Physical education, not a liberal art, required usually to secure a "sound mind in a sound body")

N.B. A mind must be "formed" before it can be "applied."

II. IF PURPOSE IS APPLICATION OF THE INTELLECT . . . TO HUMAN ENDS

Type of study	Aim of study
Manual arts and trades	Skill in a craft
Business training	Stenography, etc.
Physical education	Coaching, teaching
Domestic arts and sciences	Dietetics, teaching
Nursing arts and sciences	Nursing, teaching
Applied music—piano, voice, etc	Skill/teaching
Applied education (technique)	Skill in teaching
Technology	Engineering, etc.
Journalism	Newspaper work, etc.
Law	Legal profession
Medicine	Medical profession
Theology	Ministry-teaching
Graduate study	Research-teaching

III. IF PURPOSE IS USE OF INTELLECT IN THE FREE FORMS OF COMMUNITY LIFE

Type of community	Kind of activity
Community of Play:	
—games, sports, recreation	playing within rules
—amusements, entertainments	looking at sports, theatricals, etc.
Free communal forms:	social fellowship
—cultural societies, service	plus a common task
clubs, hobby clubs, etc.	or interest
Friendship	personal fellowship
—communal but non-organizational	through conversation

mary, while its application to technical and social uses is secondary. The *basis* of this order is Creation—God's gift of the intellect to man; the *motivation* for the Christian in the order of Redemption is the intellect in the service of God and neighbor.

AIM OF INSTITUTION	INSTITUTION IN ORDER OF CREATION

EDUCATION of the uniquely human: spiritual, moral, intellectual
 	
Nature of study is intellectual
 	
Aim is intellectual grasp on life and reality
 	
Product is the cultured/educated man
 	
Sphere: leisure/work
	(1) Pre-college —Elementary and Secondary schools
	(2) Liberal Arts College
	  a. Classroom —intellectual maturing through study
	  b. Campus —spiritual and moral maturing
	(3) Libraries, museums, etc.

AIM OF INSTITUTION	INSTITUTION IN ORDER OF CREATION
TRAINING of a skill or a function of man **Nature** of study is technical **Aim** is technical competence **Product** is the professional expert **Sphere:** work	(1) Trade schools (2) Business schools (3) Technological Institutes— engineering, art, medical (4) Conservatories (5) Professional schools—law, medicine, theological seminary (6) Graduate schools of all kinds

AIM OF INSTITUTION	INSTITUTION IN ORDER OF CREATION
Opportunities for recreation, amusement, relaxation Communal fellowship (Personal fellowship)	(1) Athletic clubs, parks, playgrounds (2) Professional sports, etc. (3) Professional theatre, etc. (4) Music clubs, etc. (5) Rotary, Lions, Red Cross, etc.

THE LIBERAL ARTS IN CHRISTIAN HIGHER EDUCATION

A CHART OF SOME BASIC INTERRELATIONSHIPS

	Rel.	Phil.	Hist.	Lit.	Fine Arts	Social Sciences	Natural Sciences
Theol.	**Credo ut intelligam—I believe that I may know.** The implications of the Christian faith for all knowledge and disciplines of knowledge are developed by **Christian Philosophy,** relating all knowledge to faith.						
Phil.	Phil. of Rel.		Phil. of Hist.	Phil. of Lit.	Phil. of Art	Phil. of Soc. Sci.	Phil. of Sci.
Hist.	Hist. of Rel.	Hist. of Phil.		Hist. of Lit.	Hist. of Art	Hist. of S. S.	Hist. of Sci.

Theology, Philosophy, and History underlie all other subjects—interpreting, relating, and/or providing a methodology of liberal understanding.

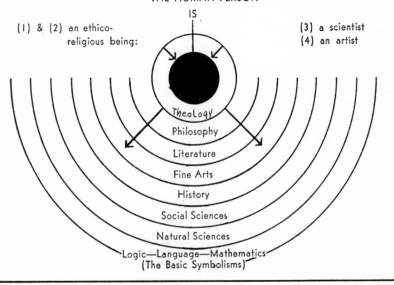

THE LAW OF THE CLOSENESS OF RELATION

The diagram below illustrates the relation of knowledge to the person. The movement is from the formal, more abstract sciences to the more personal, culminating in theology. Man is (1) a **believing, worshipping,** (2) a **loving, acting,** (3) a **knowing,** and (4) a **creating** creature of God.

THE HUMAN PERSON
IS

(1) & (2) an ethico-
religious being:

(3) a scientist
(4) an artist

Theology
Philosophy
Literature
Fine Arts
History
Social Sciences
Natural Sciences
Logic—Language—Mathematics
(The Basic Symbolisms)

THE LIBERAL ARTS IN CHRISTIAN HIGHER EDUCATION

THE BASIC OBJECTS OF STUDY

	GOD	MAN	NATURE
THEOLOGY	Biblical, Historical, Doctrinal, and Moral Theology	Theology of Man Christian Ethics	Theology of Nature
PHILOSOPHY	Natural Theology Philosophy of Religion	Philosophical Anthropology Ethics, Esthetics Epistemology (human knowledge)	Philosophy of Nature
HISTORY		Political history History of Civilization	
LITERATURE		Drama Novel Essay Poetry	
FINE ARTS		Painting Sculpture Architecture Music Dance Theater	
SOCIAL SCIENCES		Sociology Economics Political Science Education Anthropology Psychology	
NATURAL SCIENCES		(Insofar as man is a part of nature)	Biological Sciences: Zoology Botany Physical Sciences: Chemistry Astr., Geol. Physics
MATHEMATICS	The formal science of quantity as such		
LANGUAGES	Eng. and Foreign Grammar and Rhetoric (written and spoken)		
LOGIC	The formal structure of reasoning in all fields		

Chapter Seven

Concepts
of Integration
in Higher Education

A N OVER-VIEW of the history of higher education, of
present concerns in American colleges and universities,
and of the objectives of a Christian liberal arts college has indicated
the persistent presence of integrative factors in the education of
every period. Our own time is characterized, however, more by an
awareness of cultural and educational dispersal, together with the
sensed need of achieving greater integration. The awareness itself
and the sense of need mark an important shift within the past
generation.

Nels Ferré emphasizes the more than academic urgency of this
dispersion and atomization by saying that "The crisis of the university is the crisis of the world. . . ."

> The crisis of the world, on the other hand, is in large measure at-
> tributable to the crisis in higher education. The world's confusion and
> disintegration owe much to the lack of effective steering . . . and to
> the lack of dynamic leadership on the part of the universities. Is the
> university, then, to be construed as the world's keeper? No, but it
> should be the world's mind. The mind, moreover, is no piece by and
> for itself; the mind is the clarifying function in and for the organism
> as a whole with respect to all its experience and relationship. Similarly
> the university should serve as the clarifying function for the world.
>
> What, then, is the university? It is the top perspective of the educa-
> tional process, not only as a whole, but in its deliberate wholeness. It
> is not only the highest form of education, but education at the summit
> of its organic unity.[1]

[1]*Christian Faith and Higher Education* (New York: Harper, 1954), p. 233.

It is significant that the St. Olaf College faculty questionnaires reveal virtually unanimous agreement (94%) that integration is a central aim in liberal education.[2] Likewise innumerable sensitive, informed observers of contemporary higher education challenge the fissionary tendencies and call for a more cohesive ordering of the curriculum and greater relatedness in teaching. Neverthleless, one may properly raise the question: What is meant by integration in liberal education? The same disintegration which prompts the present widespread insistence upon integrative remedy results also in a pluralistic, confused understanding of educational integration itself. The task of this chapter is to present a constructive concept of integration by describing the locus of integration within the limits of liberal education and by presenting critically the major concepts of integration.

1

LOCUS OF INTEGRATION

a. *Student or Faculty and Curriculum?* It may be asserted that however isolated the teaching and however discrete the courses, educational integration nevertheless can be achieved by the student.[3] As a go-between crossing the lines of courses and departments, the student not only becomes a common channel for various subject matters but also may contribute a wider perspective to any given class. More significant is the assertion that, however cohesive the curriculum and however related the teaching, integration must nevertheless be achieved by the student himself. Otherwise educational integration is a failure.

If it is assumed that education aims at the development of discrimination, understanding, powers of mind, and knowledge *for the student,* an inescapable conclusion is that the student is the primary locus of integration. If relatedness of studies is achieved elsewhere but not within the mind of the student, the accomplishment would be significant in itself, but educationally irrelevant. It is quite proper that an educational enterprise be judged by its

---

[2]Integration in the Christian Liberal Arts College, II, 42.
[3]One Who Knows, "A Librarian Looks at General Education," *Journal of Higher Education* (April, 1953).

products—its students—and no amount of high intention and catalog statements can wash away mediocrity in educational results.

It does not follow, however, that the task of educational integration can properly and effectively be left *to the student*. Even though he is the *primary locus,* the college (curriculum and teaching) is not thereby relieved of its *prior responsibility.* The fact that some students make the marvelous, stimulating discovery that departments and courses represent a division of labor in the varied one-world of knowledge and understanding should be an encouragement to the college of teachers to facilitate a binding together of parts. The task of the college, then, involves (1) *inciting the expectation of relatedness in learning* (understanding and even remembering being dependent upon the discernment of connections) and (2) the *facilitating of educational integration* for the student through the curriculum and the substance and manner of teaching. If the college in its central task of curriculum and teaching betray a methodical anarchy, educational integration in the student is accidental and occurs in spite of the college.

Happily there is no necessary either-or in this teaching-learning process even if the teaching method emphasizes problems, gaps, and contradictions, a method aimed at driving the student to deeper levels of self-activity and of intellectual substance. The primary locus in the student and the prior and continuing responsibility of the college in curriculum and teaching are not only compatible; they are necessary foci in the ellipse of a faculty's learning-teaching and the student's whole task of integrated educational growth.

b. *Education as intellectual growth: a wide concept of reason.* It is a measure of the intrinsic fascination of teaching as well as of the towering confidence placed in the profession by the general public, that education should be entrusted with the task of developing "the whole man." There has been a growing tendency on the part of elementary, secondary, and higher education to make itself responsible for more and more of the functions formerly exercised by other social and cultural agencies. The schools not only supervise the student's growth in the basic intellectual skills of reading, writing, calculation, research, and experiment. They

118

also preside over the formation of attitudes towards food, clothing, health, and recreation, and attempt to inculcate certain basic patriotic, moral, and religious sentiments.

It can be argued that the school has been led to expand its activities because the family has largely abdicated its traditional cultural responsibilities. Yet, teachers in the area of higher education must ask themselves whether they are wise in assuming a literally boundless task. After all, education in the wider sense of forming "the whole man" goes on from birth to death. The personality in its successive stages of development is shaped and molded by the family, the neighborhood, the community, the state, the Church, voluntary cultural associations, and the media of mass communication. College education is but a small segment of this life-long process. Many fundamental moments in education have been experienced prior to the four years spent in college. Moreover, college is not the last chance of learning.

If then, college is not the first, last, or only educational opportunity, but rather a strategically located and uniquely important segment of the lifelong process of learning, it is a matter of great importance to inquire into the specific nature of the contribution made by the college to the entire process. Since the college experience is a limited portion of the whole, it has certain limited aims. The liberal arts should not attempt to do what the Church, the family, the state, and society are constantly doing for the student. Nor will the classroom seek to do for the student what is properly done for him by his participation in campus life. Liberal education does not suggest that all the levels or activities of man are of equal importance, nor does it propose to teach everything that can be known and studied.

On the contrary, a liberal education is narrow. It proposes to concentrate upon a limited area rather than to scatter its energies upon a multitude of heterogeneous studies and activities. Specifically, a liberal arts education concentrates on intelligence and its skills. By training and enlightening the intellect by means of the arts and sciences it sets the mind free. Knowing how to think, how to communicate thought, to make relevant judgments, to discriminate truth from falsehood, good from evil, the beautiful from the ugly—the knowledge of these arts should send the learner into life knowing how to learn and be interested in the world he must live in. Liberal education is, therefore, concerned with the systematic process of thought and with the systematic arrangement of the products of thought. The locus of integration, then, would be the intellectual world of the curriculum, the faculty, and the student.

This does not mean that liberal education denies that man is a moral and spiritual as well as an intellectual being, but it recognizes that in an academic setting these other aspects of personality can be dealt with only from an intellectual point of view. After all, such things as responsibility, devotion to the common good, aspiration, moral rectitude, spiritual commitment, and love for one's fellowmen cannot be communicated in their reality in the classroom. They can only come into being as the by-product of the total impact made by the intellectual substance of a course, the personality of the teacher, and the general moral and spiritual climate of the campus.

Such a forthright declaration of interest in the methods and products of the intellect exposes the liberal arts program to understandable criticism. Some fear that strong emphasis upon reason will lead to a narrow and uninspiring rationalism. Others will argue that since thinking is only part of living, an exclusive concern with the intellect marks a one-sided and inadequate approach to the education of "the whole man." These fears are valid only if reason be defined in an unduly narrow sense. Reason is narrowly defined if it is exclusively identified with thinking according to formulated rules of logic, or if it is restricted to the sort of inquiry which can be pursued through the use of the "scientific method," as that term is used by some workers in the natural and social sciences. But such narrow definitions of reason are neither required of us nor are they workable. For all but the pedant or fanatic it is plain that there are such activities as philosophical reflection, aesthetic perception, and moral judgment. In every field expert thinking is of more worth than non-expert thinking. There are matters, outside the sphere of science and the formulated rules of logic, concerning which some people have what we persistently call "insight."

120

By "insight" we mean "not guessing but a quality of vision or judgment that cuts right through appearances, a piercing apprehension of truth. If we accept it, yet dismiss it as irrational, we are forced into postulating another organ of truth besides reason, and if we reject it, we are running away from the wisdom of experience."[4]

Here there is an alternative to be faced. Either we hold to the narrow conception of reason by denying the existence of insight and the validity of reasoning that has not been reduced to rule, or we admit the existence of insight and widen our conception of reason so as to include it. It surely seems more proper to construct our idea of reason from the full range of our grasp of reality.

If we choose to work with this wider conception we will look upon reason as man's capacity to "see" the "object," to respond to the "other," to grasp what is external to himself. Virtually all philosophers have worked with this wider conception. Reason, they have held, is that in us which asks questions, believes that there are answers, and devises ways of finding these answers. "We are reasoning when we think about problems in ways that are not ruled by emotion, instinct, association, habit, social custom, and so on, but by the nature of the things thought about."[5]

The wider conception of reason implies that reason is a single and undivided capacity of man. But at the same time reason operates in a variety of modes, and it is a mistake to single out one of these modes and to equate it with reason. This is the intellectual heresy known as "rationalism." In the last thirty or forty years there has been a revolt in almost all the branches of the humanities against rationalism and a return to realism. "Let the facts themselves furnish the basis for our study." Whereas rationalism held that there was one universal and uniform method for every problem, modern realism postulates that the peculiarity of the subject-matter must determine the method of approach.

It is because reality or experience is so varied that it cannot at all points be thought about in the same way. T. E. Jessop writes:

If the aim of our thinking is not the imposition of a pattern on things but the reading off of their nature, we shall not use the same ideas in the study of electrons and beetles, and we shall not settle by the same

[4]T. E. Jessop, *Reasonable Living* (London: SCM Press, 1948), pp. 39-40.
[5]*Ibid.*, p. 41.

methods and criteria such diverse matters as the structure and behavior of the atom, the rightness and wrongness of gambling, the proper limits of state authority, whether poetry is anything more than amusement, or the status of man in the total scheme of things. In fidelity to its problems and evidence, reason has different modes of expression because the reality it confronts is diversified. If the reality thought about is of a definite nature, and is relatively limited, rational thought about it will be precise. If the reality is not definite, thought about it cannot be precise if it is to be true. And if the reality thought about is vast in the special sense of being above our present range of clear apprehension, thought can move only gradually towards definiteness, and may never reach it. In other words, knowledge can be true without being precise, so that precision, or the demand for it, cannot be an essential part of reason. Reason demands precision where it can be got, and where it is absent, still to demand it is to press not a rational requirement but a formula.[6]

So conceived, reason cannot be cut down to a single pattern. Its business is not to impose itself but to reflect its varied objects in their variety, and in doing so its procedure must take a variety of forms, and will be rewarded with varying degrees of success. Being free from prejudice (so far as this is humanly possible) and subject to external control, it will be as various as reality—spelling out "the relations of the number system, measuring the distance of a star, detecting the factors in a chemical reaction, investigating how birds manage to migrate, uncovering the hidden motives of men's deeds, divining the structure of the moral order, weighing the worth of our aesthetic, political and religious aspirations. In all those *it is still reason*. It is not a rigid yardstick, but a sensitive and resourceful instrument of mental sight."[7]

There is a legitimate kind of "rationalism," and the cultivation of it is the proper aim of higher education. The "true rationalist" is not the one who would identify reason exclusively with logic, the scientific method, or with any specialist study, but rather the man who believes that reason has a wider competence, and the universe a wider rationality or intelligibility. The "true rationalist" is the man who holds that philosophy and theology, history, literature, and art can stand alongside the sciences as ways of reading the richly diversified nature of reality, bringing to this task methods and standards that are appropriate to a larger sphere of problems.

---

[6]*Ibid.*, p. 43.
[7]*Ibid.*, p. 45.

We have said that reason is one and yet it is many. The "true rationalist," while he recognizes that reason adapts its methods of operation to the nature of the reality that is being studied, will also insist that he is one man, not three men, artist, scientist, and saint. He is the same man in his garden when he considers the lilies and wonders how to keep them from turning brown and in Church when he yields himself to God in prayer and worship. He is the same man, even if he lives in many places and relationships and at different levels of his being; and the whole business of effective living depends upon his making himself consistent and "all of a piece." He will experience tensions between aesthetic, intellectual, and moral levels of existence. But he will not seek to deny or escape these tensions or try to resolve them by a method sharply divided into categories and labelled "scientific approach," "religious outlook," or "aesthetic appreciation." Whatever the problem, the total person will face the total complex of experience in an act of understanding. Even though different areas of study require different methods of approach and yield varying degrees of certainty, there is a single intellectual thrust characteristic of the whole man. Whatever the problem, physical or metaphysical, biological or theological, he will approach it in the same way, collecting and studying the relevant evidence, testing and experimenting, reflecting and interpreting, striving like Lucretius to "seek out the causes of things." Of course the data will vary from field to field as will the specific categories of classification and interpretation, but the principles of inductive research and systematic intellectual reflection are the same in every field, thus testifying to the unity and flexibility of reason.

In thus emphasizing the unity and omnipresence of reason, we do not mean to imply that man in his essence *is* reason, nor that such movements of man's spirit as emotion, adoration, joy, reverence, and imagination are simply forms of reason or reason under a variety of names. These are genuine and distinguishable functions of the complex person. But the human person is a single entity in spite of its differentiation into so many functions. Our effort to clarify and vindicate the wider conception of reason only requires us to hold that *thought* is related to the deepest ground

123

of our being as persons. It continually penetrates to the other and perhaps deeper levels of one's being. Any intellectual construction, argument, or world-view, if it is to be persuasive, "cannot hope to persuade by logical compellingness alone, even though it must not knowingly affront logic; it must always assume, and hope to penetrate to and evoke a sense of truth which lies deeper than logic and comprehends more of the whole man as a willing and feeling as well as thinking being."[8]

We have seen that reason, the power of detecting the objective, is at work, in varying forms and degrees, in all our distinctively human experiences. Therefore, it is misleading to say that "the intellect can be overemphasized," or that the "life of reason is narrow and cold." That position could be maintained only by sundering reason sharply from insight, belief, conscience, and aesthetic judgment. In addition to the fact that such a separation could not be accomplished except by an analytical operation of reason itself, there would follow the practical result that all these other operations of the personality would have to be labelled "irrational."

In the light of this analysis, it seems clear that in submitting to self-imposed limitations, liberal education does not confine itself with crippling effect to a minute fraction of the range of fact or to one narrow level of the personality of man. Rather, by its concentration upon the student's intellectual development and upon the intellectual substance and structure of the several fields of knowledge, liberal education deals with what is essential to man as man. It restricts itself to what makes man human and through this restriction it achieves a universality. It offers deliverance from the provincial, the trivial, the customary, the capricious, and the peripheral. Liberal education does not pretend to be life. It is a concentrated reflection about the essential in a man's life. It is indeed restricted, but the restriction is a healthy one. Without it we cannot give to higher education the vital amplitude which could justify the high hopes of teachers, students, and the public. This rich world of the mind is the central concern of liberal education and is therefore the locus of integration for both teacher and student.

---

[8]H. H. Farmer, *Revelation and Religion* (London: Nisbet and Company Limited, 1954), p. 17.

2

SPECIALISM, DISTRIBUTION, CONCENTRATION, AND INTEGRATION

Integration presupposes parts which are or ought to be related. Although on good grounds one can effectively urge that liberal education is limited and ought not seek or be expected to perform the entire task of education, the range of parts may be too narrow and constricted. The basic problem here is the proper ground of self-limitation. In contemporary education specialism represents a severe, illiberal limiting of education to training in exclusive areas dominated largely by occupational and commercial interests. Specialism becomes thereby a form of extreme integration. Precisely because occupational specialism "has a skin around it" (plus an immediate cash value), it frequently stands in favorable contrast to the liberal college with its incoherence and educational haphazardness. The weakness of specialism is not its self-integration. Its weakness is in its narrow center and dehumanizing tendency.

Now specialization is more and more needed by the technical organization of modern life, yet it should be compensated for by a more vigorous general training, especially during youth. If we remember that the animal is a specialist, and a perfect one, all of its knowing-power being fixed upon a single task to be done, we ought to conclude that an educational program which would only aim at forming specialists ever more perfect in ever more specialized fields, and unable to pass judgment on any matter that goes beyond their specialized competence, would lead indeed to a progressive animalization of the human mind and life. Finally, as the life of bees consists of producing honey, the real life of man would consist of producing in a perfectly pigeonholed manner economic values and scientific discoveries, while some cheap pleasure or social entertainment would occupy leisure time, and a vague religious feeling, without any content of thought and reality, would make existence a little less flat, perhaps a little more dramatic and stimulating, like a happy dream. The overwhelming cult of specialization dehumanizes man's life.[9]

The specialist approach to education tends to regard men as social-economic functions rather than as rational-moral-spiritual persons. Even from a social point of view, a democracy cannot

[9]Jacques Maritain, *Education at the Crossroads* (New Haven: Yale University Press, 1944), pp. 19-20.

afford the feudalizing of education into specialist functional training.

Curricular distribution is the most common device used to mitigate the narrowing and technicizing results of specialism. The thought underlying distribution is that education involves appropriation of one's cultural heritage. Prior to and underneath their special functions specialists, too, are men, are human beings. Distribution aims as a minimum to remedy the partial character of specialism by introducing every student to a substantial intellectual world common to all. It is also a way of saying that integration may be achieved at too high a price, the price of dropping universally valuable areas of great richness and significance. Conant points out that

> Neither the mere acquisition of information nor the development of special skills and talents can give the broad basis of understanding which is essential if our civilization is to be preserved. No one wishes to disparage the importance of being "well informed." But even a good grounding in mathematics and the physical and biological sciences, combined with an ability to read and write several foreign languages, does not provide a sufficient educational background for citizens of a free nation. For such a program lacks contact with both man's emotional experience as an individual and his practical experiences as a gregarious animal. It includes little of what was once known as "the wisdom of the ages," and might nowadays be described as "our cultural pattern." It includes no history, no art, no literature, no philosophy. Unless the educational process includes *at each level of maturity* some continuing contact with those fields in which value judgments are of prime importance, it must fall far short of the ideal. The student in high school, in college, and in graduate school must be concerned, in part at least, with the words "right" and "wrong" in both the ethical and the mathematical sense. Unless he feels the import of those general ideas and aspirations which have been a deep moving force in the lives of men, he runs the risk of partial blindness.[10]

The influence of occupational specialism has been so great that it has affected the teaching and substance of the liberal college. For one thing it "has tended to take from the college what theoretical unity it had. It is for this reason that the college was said above to be divided against itself. Certainly, if the various fields of study do not represent a common discipline or give anything like a common view of life, then such unity as the college has must

---

[10]*General Education in a Free Society*, Introduction, pp. viii-ix.

come chiefly from imponderable tradition or simple gregarious-
ness."[11]

In teaching itself, teachers who are products of highly specialized graduate schools are inclined to reproduce their kind even
in the liberal college.

The result is that each subject, being taught by an expert, tends to
be so presented as to attract potential experts. This complaint is perhaps
more keenly felt in colleges and universities, which naturally look to
scholarship. The undergraduate in a college receives his teaching from
professors who, in their turn, have been trained in graduate schools.
And the latter are dominated by the ideal of specialization. Learning
now is diversified and parceled into a *myriad of specialties.* Correspondingly, colleges and universities are divided into large numbers of departments, with further specialization within the departments. As a
result, a student in search of a general course is commonly frustrated.
Even an elementary course is devised as an introduction to a specialism
within a department; it is significant only as the beginning of a series
of courses of advancing complexity. In short, such introductory courses
are planned for the specialist, not for the student seeking a general
education.[12]

In spite of the narrowness of specialism, its divisive effect upon
the college, and its kidnapping of non-specialist liberal education,
its value need not be denied nor should it be abolished. It should,
however, be defined as properly a function of the technical and
professional school, not of the liberal college. A limited wholeness
inclusive of the basic area of human achievement and vision should
be common to all students. The educational values of specialism
—a sense of mastery and achievement of a higher degree of
penetration—are significant aims in the customary college plan of
concentration. The "major" plan need not destroy the common
educational character of introductory courses. Even majors in an
area need the larger understanding aimed at in such courses open
to all students. For those who choose a major, there are also the
values of fulfilling individual interests and pursuing more deeply
and precisely a particular area of learning. Courses of concentration can and should contribute significantly to the coherent wholeness of the student's education. To fail in this and to become drilled
in occupational technique is to neglect the larger educational aim
and the context of the specific major area as well.

---

[11]*Ibid.,* p. 39.
[12]*Ibid.,* pp. 56-57.

SOME MAJOR CONCEPTS OF INTEGRATION IN
HIGHER EDUCATION

Every view of integration presupposes entities in possible or actual relationship to one another within a whole or constituting a whole. These relationships to one another and to the whole may be conceived in various ways with correspondingly different implications for an educational program. The major views may be called: (a) additive, (b) sampling, (c) relational, and (d) wholistic concepts of integration.

a. *Additive view*. The whole is equal to the sum of its differentiated parts. Likewise a lesser whole is constituted by the sum of its parts. The character of the whole is determined by the relative quantities of the parts making up the quantitative whole. Inasmuch as the whole is not characterized qualitatively, the kinds of parts are unlimited and, although differentiated, are interchangeable as quantitative units. Educationally this view is expressed in the course-unit system of hours and semesters and the educational whole calculated as 120 semester hours. The additive view is not found in its pure form, which would be a completely free elective system claimed by the University of Buffalo with creditable repetition of courses. Geographically or chronologically centered area courses are essentially additive with qualifications of space or time. Qualified in these ways or by requirements of distribution, quality of student work, advanced hours, and non-duplicating credit, the additive view is basic in the present conduct of American higher education. In curriculum-building under the additive view there is theoretically no limitation other than by students' interests and financial considerations.

b. *Sampling view*. In practice there may be little apparent difference between sampling and addition. Sampling, however, is based on the belief that each and any part mirrors or essentially embodies the whole. The parts may be differentiated in some aspects, but each part is a microcosm which, treated adequately, leads to a comprehension of the essential whole. This means that one part is replaceable by any other, not according to a mechanical quantitative concept, but rather on the basis that there is an essential qualitative sameness amid apparent diversity. In education this view tends to emphasize the unimportance of specific subject matter and to elevate student work habits and the role of the individual teacher. Followed rigorously this view would be the basis of a contextual wholism in which each subject pursued toward its limits would lead into and include every other subject. In practice, however, this view is most commonly found, unelaborated, in highly departmentalized colleges in which any course is considered to be as valuable as any other course and adequate without any other. Those who hold this view usually follow it in urging the educational value of their own area and deny it in its application to other areas to the exclusion of their own. Insofar as advocates of specialism assert the general educational adequacy of a highly restricted program, they are quite likely to find a rationale in the sampling view. In curriculum-building this view would support both a very restricted curriculum (emphasizing common method and/or common essential substance) or an unlimited curriculum (likewise emphasizing common method and/or common essential substance, plus variety of student interests).

c. *Relational view.* Emphasis upon the autonomy of organized parts and also upon a conceptual grasp of these parts in their partial sameness and contrast underlies the relational view. Each part is considered to have its own characteristic structure and content and is properly approached through a method peculiarly appropriate to it. Because the very term "part" implies a whole, we should rather speak of independent entities, for each area or entity is essentially self-enclosed and organized within itself. Insofar as the notion of wholeness is introduced, the relational view would be a pluralistic wholism: a federation of sovereign kingdoms —with greater or lesser importance attributed to the federation.

In the integration of higher education the relational view would include an understanding of independent areas as being more than a collection of data about differentiated objects of knowledge. Facts are not self-explanatory. A science in the sense of an organized body of knowledge comes into being not as a product of

129

immediate experience, however extensive, but by penetrating reflection on that experience, by analytical and synthesizing comparison of cognitive materials. The discernment and formulation of likenesses and differences and a larger understanding within more and more inclusive concepts constitute the guide, aim, and essential substance of the enterprise. To the degree that methodological and organizational concepts underlie each of the autonomous studies, quite naturally there arises the question of the relationship of these studies to each other through their basic organizing ideas and methods. Therefore inter-departmental courses, divisional courses, and certain departmental courses are specific reflections of the relational view, so far as commonness and contrast in ways of knowing are central amid the variation of differentiated studies.

d. *Wholistic view.* Contrasted essentially to the atomism of the additive and relational views and to the homogeneity of the sampling view, the wholistic view maintains that the whole is more than the collection of its parts. The whole, which includes the end for which the whole exists or is made, is differentiated into distinguishable parts, but these parts are adequately understood only in relationship to each other and within an understanding of the whole. The natures and functions of the parts are derivative and not autonomous. The nose with its characteristic structure and function is understood properly and fully not by itself but as the specific portion of the face and finally as a distinguishable but dependent part of the person's body. No part is adequate as a whole, nor are the parts interchangeable. Each part is important and for specified functions some parts are more important than others, depending upon the specific function of the part and upon the nature and end of the whole.

Educationally wholism is exemplified in a completely prescribed curriculum and in a program cohesively oriented by a more or less inclusive world-view or inclusive end. Insofar as specialism does not claim (as it does within the sampling view) general educational value, it illustrates a wholism cohering about a specific end. Each part is a necessary differentiated portion of a purposeful though exclusive whole. A program shaped by a fairly well articu-

130

lated inclusive world-view (as in a vigorous naturalism, Thomism, Marxism, or scientific materialism) would clearly define the end of the educational whole and also provide substantial categories of method and understanding. A curriculum aimed at common abilities (critical thinking, methodology) would be wholistic without substantial categories and content other than what is embedded in the methodological presuppositions. Educational division of labor (departments) is a legitimate aspect of a wholistic approach because of significant differentiation within the whole. Yet this is a limited autonomy circumscribed by the other parts and by the prior character and final purpose of the whole. The building and ordering of the entire curriculum would reflect the nature and end of the differentiated whole rather than the combination of victories and defeats of various individuals and departments.

4

CRITICAL ANALYSIS OF MAJOR VIEWS

a. Additive view. The proponents of this view hold that it corresponds to the radical openness of progressive knowledge, to a wide pluralism in value judgments, and to the infinite variety of student interests. It is asserted also that this view is the educational counter-part of political-social democracy in that it gives equal rights to all interests in free competition with one another. The elective system, it is specifically claimed, was the instrument for a necessary loosening up of higher education dominated at the time by traditional vested interests.

Meiklejohn criticizes this view by pointing out that the additive unit approach to education imposes mechanical, quantitative categories upon the teaching-learning enterprise and thereby destroys the organismic character of education.

> The longer one attempts to devise a liberal training by the additions and combinations of courses, the more one becomes convinced that addition is an illusion and that courses are the chimeras of an imagination perverted by the categories of mechanics. Twenty courses do not make a college education any more than twenty legs make a man, or twenty heads, or even ten hearts, two legs, and eight fingers. And in the same way three courses do not make an intellectual interest, an experience of the actual process of the working mind. Something is wrong with

131

the terms, something radically wrong with the process of combining them.

What is the trouble? It seems to me very clear that the concepts of quantity and measurement have wrecked the organic unity of the college course. In making elective courses we have felt the genuine need of uniformity and so have established units in terms of which to measure. And having established our separate units of subjects, courses, departments, we have felt free to pluck them out of the living organism one by one, to substitute one for another, and then to put them back supposing the life process to be still rushing on in spite of all our interruptions.[13]

He further maintains that learning is criticism, interpretation, and understanding through taking the fragments and finding what runs through the separate parts. The additive approach exalts informational knowledge so that teachers tend to "believe much more in subjects, believe in knowledge in the scattered sense."[14] John Ise, speaking out of the teaching of economics, corroborates this estimate that the whole learning process has become misunderstood.

Our schools and universities have largely evaded their responsibilities in this matter. The public schools have of course never dared to do much but inoculate their pupils against thinking about important questions. For fifty years our universities have steadily retreated from the field of education while adding vocational and trade schools, until today they should scarcely be called educational institutions. We are concerned less and less with knowledge and wisdom, and more and more with learning to *do* this, that and the other thing. Teachers in the public schools do not learn mathematics, French or biology, but how to *teach* mathematics, French or biology; law students do not study jurisprudence, but how to make money practicing law; most journalists do not try to learn something to write but how to write about things that they don't know; our business students do not seek to get an understanding of the economy of business as a whole, but how to run a store, or keep books, or sell insurance or oil stocks. How to *do*, that is the educational problem of our practical age. We may not understand the critical problems of the day, we may be going to hell collectively, but we're going to learn to be efficient boobs and make a lot of money on the way there.[15]

In addition to the quantifying-atomizing of education and the fostering of an inadequate grasp of its nature and purpose, the

---

[13]*The Liberal College*, p. 149.

[14]*Ibid.*, p. 74.

[15]"The Prostitution of American Education," paper presented at meeting of the Midwest Economics Association (Iowa City: Bureau of Business and Economic Research, University of Iowa, 1954), p. 5.

additive view denies or minimizes the universal aspects of men, knowledge, and wisdom, just as it accentuates individual variations in students and proliferation of the curriculum. Beginning in the high school and continuing expansively in college, the effect of the additive view and its course-unit system is to divide the curriculum into curricula of virtually independent schools. Departments tend to become more than parts of a college, and the student's work is either dominated by a department or is a succession of islands of study unconnected with most of the other islands. In this way the generic or common aspects of man, the unity of knowledge, and the relatedness of the individual's own course are all under-valued in favor of individuality, autonomy, and plurality.

The actual practice in American colleges and universities represents to a degree a serious critique of the additive, elective system and gives empirical support to the above estimate of the additive view. Experience with this system has only too well indicated that an academic version of a mechanical-quantitative position does not enhance the educational climate and that an academic version of political-social democracy leaves curriculum building and faculty growth to departmental political action rather than to conscious, deliberated educational policy and statesmanship. For these and other reasons the additive view, although still vigorously operative in American higher education, has been considerably modified in practice, and its theoretical proponents have been significantly reduced in vigor and number. As a criticism of traditionalism for its own sake and of curricular narrowness, the additive view in the form of free election has been of some positive value in American higher education. Consistency itself, however, would preclude traditionalizing the additive method and freezing its resultant divisive narrowness.

b. Sampling view. With the elective "system" sweeping the country and the curriculum expanding in extraordinary fashion, many educators became concerned about the loss of coherence and discipline in the educational development of the student and in the whole college. There seemed to be too great a likelihood that indiscriminate formlessness would result. Faculties therefore cir-

133

cumscribed the elector's freedom by developing the "major" plan of coherent work in a chosen area which, growing in importance, diminished the range and significance of whatever work was required outside the major. This became "work to be got out of the way."

Although one of the strong arguments against the older prescribed curriculum was the non-transferability of intellectual discipline, the major system represented the same underlying sampling view in that any subject for a major was supposed to be as educationally valuable as any other major subject. With the loss of significant common content, it was held that common methodology could be learned through fairly thorough study in any chosen subject. In recent years the transferable, disciplinary value of subjects has been subjected to considerable study and criticism. Although the case against transfer is frequently overdrawn, it may be pointed out that it is difficult to claim universality for a single method for all subjects. Intellectual methods in the natural sciences, social sciences, the fine arts, philosophy, and religion have similarities but hardly identity. The oddity is that the "major" plan, part of a criticism of the traditional "disciplines," embodies the same sampling emphasis on the extensibility of intellectual abilities developed in any given or chosen subject area.

Coupled with the disparagement of diversity of method in the sampling view is a lack of appreciation of differentiation in substance. This view usually exalts teaching and universality of method and asserts that any subject will suffice. Not only is differentiation in substance unduly minimized, but substance itself. Consequently the sampling concept rejects the claim that higher education should involve the appropriation of one's cultural heritage in its substantial richness and variety.

Theoretically the sampling view, holding that every part contains the essential character or structure of the whole, is a homogeneous wholism. Through each and any part, a grain of sand or a sonnet, considered properly and adequately, one can be brought to an understanding and appreciation of the undifferentiated nature and structure of the essence common to all. In practice, however, sampling has been an egalitarian atomism, deprecating not only

134

substantial differentiation but educational order and judgment as well. It has been a useful theory for the isolated departmentalism and academic utilitarianism in which each part seeks its own ends with little interest in the essential whole or in the other supposedly undifferentiated parts. The nineteenth century utilitarians realized the ethical nihilism implicit in their own philosophy and abhorred the conclusion that push-pin is as good as poetry. If value judgments and discernment of order are proscribed within the central task of the college, it is not to be wondered at that education becomes an acquiescent instrument for commercial, chauvinistic, and other interests, caring little for more inclusive and more intrinsically educational ends. One educator-administrator considered this abandonment of intra-college judgment on the part of specialist teachers to be "an announcement that they have no guiding principles in their educational practice, no principles of selection in their arrangement of studies, no genuine grasp on the relationship between knowledge and life. It is the concerted statement of a group of men each of whom is lost within the limits of his special studies, and who as a group seem not to realize the organic relationships between them nor the common task which should bind them together."[16]

Although the sampling view seems theoretically inadequate because of its ignoring variety of method and substance and the significance of educational order and relationship, and because in practice it promotes undue specialism, departmentalism, and fragmentation, it does in actuality represent a mitigation of academic anarchy and an emphasis on quality of teaching.

c. Relational view. From the standpoint that cohesiveness in the educational venture is valuable, the advantages of the relational view are that it recognizes the need for integration and that it considers educational integration to be a test of intellectual understanding through and within teachable substances.

In the additive and sampling views little prominence is given to integration as an important aim in education. An awareness is not a remedy, but the absence of awareness precludes seeking for a remedy or leaves it entirely to vagaries and chance. The rela-

---

[16]Alexander Meiklejohn, *The Liberal College,* p. 40.

tional view not only reflects an awareness of the need for binding the fragments together; it also proposes a specific way out which is within the range of the teacher—a faculty or a single instructor. One college group considering the requirements for good teaching concluded that one obvious but generally unrecognized need is that "each instructor . . . make clear to his students the methodology used in his field and how this contrasts with that used in others. Another need that became evident was a clear statement of the assumptions on which each subject rests. We were agreed that these assumptions need not be presented at the beginning of the course but by the time the course is over, the student should be aware of them. If he is not, the inter-relation of various subject-matters will not have a very firm foundation. Most of us agreed that we plunge right into the meat of our course without drawing attention to the fundamental assumptions on which this particular knowledge has been erected."

Henry Margenau's presentation of relationalism makes clear the character of this approach, that it is on the fundamental level of the central teaching task of the college.

It seems axiomatic that unified knowledge and understanding have roots that go below facts and go below language. To be impressed by this plain truth means to advocate a fourth kind of integration. The facts of our knowledge, the visible excrescences of our culture, are in a sense less important than the roots from which they spring. Lack of continuity and organization between facts, gaps between disciplines of learning, failures of understanding between people and peoples can be viewed as signs indicating places where conceptual roots, though present in the deeper soil, have for some reason not pushed up to the surface, and a probing for basic concepts may eliminate them. For it is the nature of concepts to be extensible, while facts can only fill dead spaces in knowledge. Concepts provide the texture in which facts are embedded. The picture appropriate to this point of view is a three-dimensional puzzle, in which the fragments known as facts compose the upper surface, but the surface will not hold together unless principles and concepts are filled in underneath and placed in their proper position to stabilize the surface facts.[17]

This stress on integration as a task of intellectual understanding of teachable substances for teacher and student avoids a peripheral approach to the problem in terms of campus life in all its mul-

---

[17]"Integrative Education in the Sciences," *Sixth Yearbook of The American Association of Colleges for Teacher Education—1953*, p. 134.

136

titudinous forms, however important they may be. It also avoids
the aromatic approach which emphasizes the unusual, personable
instructor, however valuable he is. Every contribution to organic
educational development is to be valued, but if the main stream
of the college as an intellectual pursuit is fragmentary, the campus
extras cannot justify default in curriculum or teaching. The relational view of integration conceives of relatedness as within the
mind of the teaching community; it also specifies the working
tactic within the sphere of subject content. The learning student
is properly considered the locus of integration, and the prior, continuing responsibility of the college (teachers and courses) is
rightly centered.

The negative aspect of a critique of the relational view most
likely would be based on a more organismic position. An assumption of the relational concept of integration is the presence of
autonomous differentiated areas or subjects. The task, then, is to
relate these areas by means of their working concepts and philosophical presuppositions. The approach to less fragmentariness and
greater wholeness is through the "separate baronies of knowledge."[18] Within each part there is a conceptual wholism which
alone makes the subject an understandable and teachable subject.
Yet the various lesser wholes, albeit on a fundamental wholistic
level, are to be related from *within* the lesser wholes, which is
analogous to expecting the accumulation of data within each
subject to yield an organized body of knowledge by squeezing the
facts. If constitutive concepts and postulates are needed in addition to data and operational formulae to make a subject possible,

---

[18]As Woodrow Wilson pointed out fifty years ago, this is the center of the practical
problem of fragmentation. "The world woke once, in that notable fifteenth century,
to find itself standing in the clear dawn of the New Learning, and the light which
then came has never since been taken away. But we have played tricks with it; we
have refracted it, distinguishing the lines of its spectrum with an extreme nicety
exceeding that of the Rowland grating, and so have brought upon ourselves a New
Ignorance. In our desire to differentiate its rays we have forgotten to know the sun
in its entirety, its power to illuminate, to quicken and expand. Knowledge has lost
its synthesis, and lies with its colors torn apart, dissolved. That New Learning,
which saw knowledge whole, shattered the feudal system of society; this New
Ignorance, which likes knowledge piecemeal and in weak solution, has created a
feudal system of learning. There is no common mastery, but everywhere separate
baronies of knowledge, where a few strong men rule and many ignorant men are
held vassals—men ignorant of the freedom of more perfect, more liberal knowledge.
We need a freer constitution of learning. Its present constitution only makes it certain that we shall have disorder and wasteful war." *The Public Papers of Woodrow
Wilson*, I, *College and State* (New York: Harper and Brothers, 1925), p. 225.

are not wholistic constitutive concepts and postulates required to relate the differentiated realms of knowledge? If the additive approach is atomistic, the relational view, although qualitatively different, is molecular in attempting to understand the parts by means of the parts themselves. An automotive parts warehouse may include everything required to make a car with the fatal exception of the idea of a car, the concept of the larger whole within which the parts have their understandable places and functions. Relationalism is at root a pluralism longing for unity and inconsistently denying the wholism implicit within the differentiated parts. In higher education the inconsistent short-circuiting of the relational view is evident in the general education movement which seeks to overcome fragmentariness on a divisional or partial divisional basis and abandons the larger labor of relating divisional study to other divisional studies in an educational whole.

d. Wholistic view. If the preceding critique seems to forget that the relational view aims to sort out the most significant content of basic human knowledge and to fashion out of it a whole or at least a smaller number of larger wholes, it is only an apparent and not a genuine oversight, according to the wholistic view. An important distinction needs to be made. The relational view may or may not, depending on the vigor of pursuit and consistency of view, press toward an understanding of the whole of reality by conceptually combining the given plurality of entities. Wholism, on the other hand, posits the primacy, actual or hypothetical, of "reality as a whole." The whole is prior and superior to any of its parts and to the sum of its parts.

The old fable of the wise men of Gotham is a piece of wholistic public relations. Wholism, the story illustrates, is required for perception and understanding. Even the simplest perception is a complex whole rather than a composite built up out of its parts. Similarly, understanding begins with an initial grasp (whether the intuition of a whole object, or a normative principle of thought, or a more inclusive hypothesis) and proceeds by rational proof or experimental verifying, guided by the very wholistic concept which is being proved, ending in an enriched insight into the whole.

Not only does the task of perception and understanding require

138

a wholistic approach to "make sense" out of what otherwise would be unintelligible, discrete sensa or experiential episodes, but it is implied by the nigh-universal theoretical and practical belief in the unity of truth. The given of knowledge, both as knowledge and as the object of knowledge, is held to be coherent, and incoherence in supposed knowledge is held to be a warning of error or inadequacy. The unity of truth does not mean actual attainment of complete, ordered knowledge and wisdom, but it signifies the conviction that differentiated reality in all its complexity is not anarchic and irrational, but is knowable in whatever possible limited way because of its universal, intelligible aspect. This is a presupposition, but a presupposition about the nature of the whole which is indispensable to understanding and not derivable from fragmentary experience. Likewise the Christian doctrine of creation implies a wholism—a reliable, orderly creation by a God of power, goodness, and wisdom, not capricious and arbitrary. Objective knowledge, therefore, as a coherence of valid inferences and objective knowledge as intelligible discovery is based on the wholistic conviction that truth and reality are an ordered whole, potential for knowledge. Insofar as existential surds, intellectual contradictions, and gaps of ignorance characterize our understanding of thought, of ourselves, and of the world, the conviction of ordered unity generates the intellectual passion underlying artistic creativity, philosophical reflection, scholarly research, and ethical endeavor, and is not absent even in religious faith.

The international concern with the "university question"—How did the university cease to be a uni-versity and how may it renew its coherent character?—has evoked numerous claims that this can be achieved only by conscious recognition of the wholistic approach. Historically metaphysics and theology have been the means whereby a rational and practical order in the university has been attained.

Why is it that the chief characteristic of the higher learning is disorder? It is because there is no ordering principle in it. Certainly the principle of freedom in the current sense of that word will not unify it. In the current use of freedom it is an end in itself. But it must be clear that if each person has the right to make and achieve his own choices the result is anarchy and the dissolution of the whole. Nor can we look to the pursuit of truth for its own sake to unify the higher learning. Philistines still ask, what is truth? And all truths cannot be equally important. It is true that a finite whole is greater than any of its parts. It is also true, in the common sense use of the word, that the New Haven telephone book is smaller than that of Chicago. The first truth is infinitely more fertile and significant than the second. The common aim of all parts of a university may and should be the pursuit of truth for its own sake. But this common aim is not sufficiently precise to hold the university together while it is moving towards it. Real unity can be achieved only by a hierarchy of truths which show us which are fundamental and which subsidiary, which significant and which not.

The modern university may be compared with an encyclopedia. The encyclopedia contains many truths. It may consist of nothing else. But its unity can be found only in its alphabetical arrangement. The university is in much the same case. It has departments running from art to zoology; but neither the students nor the professors know what is the relation of one departmental truth to another, or what the relation of departmental truths to those in the domain of another department may be.[19]

The fundamental problems of metaphysics, the social sciences, and natural science are, then, the proper subject matter of the higher learning. These categories are exhaustive. I have used the word metaphysics to include not only the study of first principles, but also all that follows from it, about the principles of change in the physical world, which is the philosophy of nature, and about the analysis of man and his productions in the fine arts including literature. The social sciences embrace the practical sciences of ethics, politics, and economics, together with such historical and empirical materials as may be needed to supplement them for the guidance of human action. The theoretical principles of ethics, politics, and economics are, of course, principles of speculative philosophy. The principles of ethics, theoretically considered, are to be found in metaphysics. In ethics itself the same knowledge is viewed in the practical order. To speak of ethics, politics, and economics as practical philosophy is to indicate that they are philosophical knowledge organized for the sake of action. In the law we have a practical application of this body of practical principles. By the natural sciences, I mean, of course, the study of nature. The natural sciences derive their principles from the philosophy of nature, which in turn depends on metaphysics. In the study of them such recent observations as serve to illustrate, exemplify, or confirm these principles must be included. Medicine and engineering are applications of this whole body of knowledge.

By constructing a university in this way it can be made intelligible. Metaphysics, the study of first principles, pervades the whole. Inseparably connected with it is the most generalized understanding of the nature of the world and the nature of man. Dependent on this and subordinate to it are the social and natural sciences. In due subordination in the teaching of these we include historical and current empirical material. Such material ceases to be the whole of these sciences as studied in the university and becomes instead an aid in understanding

---

[19]Robert Hutchins, *The Higher Learning in America*, pp. 94-95.

their principles. In a university like this it should be possible to get an education; it is possible to get one in no other way, for in no other way can the world of thought be presented as a comprehensible whole.[20]

This view is condemned by some contemporaries as based on the untenable assumption of static "antecedent being," an essential given realized in particular things. John Dewey has been the foremost American critic of antecedent being in contemporary thought and in educational philosophy. Nevertheless, he and a host of followers and collaborators have upheld a wholistic interpretation of existence, knowledge, and education.

There is in thoughtful literature of the times evidence of a growing belief that an effective understanding of nature, including human nature, requires an attention, heretofore neglected, to an aspect which, differing for each different case, may be called "the whole". This newer way of seeing nature involves a new method of study. The literature concerned with this point of view may, on the one hand, be seen as a protest against a method of thought variously described as "atomistic," "elementistic," "mechanistically analytic," and "materialistic," and, on the other hand, as a suggestion of a positive new program of attack in the various fields of thought.[21]

Whatever the incidental and more central divergences and conflicts there are between these two important schools of educational philosophy, it is more than interesting to note the wholistic emphasis in both. Some scholars point out that in spite of his aversion to metaphysics, Dewey substitutes a futuristic hypothetical metaphysics for the structured objective metaphysics of the Greeks and Aquinas. The integrated, intelligible whole is therefore an achievement to be made rather than a given to be discovered. In both instances, however, there is a wholistic emphasis in contrast to autonomous pluralism as the framework for knowledge and education.

In the negative criticism of wholism there are two observations most frequently made: it is dogmatic in character and a deterrent in effect. The first understands wholism as an unwarranted imposition of pretended knowledge. Not only, it is held, is our knowledge incomplete, but there are the hurdles of undiscoverable common error and of limited human intelligence. A coherent

---

[20]*Ibid.*, pp. 107-108.
[21]E. V. Sayers, *Educational Issues and Unity of Experience* (New York: Teachers College, Columbia University, 1929), p. 38.

whole is no doubt possible for God, but we are finite and temporal beings. Our knowledge, therefore is piecemeal and even distorted. It is subject to change and even to repudiation as knowledge grows. Because of this, dogmatism—unfounded, premature, presumptuous, unwarranted assertion—is necessarily the characteristic of any wholism which claims knowledge with larger, more fundamental categories than those of common sense and of the methodologies of the various disciplined studies. If there are such inclusive, basic categories of thought and being, they will be emergents in the future of the race.

The second main criticism expresses apprehension that scholarly freedom will be impaired by any wholistic approach. The natural sciences, as Russell maintains, developed only when there was a divorce of ethics and knowledge. Autonomy of thought and research are endangered by any critical intrusion of extra-disciplinary concepts and values. Domination of education by political authoritarianism in Germany may be cited as a contemporary warning against the constrictive effect of any kind of wholism on intellectual activity and discovery. Only in practical and ideological freedom is the significant pursuit of truth possible.

5

QUALIFIED RELATIONAL-WHOLISM

Each of these four major concepts of integration has theoretical and practical advantages and disadvantages. How is one to evaluate them? The most important criteria seem to be the nature of experience, knowing, and understanding, the character of the world of knowledge and wisdom, and the goal of the liberal education enterprise. The additive and sampling views are in theory or in practice basically atomistic. The relational and wholistic views are in varying degrees basically comprehensive and integrative. On the assumption that liberal education aims at an intellectual cosmos, an intellectual map of the world, in the curriculum and *for* the student, rather than a possibly chaotic collection or accidental cosmos, the conclusion of this study is that educational planning should be wholistic rather than atomistic. The configurative character of experience, knowing, and understanding

142

also substantiates a wholistic approach, as does the inter-related, inter-dependent character of man and the world as objects of knowledge.

The case for wholistic integration in the task of knowing and understanding need not be labored. In the specific academic studies there is wholistic integration or there is no *scientia,* no science, no organized body of knowledge to be learned and taught. Likewise an atomistic, collective approach is inadequate in perception itself, in aesthetic contemplation, in personal ethical life, in religious devotion, and in social existence, just as it is inadequate in the world of intelligence and understanding. The principle of contradiction in thought and the conviction of the unity of truth underlie our thinking and our pursuit of knowledge and wisdom. Understanding irreducibly involves discernment of the relatedness of parts to each other within a whole and an apprehension of the whole qualitatively distinguishable from the mere presence of its parts. If relatedness and wholism characterize the ordinary life of the mind, individual and social existence, and the specific academic studies, it seems reasonable to conclude that formal education, especially on the higher levels of conscious reflection and intellectual formulation, should aim at an intellectual whole *in* the curriculum and *for* the learning student.

A number of serious issues are involved in wholistic integration. These are of such importance that in recognition of them this constructive statement on integration should perhaps be called a *qualified wholism.* The qualifications, based on the nature of the whole and on the character of knowing, distinguish this view from a fused, static, dogmatic wholism, while it maintains the essentially inescapable non-atomistic approach and the potential fruitfulness of a relational-wholism. The three major issues requiring clarification are (a) variety and unity, (b) freedom and imposition, and (c) growth and fixity.

(a) *Variety and unity.* Sampling has been described as theoretically a homogeneous wholism and in practice an atomism. In theory it denies significant differentiation. Therefore in education one subject would be interchangeable with any other subject and would be adequate without any other. Wholism, on the other hand, emphasizes that within the whole there is an important distinctiveness of the parts: chemistry is not poetry, philosophy is not history, the individual is not the family or the state, the tongue is not the heart. Each, although related significantly to the others, has its differentiating characteristics, structure, and substance. Each has its differentiated role in relationship to the others and within the whole. In terms of this or that smaller or larger function each has its greater or lesser importance, depending on its function or purpose. Wholism, therefore, emphasizes that homogenizing and universal interchanging do violence to the parts and ignore the nature and purpose of the whole. On the other hand, wholism would point out that the organismic character of life and education implies the partiality of any part; it is limited; it is in a sense a whole but it is not the whole. Its function is a related, derived function. Its place is in a context which does not dissolve the part into its antecedents but rather gives larger meaning to the limited, distinguishable part.

If a wholism is conceivable as a night in which all cows are black, this would be a homogenized wholism, instead of the qualified wholism here proposed. A qualified relational-wholism, avoiding chaos, on the one hand, and a monolithic fused unity, on the other, both as being descriptively inaccurate and normatively undesirable, maintains the real significance of a differentiated unity, characterized by variety and contrasts, existential contradictions, commendable alternatives, gaps in knowledge, and qualitative levels of being, with discernible relationships between the parts and an envisionable whole comprehending the parts and shedding larger meaning upon them.

(b) *Freedom and imposition.* One justifiable fear of a wholistic approach in education is that an immature, premature, constrictive caricature may be thrust upon the relatively autonomous disciplines, thus robbing them of their vitality and openness—a kind of bureaucracy of the mind with loose-leaved operating rule-books distributed from headquarters. The temptation here is to think in political analogies of dictatorship and oligarchy. This is misleading, however, inasmuch as the world of knowledge and wisdom is not basically a world of force, persons, and power groups.

144

Within the limitations of political analogue, one may, however, illustrate an aspect of the qualified wholistic view by pointing out that democracy does not imply anarchy, the war of every man against every man, in which life is "solitary, nasty, brutish, and short." Nor does it imply an automatic harmony without effort to achieve the greater good. Freedom is a limited freedom; otherwise, it tends centrifugally towards chaos. Freedom maintains plurality of origination, together with a commonness of responsibility and relatedness in a whole. Our analogy breaks down in numerous ways, not least in that specific studies are not sacred personalities but divisions of labor in differentiated object areas, approaching limited aspects of nature, man, and God with distinguishable methods. Nevertheless, if political-social freedom is abridged where the next man's nose begins, so, too, departmental autonomy is abridged by the other parts. Further, the world of knowledge constitutes a whole in a way which goes beyond even the wholeness of an organized democratic society, which also has significance above a collection of individuals. The universe of knowledge and wisdom, like the object of knowledge, is a given, not a product of social contract. It has its variegated unity of structure of thought, its substance of creative vision, and the patterns of that which is known. The relative autonomy of the various disciplines is freedom of pursuit, not a freedom from the findings and constructions in other studies, nor from normative thought, nor from relatedness in a meaningful universe of knowledge and wisdom.

Qualified wholism would not be a dogmatic imposition, but it would rather be a fruitful dialogue within more inclusive ranges, correcting the partialities of limited parts and methodologies, an undertaking pursued under critical norms of coherent understanding and within the substance of experience, reason, and faith. Imposition is, properly understood, a political category and in the world of mind is the result of coercion from outside this world, from the realms of social, governmental, and ecclesiastical powers. The best defense against external coercion is not intellectual chaos but a vigorous, coherent intellectual life conscious of the integrity of knowledge and wisdom.

A qualified wholism does challenge radically autonomous positions such as empiricism, rationalism, fideism, aestheticism, scientism, materialism, and spiritualism, as it challenges any claims to total independence by any department or study. But this is within the universe of knowledge, incomplete and varied, yet with its criteria and its varied substance. Academic freedom means responsible scholarship in a community of scholars within this universe of knowledge. Vigorous research and thought are stimulated by mutuality within this community which is fruitfully bound together by an intelligible insight into the larger whole of knowledge and wisdom.

(c) *Growth and fixity*. A qualified relational-wholism cuts through the extreme Heraclitean assertion that knowledge grows from day to day and therefore no coherent intellectual map of the world is possible or reasonably desirable. A dogmatic, static wholism would ignore both new creative vision and intelligible discovery, but this is not a necessary aspect of wholism. Rather a qualified wholism affirms that there is quantitative change in knowledge and re-formation of understanding through creative contemplation, critical conversation, and experience.

Likewise qualified wholism affirms the stabilities of knowledge and wisdom. Without a slavish historicism, it would challenge the conceit of modernity, which in extremes might claim total newness; and it would point out that growth in knowledge and understanding depends upon deep stabilities. Even the Copernican and Kantian revolutions, the Protestant Reformation, and the modern development of the natural sciences were not entirely novel but had profound roots in the Greek-Hebraic heritage. Change itself is perceptible only by virtue of stabilities within change, and in the practical sphere deliberate change is possible only on the basis of constancy.

Part of the genius of wholism is its non-reductionism, which precludes precisely the over-simplifications which usually deny diversity, freedom, and growth, while at the same time it undergirds the significance of man's knowing enterprise and forwards its movement.

In its inclusiveness wholism is critical of partiality, and in its

146

emphasis on the unity of truth and the interconnectedness of parts it points beneath superficiality. In addition, as a working instrument of knowledge it has a positive suggestiveness in at least two ways. The first is illustrated by the wholism of the hypothetico-deductive method of the experimental sciences. Experience, otherwise random, is directed and harnessed by the wholistic hypothesis and constitutive concepts. Secondly, by virtue of a larger vision of the whole, it encourages interdisciplinary reflection and critical conversation, revealing the similarities, contrasts, and contradictions which are the very life of scholarly pursuit and growth in knowledge and understanding

6

QUALIFIED WHOLISM AND MOTIVATION IN LEARNING

Rooted in the unity of truth, in the intelligible character of the world (however our knowledge is limited by gaps and contrasts), in the organic nature of perception, knowing, and understanding, in the integrated structure of specific studies, and in the fruitfulness of a more inclusive apprehension of the larger whole, the interdisciplinary integration of relational-wholism is also of importance in the motivation of both teaching and learning. Whitehead observes that too much education is "a rapid table of contents which a deity might run over in his mind while he was thinking of creating a world, and had not yet determined how to put it together." The result is "the fatal disconnection of subjects which kills the vitality of our modern curriculum."[22] Arthur Compton, out of a life of teaching, research, and university administration, judges that the sketching of an intellectual map of the world is our most urgent educational need.

Strong, exciting teaching and strong, exciting learning (to use Kenneth Brown's phrase) are intrinsically related to an eradication of this fatal disconnection and to this mapping of the intellectual world. Understanding for teacher and student requires connectedness of parts and a vision of the whole. The learning pursuit for both teacher and student is enlivened by the perception of signifi-

---

[22]*Aims of Education,* pp. 10-11.

ćant coherence and contrasts or contradictions. When both student and teacher have a conscious expectation and task of an intellectual map of the world, motivation is engendered both by the high aim and by the excitement of discovery as one moves further and deeper. A "course" is no longer an independent entity worth "three hours credit" but a significant portion of the educational curriculum or venture ("curriculum" means "course"). Then both student and teacher can have the satisfaction of the craftsman and artist dealing with a moving whole rather than the truncated experience of the assembly-line worker. The specific studies are no longer units to be got out of the way, but important portions contributing to the whole educational development and illuminated by an understanding of the larger whole.

In addition to the stimulating power of intellectual design, the student should know the encouragement which comes from development of intellectual power: the ability to read and listen understandingly, to apprehend presuppositions and inferences, to think in valid comprehensive categories, to grasp the wider relevancy of ideas and events. The development of such powers is directly related to conscious pursuit of integration on both departmental and inter-disciplinary levels.

Students do make these enhancing discoveries and do develop these powers whatever the curriculum and teaching might be. They should not be robbed of their participation which makes the achievement *their* achievement. But it should not have to happen quite apart from curriculum and teaching or in spite of them. Interdisciplinary integration and perceptive, relational teaching can create an expectation and illustrate the genuine possibilities of the pursuit, which are only occasional if the task of the college is not actively conceived and structured as an internally related whole.

7

INTEGRATIVE MEANS

Whatever valid claims may be made for the integrative value of dormitory life, regularized arrangements for meals, extra-curricular activities, church and chapel, and personal relationships, the liberal arts college with its central intellectual task of teaching and learning must face the problem of integration as having its locus within curriculum and teaching. Insofar as "the intellectual climate" of a campus is stimulating and integrative, it is itself largely the creation of the educational aims of the college and of what actually goes on in the classroom. A study, therefore, of integrative means is properly centered on the teachable structures, substances, and methods which constitute the stuff of the educational transaction. There certainly are imponderables in good teaching, but these are not amenable to selection, formulation, and propagation; whereas the college as a community of teaching scholars is responsible for what and how it does what it does. If integrative means cannot be found here, the college as a college leaves educational coherence to the periphery of its life and neglects it where it is most likely to be found, precisely where the college can do something about it within its central task.

What are the most suitable integrative means? The Harvard study points out four (Religion; Western Culture; Change: Contemporary Problems; and Pragmatism and Natural Science) and finds all of them impracticable, intrinsically deficient, or too narrow. Claims have been made for specific studies: especially for theology, history, philosophy, literature, fine arts, and the natural and social sciences. These claims are based on method, scope, and content and on the effectiveness of specified subjects for specified purposes. Reorganization of courses and of patterns of teaching are urged as integrative within broader divisional areas. Faculty education or re-education in the direction of common concepts and fundamental distinctions has been advocated. Senior seminars, comprehensive examinations, and senior essays are among the more specific devices in use and widely recommended.

The concept of integration which animates positive concern for educational coherence is important in the evaluation and choice of integrative means. A qualified relational-wholism would stress (1) clarification of the intellectual purpose of the whole college enterprise, (2) teachers' awareness of the relatedness of their portions to the entire educational venture, (3) the importance of order in the curriculum, (4) a functional understanding of the

149

various departments and parts of the curriculum, and (5) any methods which would aid students to participate in the intrinsically valuable and practical task of sketching a coherent understanding of man in his basic relationships. "Thus *the search continues* and must continue for some *over-all logic*, some *strong*, not easily *broken frame* within which both college and school may fulfill their at once diversifying and uniting tasks. This logic must be wide enough to embrace the actual richness and variegation of modern life—a richness partly, if not wholly, reflected in the complexity of our present educational system. It must also be strong enough to give goal and direction to this system—something much less clear at present."[23]

---

[23]*General Education in a Free Society* p. 40.

PART THREE

Integrative
Means

Chapter Eight

The Integrative
Potentialities of
Specific Academic Studies

A SURVEY of twenty-one college and university self studies carried on in 1953-54 with the aid of grants from the
Fund for the Advancement of Education indicates a miscellany of
concerns in the various institutions. Coherence, the provisional
study states, is nevertheless "the pervasive problem." "Each of the
self-studies reflects in some way a concern for better integration
in higher education."[1] The self study report of Baldwin-Wallace
College in stating the aims of a Christian liberal arts college declares first that liberal education "can be described as a search
for coherence of knowledge. . . . Therefore, the liberal arts college
sees as its unique task that of providing the student with an over-
all view of man's accumulation of knowledge interpreted in terms
of coherent meaning."[2]

This wide-spread interest in the educational task "of the college
as a whole," or, more accurately, "within the curriculum as a
whole," does not necessarily verify the majority judgment of the
St. Olaf Faculty (94% of those answering question IIA of the
Faculty Questionnaire)[3] that integration is "a proper central aim
in liberal arts education." Yet it does indicate a significant com-

---

[1] *Draft College Self Study Report* (New York: The Fund for the Advancement of
Education, 1955), p. 30.
[2] "Philosophy of Education," Chapter III of "Self Study, a report on education
as practiced and projected at Baldwin-Wallace College," *Association of American
Colleges Bulletin,* October, 1955, p. 454.
[3] Cf. *Integration in Christian Higher Education,* Volume II, Appendices, p. 42.

153

munity of educational judgment which accents a critical need aggravated by specialization, occupationalism, departmentalism, and curricular expansion.

Integration in this sense is focused upon "an understanding of the relatedness of courses, of areas, of the entire curriculum." Integration can also be thought of as integration of the personality, as structural integration of the college as an operating group (students, teaching officers, administrative officers, trustees, Church Board of Education) in its legal and organizational aspects, or as integration of "campus and classroom." Although the importance of these various localizations of integration is recognized, this study of educational integration has been concentrated upon that central activity without which a college may still exist as an institution but would essentially cease to be a college: the teaching-learning enterprise. Therefore, educational integration must be considered first in the area of "teachable structures and substances," because this is the core-stuff of the college and because this is where the collegium of professors can most directly and effectively do something about realizing its educational objectives.

Educational integration as penetrating relational understanding is rooted in the prime conviction of the *universe* of truth, in spite of the incompleteness of truth as known, in spite of human error and partialities, in spite of the paradoxes of understanding, and in spite of the tragedy and mystery of existence. This universe of truth consciously explored is the proper central sphere of the college and distinguishes it from a church, a housing settlement, a factory, a technical institute, a finishing school, a training center, a marriage mart, or a reformatory. A college drifts away from its essential character when there is a shift from central concern with this sphere and from pre-occupation with that which it can best do: the awakening of critical, creative intellectual powers, the development of an intellectual grasp of experience and reality, and the sharpening of discriminating judgment of values. Whatever other valuable kinds of integration are achieved, the college in its primary intellectual task ought not be careless, consciously or by default, within its primary area: the knowable realm of the good and the real.

Given coherence in understanding as a shared educational

154

objective, we still have the problem of discovering the integrative means most adequate to achieve this goal. There have been numerous educational experiments in the United States during the last two or three decades, some of which are discussed in succeeding chapters. Some of them have involved extensive institutional reorganization, remodeling of the traditional curricular pattern, and the introduction of numerous new courses and instructional divisions. Without passing judgment here on these approaches to integration and other problems, we propose to consider the question of integrative means from the standpoint of the integrative potentialities inherent in the teachable structures and substances of academic studies offered in a Christian liberal arts college like St. Olaf.

Such an approach betrays some unelaborated conclusions: (1) that there *is* an important measure of educational coherence in our program of Christian liberal education because of the kinds of courses usually offered, however much disintegrative tendencies have dispersed educational thinking and practice even in the liberal arts college; (2) that every subject customarily taught in the best contemporary liberal arts colleges is a differentiated part of the whole curriculum and can in some way and to some degree be integrative beyond its own borders; (3) that the individual instructor's awareness of the educational aims of the curriculum as a whole and of his own subject's integrative role is a *sine qua non* of educational integration no matter what is done within the whole curriculum and by other instructors and departments; and (4) that there may be unrealized or educationally unexploited integrative means intrinsic to academic studies now offered.

Inasmuch as there is valid differentiation of the curricular whole into its significant parts or subjects, so that no one study in liberal education is mechanically replaceable by another, our question of integrative means includes a corollary question: are there academic studies from which comparatively larger integrative contributions can legitimately be expected? George Santayana once lamented that Harvard was like a Noah's ark, with each of the professors sticking his head through his own porthole in the ark and with no more communication between them than between a milkmaid and a cow. The criticism implied is not of differentiated positions and

155

concerns but of inadequacy of communication between portholes and of no one's being concerned about the ark (except Noah—the Dean or President?). Without making one large porthole or eliminating all but one, our question asks whether some places on the educational ark can properly be expected to provide larger views of the ark and a more commodious setting for deliberate conversation about the whole ark and its journey.

Differentiation of subject matters within the teachable substance of the Christian liberal arts college implies differentiation of functions under the objectives of the college as a whole. If it is judged educationally valuable, for example, that every student should be competent in the use of his mother tongue, it is legitimate to expect every course and department and teacher to contribute to this end and to expect a special contribution from formal teaching of English. In fulfilling the objectives of the requirement in the natural sciences and mathematics, formal instruction in these areas should be expected to carry disproportionate functional responsibility, with other instruction making a greater or lesser contribution as the nature of method and subject matter permits. Likewise with regard to fulfilling the objective of integration we have the question: are there relatively differentiated functional responsibilities? Are there diverse levels of integrative contribution which can legitimately be expected from the various studies?

This has nothing to do with academic dignity or with the equal honor of vocations. Nor is it a matter of departments or persons, except insofar as division of labor has formally lodged certain tasks in certain hands within an organized working group. Even then it is not a matter of departmental possession but rather of the intrinsic potentialities inherent in the level, method, structure, substance, and conscious aims of the specific study itself.

Therefore, the attempt here to discover the integrative potentialities in present academic studies is analytical and systematic and is directed at the studies themselves. The objects of critical analysis are not the subjects as they are actually taught at St. Olaf or at any other particular college. The basic objects of scrutiny here are statements on the integrative roles of specific studies prepared by the various departments of St. Olaf College.[4] As requested, how-

---

[4]These statements appear in Volume II, Appendices, pp. 55-161.

ever, these statements are not essentially empirical descriptions of these studies as now taught but formulations of the inherent integrative character of the "teachable structure and substance" of the specific subjects.

1

ANALYSIS OF DEPARTMENTAL STATEMENTS

A careful reading of the departmental statements reveals the presence within the faculty of a larger measure of agreement concerning educational aims and methods than one might have expected in view of the occasional sharp clashes between teachers and between departments over curricular policy. Some of the statements utilize the fact that the majority of the faculty and administration "consider educational integration to be a central aim in the task of the Christian Liberal Arts College" as a premise from which to proceed to constructive suggestions. It would appear that positive motivation does exist for a deliberate and concerted attack upon the problem of fragmentation and it would also appear that something like a common mind exists with respect to the curricular ingredients and relationships required for a college-wide effort at integration. In some statements, explicit reference is made to the different levels on which integration occurs, and in others these levels are acknowledged implicitly. In any case, it is possible to arrange in a systematic order the claims and implications endorsed by the faculty.

The statements are unanimous in affirming that no one area of study can provide a complete education, nor can any subject stand alone. The Home Economics statement may be allowed to speak for all departments when, after listing its goals, it says: "Home Economics cannot do this alone and thus there must be a well integrated program at the college level."

The interrelationship of areas of study is assumed both as a fact and as an ideal, and it is accepted as a specific task in the great majority of the departmental statements. But it is important to notice that the several departments do not speak about integration in exactly the same way. Most of the writers claim that their subjects coordinate materials and methods which are contributed

157

by other areas of study. Thus, the majority of studies acknowledge dependence upon a few basic subjects.

Within the area of dependent studies, different types of integrative achievement may be distinguished. First, there are those subjects which claim to give exceedingly valuable, if not indispensable, aid to the understanding of the total human situation by the *inspection* of *one phase* of man's life. For example, concerning Chemistry it is stated that "everything in the physical universe has a chemical aspect, i.e., its substance"; consequently a study of the composition and laws of substance gives one invaluable understanding of his total situation. The Biology department's statement says that "a student should gain an understanding of life from the standpoint of the basic living substance." A similar claim is made in the statement, by the Norwegian department, in which the valuable distinction is made between subjects that have wide-scale coordination as their goal and those that provide "contributive elements" which "may not strictly be called integrative." It is said that a "national language is the most distinctive part of the national spirit." If one is to understand his nationality and that of others, he must do so through the medium of language. Language, is, then, an aid to the understanding of the human situation because it enables the student to inspect that situation from the standpoint of one of its fundamental aspects. It is said in both the German and the Romance Language statements that such study releases one from the "provincialism" of "cultural isolation." Economics promotes an understanding of life by focusing attention upon the complex of such factors as resources, management, production, and consumption of the goods and services required for community life. Psychology is said to contribute toward an understanding of the total picture of human life by fixing upon the single aspect of "personality growth," and Sociology aims to achieve the same result by centering upon "human social behavior." These examples are sufficient to indicate that several subjects claim to be integrated and self-consistent approaches to a single aspect of reality, although they do not claim to be able to replace one another or to coordinate the findings of the other areas of knowledge, except insofar as those findings furnish data for some other particular study. These subjects are, then, correlative with one another and depend in various ways upon the stream of human experience, which each subject examines in terms of one of its fundamental aspects.

Certain other subjects do not claim to discover or analyze data furnished by any particular aspect of reality. They are almost completely dependent upon the studies mentioned, and upon others to be examined shortly, and claim primarily to provide a point of focus for the integration of methods and materials drawn from other areas. For example, the statement of the Music department asserts that "the musical experience" provides a point upon which one can bring to a *focus* the knowledge and skills gained through broad human experience and an acquaintance with the total curriculum. By producing a point of focus in a type of self-expressive action, Music is "an aid in the development of an integrated personality." Apart from the "musical experience" it is not claimed that Music contributes values or concepts which are peculiar to itself, and it is clear that the end-product is to be found in a person rather than in any extensible systematic structure. The musical experience is a composite of "physical, intellectual, moral, and spiritual" experiences. Classroom work within the area of Music presupposes a knowledge of Philosophy, History, Religion, Literature, Geography, Natural Sciences, Social Sciences, and Art. The Home Economics statement lists goals which involve a knowledge of moral values and data within the areas of the social and natural sciences. Since these values and data are used but not originated by Home Economics as such, it is proper that the statement should read: "Home Economics draws upon all areas of learning and brings them to focus upon the home." The Nursing Program statement affirms that through "the intellectual and moral vision gained from sharing in the cultural heritage of the liberal arts," the nurse will be aided in her task of "ministering to the patient's total needs." The nursing candidate should possess knowledge in the areas of the Natural and Biological Sciences, the Humanities, History, Psychology, Sociology, Language, and Religion. The data from these fields are used by the Nursing Program for a specific purpose. The same can be said of the claims made in the Speech, ROTC, and Physical Education statements. Each provides a point of focus in a type of action, so that the integration is achieved in a personal product rather than in a unique intellectual structure. An examination of the statements issued by the Art, Speech, ROTC, Education, Economics, Physical Education, and Political Science departments will reveal that, at least on certain levels of course offerings, these areas "draw upon" a wide range of values and data which are supplied by other areas of study and are brought to a focus in the preparation of the student for some type of action or self-expression. In this sense the fields just noted are more dependent upon supporting courses than are the subjects discussed under the first heading (Biology, Physics, Chemistry, Language, etc.).

A third type of integrative operation within the general grouping of the more or less dependent subjects is found in the claim that a certain subject is a *place* which provides an "opportunity," "laboratory," or "proving ground" within which values, substance, and methods contributed by other subjects may be observed in practice. This place is said to be desirable, but not indispensable, since another study could also illustrate the values, substance, or methods. The stress here is not upon an action, as in the second group, but upon concepts and methods which are useful in many areas. For example, it is said that the scientific method "can be introduced in admirable fashion in the teaching of chemistry." The Mathematics statement declares that the appeal to "definition, axiom, assumption and hypothesis can be demonstrated in other fields, but outside of the discipline of formal logic, there is no clearer demonstration of these than in mathematics." The Physics department states: "The study of mathematics can be and is made more stimulating by applying it to physical problems." The statement about Romance Languages argues that the truly foundational concepts of nature, man, and God, with which the "Queen Disciplines" of "theology and philosophy" are specially preoccupied, may be examined profitably in Area Study programs which "serve as successful examples of a very real kind of integration." It is said of both Psychology and Sociology that they represent specialized or focused uses of the general method of scientific thought.

The statements which acknowledge that their subjects "draw upon" or illustrate methods, data, or concepts supplied by one or several other studies, cite very similar lists of such sources. In al-

160

most every case, the "inspectional" type of subject is mentioned (Psychology, Economics, Sociology, Language, Physics, Biology, and Chemistry). But another type of subject is also mentioned. Generally speaking, dependence is acknowledged upon Logic, Mathematics, Philosophy, Scientific Method, History, and Religion. This latter group of subjects is evidently regarded as fundamental in some special sense.

This judgment tallies with the claims made about the subjects themselves. The Physics statement, for example, acknowledges that "physics is based upon mathematics." Mathematics, as a study of purely formal relationships, is not said to be based upon any other method or data. Mathematics presupposes only the rational capacity to comprehend "basic concepts" and to appreciate "significant meanings" and it is a matter of indifference as to what sort of substantial content is being subjected to mathematical analysis. Mathematics is thus an indispensable "tool subject" for work in the areas of "astronomy, biology, chemistry, geology or physics."

Although Philosophy is usually regarded as a synoptic study, the Philosophy statement points out that "philosophy, in its analytic function, includes metaphysics, epistemology (and logic), and the study of values." Philosophy is a peculiarly basic type of study since it is an "approach to three major areas—to being, knowing, and value" (ontology, epistemology and logic, and axiology). Philosophy, in the form of logic and epistemology, studies the presuppositions of the special sciences, and indeed, "of every cognitive encounter." Since "the act of knowing is an act dealing with being and values," it is, in its critical function, a foundation even of the studies usually regarded as basic.

History, like Mathematics and the Scientific Method in general, can claim to be peculiarly basic since it is a specialized form of logical procedure. The statement from the History department declares that "past events become history only after they have been correlated into a meaningful sequence." Again, it is said that "the historian must approach his task with relative detachment and a minimum of prejudice if he is to fix his subject in proper relation to what preceded and what followed it." It is the task of History, then, to place remembered events within a temporal sequence. This method of approach is not borrowed from any other

161

discipline, although it is used in nearly every field of knowledge. The point is that any such temporal relating constitutes an historical operation.

The Scientific Method may also be regarded as a specialized type of logic, since, with specific modifications, the process of systematic rational procedure is essentially the same in every field. It is therefore not dependent upon those other fields but enjoys an independent, and therefore basic, status. Mathematics, History, and Scientific Method are basic to other studies in the same sense in which formal logic is basic to the specialized types of logic.

Language is similarly a basic type of study. In the statement about Romance Languages it is maintained that "theology and philosophy are the main integrating fields in the final analysis," but neither these nor any other disciplines could exist without "their expression in language." Language is not only the universal and elementary vehicle of human expression, but "creative literature" can give "dramatic impact" to any expressed substance. Language is, then, an independent cultural entity which "mediates virtually every kind of learning" (German statement).

The constant reference to Philosophy as a subject which is "drawn upon" by the dependent studies indicates more than that logic is the "formal point" at which "all sciences meet." It also recognizes that Philosophy is a deliberate and systematic study of the whole of knowledge and experience. It examines the principles or presuppositions not only of reasoning but of all being and knowing. Consequently, "philosophizing" occurs in every subject, and it is independent of the subjects themselves.

Religion (theology) is cited in nearly every statement as a source of ethical norms and as a witness to the Object of Faith which gives a dynamic and practical unity to all of life. Although Theology uses the common rational method studied in Logic, works with the presuppositions regarding being and value studied in Philosophy, and draws upon historical data, it is an independent study in the sense that it is its special task to affirm and explain the basic truths involved in the Church's proclamation. It may be said then that Logic, Language, Philosophy, History, and Theology are independent studies upon which other studies depend for method and some basic kinds of substance.

We have observed that the departmental statements make assertions which may be separated into categories claiming that certain studies achieve the coordination of knowledge in terms of the *inspection* of one fundamental phase of experience, or in terms of a certain *type of action*, or in an *opportunity* to observe methods and values which are derived from other studies, and those which achieve coordination in terms of method or substance on a basic or more *independent level*. Finally, there are those subjects which claim to coordinate studies in terms of a *unified intellectual perspective*. The Music, Romance Languages, Philosophy, and Religion statements say or imply that all knowledge should be coordinated in terms of the all-embracing concepts of "nature, man, and God." Subjects which aim to interpret or express the data from all fields in terms of these concepts possess a peculiarly comprehensive or integrative value. Such claims are made by History, Literature, Philosophy, and Theology, and by those subjects which offer a history or philosophy of a certain area of knowledge or action, such as History of Art, History of Music, History of Literature, and Philosophy of Science. It would seem, then, that these subjects appear at the beginning of the scale of studies as furnishing the basic procedures or contents upon which the more dependent studies may draw, as well as at the end of the scale where they interpret or express in more inclusive categories the data provided by all the fields of knowledge.

2

SYSTEMATIC FORMULATION

Firstly, in the statements made by the various departments, the great majority of them suggest that they both *draw upon* other fields and *contribute* to others. The statement of the Biology department is representative, wherein they speak of those subjects which are utilized in Biology (Chemistry, Mathematics, Philosophy, Physics), those which integrate reciprocally (Economics, History, Political Science), and those which require Biology as a basis to their study (Home Economics, Nursing, Physical Education, Psychology, Sociology).[5] Similarly, the Physics department states that

---

[5]Vol. II, Appendices, p. 97.

it contributes to Chemistry, but draws upon Mathematics.[6] Comparable statements could also be cited for the Social Sciences,[7] for the fields of Literature and the Arts, and for History, Philosophy, and Theology. In some way or other all these fields contribute to other fields and also draw upon others, some to a lesser and some to a greater extent. This *receptive-contributive* relationship (whether from and to the same fields, or from some and to others) is then a kind of integration, whereby various fields are coordinated to some extent for the purposes of a particular field. This level of integration might be simply called *coordinating*—which may largely be an unconscious operation, for teaching in most fields coordinates to some degree without pointing to the fact that it does so.

Secondly, some fields emphasize especially how they draw together a vast wealth of other fields in view of the end sought in the specific field. Since a person pursuing studies in that field must then *focus* his work upon this end, he achieves a kind of integration of his studies. It should be noted that integration here is spoken of in terms of the person and not so much of knowledge as such. These areas constitute an *occasion* where the student may bring his studies together in a focus, and doubtless other studies could argue that they too contribute to the integration of the person in this manner.[8] However, these particular studies—chiefly Air Science, Home Economics, Music Education, Nursing, Business Education, and Speech—argue that they help to integrate the person because of the way in which they draw other studies together into the goal of their study, whether this goal be the training of future airmen, nurses, musicians, homemakers, good public speakers, and the like. Thus the department of Air Science speaks of its objective being "to produce graduates who are capable of using all the knowledge at their command in the performance of their jobs."[9] The Speech department refers to the fact

---

[6]*Ibid.*, p. 125.

[7]*Ibid.*, pp. 132, 144, 148, 156, 159-60.

[8]Thus a student majoring in any given field must bring to bear on that *specialization* all that he can from other fields. Furthermore, all studies are disciplines, and a student can enjoy the disciplining of mind in any field, so that all studies contribute to this end. Or all studies pursue *truth* as an end, and all studies contribute to this end. Specialization, discipline, truth as goal—all can be integrating for the *person*, although they may communicate no integrative intellectual substance and thus do not integrate studies *per se* with one another.

[9]Vol. II, p. 93.

164

that Speech enables a student to integrate all his studies in oral communication,[10] and also how Speech itself uses principles and methods from other departments.[11] Home Economics states that its study "draws upon all other areas of learning and brings them to a focus upon the home."[12] The statement of the Nursing department points out the way in which other studies contribute to the making of "an able and professional nurse."[13] Physical Education focuses upon the health of the individual as its end, utilizing the insights of several fields, chiefly Biology and Medicine.[14] These fields, therefore, either speak of their integrative role for their majors, or for all students in a practical sense (as public speaking). They are integrative primarily on a receptive level, then, and because they *focus* on some particular function of the person (nursing, homemaking, public speaking, musical performance). Consequently it is not stated that other studies use them, nor do the statements about other studies speak of drawing upon them for intellectual substance. Thus we might call this kind of integration the *receptive-focal* type.

So far, then, two levels can be seen. All disciplines draw upon others. But some are (1) *receptive-focal;* whereas others also contribute substantially to others, and can be called (2) *receptive-contributive* studies. If some primarily receive, and others both receive and contribute, the question arises as to whether there are any (3) *basically contributive disciplines?* Such disciplines would constitute the third level of integration, and a fourth level will appear when we ask if there are not disciplines whose very nature it is to view the whole of knowledge and culture, and in this synoptic manner relate disciplines to one another.

Thus, thirdly, are there disciplines whose nature is almost solely *contributive or basically contributive?* We can perceive at the outset that, if there are such, they would have to be studies of an almost *formal* nature—that is, not dealing so much with the substance of knowledge as with the forms in which knowledge must be cast. Such studies would also be *non-derivative*—not derived from other

[10]*Ibid.*, p. 83.
[11]*Ibid.*, pp. 84 f. Speech is also a part of language study; for its role there, *vide infra.*
[12]*Ibid.*, p. 103.
[13]*Ibid.*, pp. 111-114.
[14]*Ibid.*, p. 115.

studies—and thus basic to other studies. This level of integration becomes especially important, because such basic disciplines relate to all fields and in essentially the same way. These disciplines are Logic, Language, and Metaphysics. Let us examine them one by one.

The *first* of these, Logic, is the study of valid thinking, and thus is presupposed by all fields of knowledge. As the self-study report at Baldwin-Wallace College has stated—

> Logic . . . is an indispensable tool for each field of knowledge in its search for truth. Understanding of and skill in the use of principles of Logic are, therefore, central to understanding and using any rational method of inquiry.[15]

Or as Professor Mueller of Oklahoma says of Logic: "It is the *formal unity* of all scientific training," and "logic, therefore, is a prerequisite for all branches of learning."[16] Logic is a non-derivative field, drawing upon no other, but contributing to all and integrating all, although in a *formal* sense. In this connection one can also mention the various "specialized logics," or the various methods of reflective inquiry. Among these would be the Mathematical Method, the Scientific Method (or Methods, as some prefer), the Historical Method, the Artistic Method, the Literary Method, and the Philosophical Method.[17] Here the kind of object studied helps determine the specifically appropriate method of study. An event in history, an event in nature, and an artistic event are not equivalent—yet as objects of study and teaching they have some rational structures in common, as do the methods, although they must differ because of differences between the natures of the objects studied.

The *second* kind of non-derivative study is Language. While it is true that without logic language could not be studied as a science, it is just as true that without language logic could not be expressed. Logic and Language are thus closely interrelated, the one dealing with the structure of correct thinking, and the other with the structure of the instruments of thought—words. Since the structure of correct thought is logically prior to the symbols with which it is

---

[15]P. 455.
[16]*Education Limited*, pp. 63 and 67. Italics not in the original.
[17]Cf. F. C. S. Northrop, *The Logic of the Sciences and the Humanities* (New York: Macmillan, 1947) and the Baldwin-Wallace Report, p. 455-456.

expressed (not psychologically prior, for we learn language first), Logic is more basic. But Language shares in the same non-derivative quality that Logic has. It does not draw its subject matter from other fields, but it is used by all other fields. Without language no knowledge could be expressed or communicated. Language includes both the grammar and rhetoric of the language, and as to the latter, both oral (speech) and written rhetoric. Thus Language, like Logic, integrates in a *formal* way, but in a verbal, not conceptual way. In either case we do not deal with integration of substance but with the formal "backbone" of all studies. Grammar, Rhetoric, Logic—the old classical "trivium"—are, as one writer put it, "right reason joined to cultivated expression."[18]

The *third* kind of non-derivative study is Metaphysics. This study has been variously defined, but as basic we can define it as the study of the presuppositions of being and knowledge. In relation to the whole field of knowledge every thinker builds upon suppositions—fundamental suppositions—about reality as such and about the possibility of knowledge itself.[19] If we ask questions, we suppose they can have answers. We suppose that reality is such that it is knowable. Metaphysics inquires, then, into the nature of reality (or being, as some would prefer to call it) and the nature of knowledge—both of which are presupposed in all other fields. These two problems run in a tight circle, for to believe that our senses are fit instruments for finding out what sorts of things there are in the world really depends upon what we believe are the sorts of things in the world. The field of Metaphysics is, of course, a field of controversy, and as a result in a Christian college the orientation of *faith* enters as the starting point or "key"-category. This would involve Theology to the extent to which one complements the faith by rational understanding and expression. Thus ultimately the Trinitarian God who created the universe through His Word (Greek "logos") in the unity of the Holy Spirit is the guarantee of the rationality and reality of the universe, but

[18]J. E. Wise, *The Nature of the Liberal Arts* (Milwaukee: The Bruce Publishing Co., 1947), p. 188.

[19]Paul Tillich emphasizes the importance of using the term "reality as a whole" and not the "whole of reality." That is, metaphysics as a basic study does not aim to piece together the conclusions of all studies to make an encyclopedic picture of the whole of reality, "but to study the basic categories and structures of reality as a whole." *Systematic Theology*, I (Chicago: University of Chicago Press, 1951), p. 18.

this theological ground is no substitute for the analysis of the structures and categories of reality and knowledge as developed in metaphysical study. Metaphysics is here spoken of, then, as *philosophia prima* (first philosophy), the study of first principles, and not as "world-view." In terms of the latter Metaphysics will appear again in our fourth level, but as the study of first principles it shares the quality of Logic and Language—it is more formal and abstract in nature and related to all disciplines as the study of the presuppositions of being and knowledge.

Lastly we turn to the *fourth* level where in addition to the *receptive-contributive, receptive-focal,* and the *basically contributive* levels we speak of those disciplines which intentionally regard the whole of knowledge and reality as one of their specific tasks. Here we come to the so-called *synoptic studies*—namely, History, Philosophy, and Theology. By *synoptic* is meant "seeing together"—studies which in addition to their own problems also try to see things connected together as a whole. These studies are not accidentally synoptic—in intention, method, and substance they are synoptic. That is to say, they intend to view all things and all knowledge together; their methods are inclusive, not exclusive as with the special sciences; and the substance of their subject matters includes synoptic interpretation and understanding. It is likewise a characteristic of these areas, although more specifically History and Philosophy, that they can underlie and "methodize" any other area of knowledge. Thus we have "History of Art" or "History of Science," or "Philosophy of Science," and "Philosophy of Art," and the like. This characteristic is also revealing of the synoptic role these studies have. Theology uses chiefly the methods of History, Philosophy, and Linguistics, as we shall soon see.

History achieves synoptic integration by relating things temporally. The historical approach can be utilized in any discipline. Its function is perhaps least discernible in the natural sciences, but it becomes very important for the social disciplines inasmuch as society is greatly affected by the time process. History becomes uniquely important for the humanities as the context in which great works of art, great philosophical and religious teaching have an enduring significance. Here a study of the past is absolutely essential. Lastly, History comes into its own when the historian weaves together the isolated strands of cultural, political, economic life into as concrete a view of the historical process as possible. How he interprets history depends on his own philosophical-theological orientations, which shows the coordinating function which history also has. Thus the method of History is inclusive, and it "sees together" chronologically.

Philosophy, which is a wider study than Metaphysics and Logic (already discussed), achieves synoptic integration by relating things systematically. A philosophical approach can be used in any discipline, insofar as the presuppositions, methods, and basic concepts of each discipline and group of disciplines are fundamentally examined. Thus there are such studies as Philosophy of Science, Philosophy of Art, Philosophy of History, and the like. A Philosophy of Culture will seek to show essential interrelationships among all areas of culture, including the relationship of the various special sciences. Problems of the nature of being, knowledge, and value all enter the picture, and all culminate in the metaphysical attempt to give a coherent and reasonable account of reality and of human experience as a whole. Metaphysics is thus at two levels—both the non-derivative and the synoptic levels. In the latter sense perhaps the term "world-view" could be used to distinguish its wider extension from the ontological-epistemological task of Metaphysics in its non-derivative sense. All sciences contribute to the philosopher's task of formulating a world-view, but, as pointed out before, not in the sense that the philosopher aims to compile an encyclopedia. Thus Philosophy has its coordinating function too, and especially in relation to Theology, because the "key"-categories or "clue"-concepts originate for the Christian thinker in this realm. But the philosopher cannot ignore historical development either, and thus History and Philosophy complement each other—there is History of Philosophy and Philosophy of History. The method of Philosophy is an inclusive one, for it deals with total meanings, questions of purpose and value, and consults the data from all experience.[20] It seeks synoptic interpretation on the basis of principles.

Lastly, Theology does not ask the question about reality as a

---

[20] Cf. Baldwin-Wallace Report, p. 457, on relation of Philosophy to the special sciences.

whole in the way in which Philosophy does, for it turns to a study of the relationship between the source of reality, God, and this reality, and especially of the purpose for man within it. Thus Theology must draw upon Philosophy for the categories, laws, and concepts of reality, as well as upon History, Philosophy, and Linguistics for its methods of study. But Theology looks to revelation for its source of knowledge, adding a dimension, then, not to be found in other disciplines, although as a science it works with the methods of other studies. As someone put it: "Theology is philosophy with a given." It is this "given," the revelation of God, which adds something *substantive* to the philosophical interpretation, namely, the relation of all things—knowledge, man, and reality—to the Trinity of Christian Theology. This is a new level and a unique position from which to view the integration of all things. However, Theology's task is essentially the self-reflection of faith on the Biblical revelation and the proclamation of the Church in order to purify that proclamation. It is a task primarily for the Church. Insofar as this faith relates to the fields of knowledge perhaps we would have to agree with the Swiss theologian, Emil Brunner, when he writes that

> the coordination of the various spheres of life is the task, not of the theologian, but of the philosopher. But if this coordination is to take place from the standpoint of the Christian faith, then we need precisely a Christian philosophy.[21]

In conclusion, then, we have now seen four levels of integration of the teachable substance of the Christian liberal arts curriculum: *basically contributive, receptive-contributive, receptive-focal,* and *synoptic*. From a practical standpoint the final integrating point could well be that of ethics, for it brings all knowledge and all experience to one focal point: human action under a norm. However, this is not an integrative study in itself for other studies, but rather for the *person*. Yet it is not an idle dream to see the gamut of the curriculum run from logic to ethics—*from* the form of knowledge *through* the differentiated-integrated intellectual substance *to* the norms of human action.

---

[21]*Revelation and Reason*, p. 395.

Chapter Nine

General Education
in the Humanities

S O WHILE it broods upon its own improvement, as it always
does, education can afford to ponder programs of being no
less deeply than schedules of doing," says Mark Van Doren,[1] and
points to "the absence of intellectual design"[2] as being the one in-
tolerable thing in education.

In a clearly practical sense, education in the liberal arts should
be an education in what Jacques Maritain calls the "artistic" rules
of good thinking or in the "attainment of indispensable means."
It is further recognized that there are two other general needs: 1)
the mastering of a common body of information, at least in the
rudiments of each of the great disciplines of learning, which
together constitute the foundation of the educated mind; and 2)
a perception for the undergraduate of a larger unity, more coherence, and therefore more meaning in his course of study—"a
reasonably deep and clear feeling about the bearings upon one
another, and upon his own mind, of three things, to name no more:
art, science, religion."[3]

Though "in a sense, good education is always both general and
special," the courses in basic general areas of study are especially
designed to prevent the "whole from being lost in one of its
aspects." Contrary to the belief of many, *general education* does
not mean education for the many; nor is its intent to bring to-

[1]*Liberal Education,* p. 5.
[2]*Ibid.,* p. 10.
[3]*Ibid.,* p. 11.

gether a little of this and a little of that within the compass of a single course. Rather, as the term is used in the conventional college program it is, in the words of John F. A. Taylor, "to make the issue of education, philosophic." Perhaps the highest goal "of any specialized group of thinkers should be the discovery of ideas and principles which may be added to man's common stock, with applications that transcend the field of their discovery."[4]

To serve its purpose ideally, a general course would be oriented from the point of view of root factors common to those disciplines and followed through meaningfully within a structural unity. It is generally admitted that such "underneath the surface" relationships do exist. It is likewise more commonly denied than not that such relationships are apparent to the student. In the view of the proponents of general education it is the particular business of general education to discern these relationships and to make them visible by design. The mind of the student cannot be relied on to establish them.

1

OBJECTIVES IN THE TEACHING OF THE HUMANITIES

Freed from the formal limitation of being a discipline in higher education as distinguished from the disciplines of the natural sciences and social sciences, the humanities, says David H. Stevens,

are the embodiments, in forms that all can understand, of the learning, experience, and expression of humanity.

They put upon every individual a compulsion to use whatever he gathers from humane experiences in his every act and expression; this natural necessity of personal identification with what we learn of mankind, creates new life out of the old. The humanistic way is always out of what was past and what is present. . . . Each person enters into that way when he realizes that he himself is part and product of all that the humanities signify. . . .

Through people all humanistic disciplines have influence upon individual men and women, and so upon their conduct in life. What the scholar and teacher give and do is influential in world affairs, by example and guidance toward the human values of all time. Their usefulness in that world is a matter in need of study and description.[5]

---

[4]Hoyt Hudson, *Educating Liberally* (Stanford University, California: Stanford University Press, 1945), p. 42.
[5]*The Changing Humanities* (New York: Harper and Brothers, 1953), Intro., pp. ix, x.

That there should be a vital connection between the important and nearly universal interest in the destiny of mankind and those subjects which are traditionally concerned with human purposes and values is natural. It is not disputed that a proper study of mankind is man. Within the formal framework of education, however, the subject matter of the humanities as study material of great consequence to the individual and to society is by no means generally viewed in the perspective nor pursued with the respect and sense of significance which it merits. At times such study is openly attacked as useless, trivial, or as a luxury. Left to election by the undergraduate it is, either by the exigencies of curriculum requirements or by the will and interests of the student, passed by. In the view of President Nathan Pusey of Harvard, the humanities—literature, languages, philosophy, music and the other fine arts—are elected by too few college students. "A college," he warns, "in which the Humanities are weak runs the risk of being less liberal than it should; for our full humanity is best quickened and developed through imaginative grasp of subtler experiences of individuals as revealed through arts and letters."[6] Vision lacking, the student sees in these studies no source of wisdom. But "wisdom is the fruit of a balanced development. It is this balanced growth of individuality which it should be the aim of education to secure. The most useful discoveries for the immediate future would concern the furtherance of this aim without detriment to the necessary intellectual professionalism."[7] Any program which omits the study of man as a human being "with extra-scientific concerns" will fail to make its contribution to the "balanced growth of individuality which it should be the aim of education to secure."

Though a step in the right direction, the distribution-concentration type of program, intended to ensure the student's contact with the major divisions of knowledge, did not eventuate in a learning more meaningful and vital for the student. It failed to lead him to grasp the significances of and within these broader fields, to realize their importance, and to see their relatedness within themselves and to each other. In speaking more particularly

[6]Quoted in "News and Ideas," *College English*, XVI (May 1955), 517.
[7]Alfred North Whitehead, *Science and the Modern World* (New York: New American Library, Mentor Book, 1925), p. 197.

173

of the humanities, for example, Fred B. Millett in *The Rebirth of Liberal Education* says that if it were not for an abundance of evidence that dissatisfaction with the achievement of the humanities in the liberal arts has been taking "a practical and dynamic form, the prospects for the humanities would look dark indeed."[8]

On what basis do the humanities as a discipline distinguish themselves from the sciences? In answering the question "Are the Humanities Worth Saving?" Joseph Wood Krutch thinks the air might be cleared by this broad distinction of their subject matters:

> By science's more modest practitioners we are sometimes told that its subject matter is *all objectively verifiable truth,* and that its method is *experimental verification.* It deals with what can be proved and, especially, *with what can be measured.* Could we then define the humanities by stating a simple opposite? 'Humane learning and humane studies are those which concern themselves with what cannot be experimentally verified and is not susceptible of measurement.' . . .
>
> But unless we are willing to affirm boldly that there is a large area of elusive truth which it would be fatal to neglect but which, nevertheless, cannot be dealt with by any scientific method; unless we are willing to admit also that in this area doubt and dispute must rage, perhaps forever, because what is included within it cannot be measured or subjected to controlled experiment, then there is little use in 'defending the humanities,' because there is little left to defend. . . . If we permit ourselves to contemplate the truths which cannot be verified and the values which cannot be measured we may well wonder that any age dared to neglect them.[9]

In educational programs the subject fields most commonly included in the humanities are literature, the fine arts, philosophy, and history. Viewpoints pertinent to their common bond may be seen in the following:

FOR LITERATURE:

> Our education needs . . . to create men and women who have received from the past and from the present, both from their own country and from foreign lands, a true enlargement of mind and emotion; who have had more than fleeting glimpses of that beauty and truth and goodness which is as much man's claim upon the world as is his claim for food and water, air and sun; who have known sympathy, compassion, and toleration. . . . Because literary studies have as their end the enrichment of personal values they are the partners, not the rivals, of all the sciences that advance human life.[10]

[8](New York: Harcourt, Brace, 1945), p. 22.

[9]*Saturday Review,* June 4, 1955, p. 23.

[10]Howard F. Lowry, *et al.,* "Literature in American Education," Report of a Special Committee, Commission on Trends in Education, Modern Language Association of America (1943), p. 13.

In alluding to an earlier lecture, Alfred North Whitehead says:

. . . I developed a parallel line of argument, which would lead to a system of thought basing nature upon the concept of organism, and not upon the concept of matter. In the present lecture, I propose in the first place to consider how the concrete educated thought of men has viewed this opposition of mechanism and organism. It is in literature that the concrete outlook of humanity receives its expression. Accordingly it is to literature that we must look, particularly in more concrete forms, namely, in poetry and in drama, if we hope to discover the inward thoughts of a generation.[11]

FOR THE OTHER FINE ARTS:

. . . Great art itself is a mirror of man, not only in what it *says* but in what it *is*. In its *stylistic* changes it records man's changing and maturing sensibilities. In its *content* it mirrors man's idea of himself, that which gives his actions meaning and enables him to live under the burden of a world view that increases continually in complexity and magnitude. Creative vision of *form* dormant in raw material and its realization by means of tools and techniques not only reflect man's inborn creativity but are its foremost example. Our age-old habit of creating order and perfection in our art may be considered a luxury and even an idle pursuit from the standpoint of a *utilitarian* interpretation of life. But in this luxurious idleness man reaches down to the foundations of his being.[12]

FOR PHILOSOPHY:

What is wanted, and what I have striven after, is a sympathetic study of main ideas as seen from the inside. If my view of the function of philosophy is correct, it is the most effective of all the intellectual pursuits. It builds cathedrals before workmen have moved a stone, and it destroys them before the elements have worn down their arches. It is the architect of the buildings of the spirit, and it is also their solvent: —and the spiritual precedes the material. Philosophy works slowly. Thoughts lie dormant for ages; and then, almost suddenly as it were, mankind finds that they have embodied themselves in institutions.[13]

FOR HISTORY:

. . . The student acquainted with history lives in a world of many dimensions, a world of human experience that extends across the centuries. History illumines man's spiritual nature as well as records his secular achievements and failures; it is no accident that nowhere is the sense of history stronger than in the ancient Christian Church. By walking in other streets with men and women of other times, the student of today can best take the measure of his own life and his own

[11]*Science and the Modern World*, p. 76.
[12]Arnold Didier Graeffe, *Creative Education in the Humanities* (New York: Harper and Brothers, 1951), p. 73.
[13]A. N. Whitehead, *Science and the Modern World*, Preface, pp. viii-ix.

age. Hereby he best becomes aware of his own dignity and worth, his own duties and responsibilites, as a human being.[14]

Courses illustrative of the more recent approaches to general education in the humanities cannot be set off against each other in mutually exclusive frames, but it is possible by abstracting some common features among these greatly diversified programs to distinguish four or five dominant motivations. Concurrently it will be obvious here as elsewhere that the drive toward a dominant objective in any one pattern can and undoubtedly will have as concomitant results the attainment of some of the ruling objectives of the others. Summed up in generalizations, some forty or fifty individual statements of objectives in this volume would include: the acquisition of significant insights, the perception of deeper meanings; familiarity with a necessary body of knowledge; the broadening of the mind, the enlarging of the outlook; the discernment of quality, of value; the ability to discriminate, to evaluate critically; preparation for meeting individual needs, immediate and anticipated.

2

TYPES OF COURSES

Evidence of the prospects for more "practical and dynamic forms" for the teaching of the humanities noted by Professor Millett, and the extent of the progress made by 1948-1949 in the establishment of basic or general courses in the area may be judged by a series of accounts solicited by Earl J. McGrath, then U.S. Commissioner of Education, from nineteen institutions carrying on such work. The institutions were arbitrarily selected and included state universities, large private universities, land-grant colleges, men's and women's colleges, private liberal arts colleges, and junior colleges. The purpose was to make information about such programs available to interested institutions. The accounts sent in, together with a chapter on trends, were published in a single volume, *The Humanities in General Education*, under McGrath's editorship in 1949. What follows in this section will be

---

[14]H. H. Kimber, "The Humanities in General Education at Michigan State College" in *The Humanities in General Education*, ed. by Earl J. McGrath (Dubuque, Iowa: Wm. C. Brown Company, 1949), p. 70.

176

an attempt to suggest, largely by quotation, the general patterns in viewpoints and procedures of such humanities courses as were then in progress.

Though the relatedness of all the subject matters which may be and are variously included under the name of the humanities is not difficult to see, a decision concerning which departments are to be brought together for the purposes of a course is necessary. The courses of the nineteen institutions mentioned above show the inclusion of from one to five of the following departments: literature, languages, philosophy, history, religion, music, visual arts (including architecture, dance, drama), English composition, communications, psychology. Literature is emphasized in all but one, which confines itself to history but is followed by a course in literature and the arts; the visual and tonal arts are included in twelve; philosophy in eleven; history in six, religion in two; psychology in one. Though some of these disciplines are claimed by the social sciences, it is clear that they also stand in an intimate relationship to the humanities.

The three major patterns of approach are:

a. *Historical and Cultural.* Concern: "to provide for the student some broader understanding of his cultural heritage and some enlarged cultural perspective in his own view of life." In this approach literature and the arts are used as historical evidence.

b. *Philosophical.* Concern: 1) student's need to be brought "face to face with the great issues of living that man has had to confront in the past and must face today"; *or* 2) "student's present problems of living and thinking" rather "than with his education in the great tradition." In this approach literature and the arts are used as expressions of philosophical insights.

c. *Aesthetic.* Concern: "to acquaint students with the best works in literature, music, and the visual arts, to provide some understanding of the aesthetic principles and techniques in terms of which intelligent appreciation of the arts is possible, and to develop some competence in the use of these principles."[15] In this approach the arts are viewed as constructed things.

---

[15] Robert F. Davidson, "Trends in the Humanities in General Education," *ibid.*, pp. 290-292 for statement of objectives in all three approaches.

A sampling of descriptive materials from the courses offered in five of the institutions reporting in *The Humanities in General Education* may help to illustrate the intent, *modus operandi,* and the potentialities in the differing approaches to the problem of values. These will not necessarily appear in the order of their occurrence within the individual account.

a. *The Historical and Cultural Approach*

These courses frequently appear under the simple title of *Humanities* and a number, though at times they bear more closely descriptive titles such as *History of Civilization, Culture Epochs,* or *Our Cultural Heritage.* Their general emphasis is upon the forces which have shaped Western civilization. The development is chronological, incidentally the most common of all orders, whatever the approach. More than three-fourths of the courses reported in *The Humanities in General Education* use it. Its choice as a sequence represents the viewpoint expressed by Wesleyan University: "We felt that the historical organization gave the course greater unity and provided richer opportunities for appreciating the liberal enterprise as the continuous effort to grapple with recurrent fundamental problems."[16]

There is also more general agreement on the aim of a historical-cultural approach to the humanities than on any other: namely,

. . . It is generally felt that the typical college student needs to be released from slavery to the purely contemporary, and that to accomplish this the limited outlook of our own age and society must be enlarged and broadened by a knowledge of history and by the understanding which such a knowledge provides of man himself and of his creative achievements. Until a student has in some measure at least made the great cultural achievements of the past his own, it is obvious that he cannot live fully and intelligently today.[17]

Because of the conviction that the earlier historical-cultural survey attempted too much and therefore defeated its purpose by becoming superficial and "too full of undigested detail," present courses now select four or five periods in the development of Western civilization for more careful study. This trend is illustrated in the courses given in the universities of Arizona, Florida, and

    [16]Norman O. Brown, "The Humanities at Wesleyan University," *ibid.,* p. 33.
    [17]Robert F. Davidson, "Trends in the Humanities in General Education," *ibid.,* p. 290.

Wisconsin, in Wesleyan University, in Reed College, and in Michigan State College.

Three illustrations of the historical and cultural approach follow:

(1) *The University of Florida*[18]

COURSE: Our Cultural Heritage. The Humanities in Contemporary Life. A Year course.

DISCIPLINES: literature, philosophy, the arts of Western civilization.

OBJECTIVE:

To provide for the student a wide and appealing first-hand acquaintance with literature, philosophy, and art that has some genuine claims to greatness, and likewise to encourage him to face for himself the issues which such works raise. This has meant a sparing use of secondary sources, a determined effort to find original sources which will serve our purpose.

ORGANIZATION:

First semester: Our Cultural Heritage
    Unit I. The Greek View of Life
    Unit II. The Medieval and Renaissance Views of Life
    Unit III. Rationalism and the Romantic View of Life
Second Semester: The Humanities in Contemporary Life
    Unit I. The Practical and the Idealistic in Our View of Life
    Unit II. The View That Life Is Dominated by Passion, Not
        Directed by Reason
    Unit III. The Welfare of the Group as the Basic Concern
        of Life
Material suggesting principles and procedures:

First Semester: The material used during the semester is organized in a chronological framework but an attempt is made to integrate it more effectively in terms of the view of life or sense of values which inspires and unifies the literature, philosophy, and art included in each unit. Five creative periods in our cultural heritage have been selected for study and the relationship between these periods has been emphasized in the three units into which the work of the semester is divided.

The sort of thing we have tried to do in the selection and integration of material can readily be seen in the unit, "The Greek View of

[18]Robert F. Davidson, "The Comprehensive Humanities Course at the University of Florida," *ibid.*, pp. 55-68.

Life." The Age of Pericles in Athens has been taken as the focal point in this unit both because of its enduring contribution to our cultural heritage and because of its obvious relationship to the issues we face today. Homer's *Odyssey* (Books V-XII) and Sophocles' *Antigone* are read to acquaint the student with creative and influential literary expressions of the view of life that characterizes the Age of Pericles and also to focus his thinking upon certain perennial religious and political problems which these books raise. Athenian democracy is surveyed and contrasted with the totalitarian state in Sparta to provide historical and social background for our discussion of these issues. An illustrated lecture and subsequent class discussion, emphasizing especially the Parthenon in Athens and the sculpture of the Golden Age, not only indicates the place of the arts in the Greek view of life but provides opportunity also for detailed analysis of the greatest achievements of Greek art. Finally Plato's *Apology* is read, and his *Republic* and Aristotle's *Ethics* are discussed, to afford a careful philosophical consideration of the dominant ideals and values in the Greek view of life at its best.

Throughout the unit attention is given to the implications for our day of the view of life presented here as well as to the details of its literary and historical expression. A consistent effort is made likewise to treat literature, philosophy, and the arts in proper historical perspective as closely related expressions of an underlying sense of values by which all life and thought is molded. In this fashion we have tried to avoid the fragmentation and narrowness of the usual introductory courses where each subject is studied in comparative isolation. Above all else we have sought to leave no gap between the study of our cultural heritage and the daily needs of ordinary men and women. This is not a course for the specialist but one designed as an integral part of a program of general education. The enduring values and the ultimate ends of human life, the things that are worth living for, struggling for, and if need be, worth dying for, these things have been the concern of the great masters of reality in every age. We have tried to make them the central concern and the integrating principle in the study of "Our Cultural Heritage."

Second Semester: To live effectively, however, we must live in the present not in the past. We must see clearly the relevance of inherited ideals and values to crucial issues of life as we know it today. Hence the second semester of our course we devote to a consideration of "The Humanities and Contemporary Life." Here many conflicting patterns of interpretation may be found.

The three units in the work of the semester suggest in more specific fashion the major conflicts of value around which our treatment of "The Humanities and Contemporary Life" has been organized.

. . . the second unit will indicate both the kind of material we have included in the course and the way in which we have sought a functional integration of this material in terms of student need and experience. The conflict between reason and appetite in contemporary life is portrayed with directness and clarity in Somerset Maugham's *Of Human Bondage* and Eugene O'Neill's *Anna Christie*. We discuss these two works in detail, seeking both to increase the student's understanding of modern fiction and drama from a literary viewpoint and also to present to him in vigorous and challenging fashion the underlying conflict of values found here. The thought of Schopenhauer provides us with a philosophical discussion of the same issue, remarkably contemporary in insight and equally provocative. The work of certain outstanding modern artists, men like Cezanne, Van Gogh, Picasso, Dali, Maillol and Lipschitz, has been selected to introduce the student to modern art. Here he finds a reflection of the same conflict of values seen already in literature and philosophy and also an excellent insight into the spirit and character of modern art itself. As a concluding assignment each student is asked to write an essay in which he attempts to evaluate for himself the interpretation of life in terms of appetite, impulse, or will, seeking to determine both its elements of validity and its limitations as a sound and workable view of life.

A comprehensive general education program has been in operation at the University of Florida since 1935. At present [1948] these courses are organized under a separate college known as the University College. Every student is registered in this college during his first two years and is required to take all of the six comprehensive courses as a part of his regular program, regardless of any later plans for study. The courses are handled by a chairman and an appointed staff. An effort is made to secure men with broad training and wide interests for the humanities staff rather than those preoccupied with scholarly research, and a type of in-service training has been developed. "Staff members trained in the particular fields under consideration have led the discussion of material to be used each week, describing . . . their own plans for actually handling this material in class," the principal concern being to discover how they hoped to make the assignment meaningful to their students. "It amazed us all to see how far and how fast we have been able to go in handling effectively the various materials included in our program." Each instructor takes the same group of students through the work of the entire course.

The report admits the persistence of problems throughout the development of the course as a whole. The most difficult of these had proved to be the achievement of integration, one of the major and continued aims. With the inclusion of traditionally distinct fields had come a temptation to compartmentalize. In the hands of an "unimaginative instructor" the otherwise natural and helpful chronological order in "Our Cultural Heritage" had resulted in a wrong emphasis and a failure to achieve the enlarged insight

181

and understanding wanted from the course. In the earlier years students had complained that the course included too much material for so short a time, also that it failed to relate the material effectively to their own experience. How the effort to avert their first criticism had been met, has already been stated. In consequence of their second criticism, the staff had turned more and more to the functional approach, trying to relate the material directly to student interest and experience.

(2) *Wesleyan University*[19]

COURSES: Humanities 1-2; Humanities Laboratory. Required freshman year. Eight credits.

Humanities 3-4. Elective in sophomore, junior, or senior year. Six credits.

DISCIPLINES: literature, philosophy, the arts.

OBJECTIVES: Humanities 1-2; Humanities Laboratory. The foundation for the content of Humanities 1-2 is the belief that the best way to make freshmen aware of the true nature of a liberal education is "tied up with" awakening them to an appreciation of the "breadth and depth of the greatest minds in our Western cultural tradition," for the qualities by virtue of which they are regarded as classics are the qualities which are characteristic of a liberal education. The primary content of the course therefore consists of readings from the classics of Western thought and literature ranging from ancient Greek drama and the Bible to Whitehead's *Science and the Modern World*. The purpose of the Humanities Laboratory is to stimulate freshmen to an awareness of the possibilities inherent in aesthetic experience. Through systematic discussion it introduces the student to the basic principles involved in aesthetic creation; it also gives him opportunities for practical experience and experimentation in one of the arts.

ORGANIZATION:

Humanities 1. The sequence below shows the materials of the course, together with the timing of lectures and discussion periods. There are very few lectures. No syllabus is provided. (The lecture

---

[19]Norman O. Brown, "The Humanities at Wesleyan University," *ibid.*, pp. 30-41.

topics are distinguished by quotation marks; readings for discussion by italics.)

1. "Athens and America"

2- 3. Aeschylus, *Prometheus Bound*

4- 5. Sophocles, *King Oedipus*

6- 7. Euripides, *Medea*

8. Aristotle, *Poetics I-XV*

9. Hour examination

10. "Greek Philosophy"; Plato's *Apology*

11. Plato, *Crito*

12-13. Plato, *Symposium*

14-17. Plato, *Phaedo*

18. Aristotle, *De Anima,* II (Selections)

19-23. Aristotle, *Ethics,* I, II, VII, X

24. Hour examination

25. "The Old Testament"; Genesis, I-III, VI-VIII

26. *Exodus,* I-VI, XII-XX

27. *Amos,* I-VIII

28. *Isaiah,* XL-LV

29-30. *Job,* I-XV, XXII-XXXI, XXXVIII-XLII

31. "The New Testament"; Luke, I-XI, Matthew, V-VII

32. *Luke,* XII-XXIV

33. *John,* I-III, VIII-XVII

34. *Romans,* I-VII, XII-XIII; *I Corinthians,* XIII

35-37. *Marcus Aurelius* (Selections)

38. "From Paganism to Christianity"

39-44. Augustine, *Confessions*

Humanities Laboratory, first semester. A portion of the schedule beginning with period 4 illustrates the type of program. Note the references to section work.

Group meeting	Section meeting
4. Athletic demonstration and dance interpretation of athletic demonstration.	Art as Imitation I
5. Athletic demonstration repeated; criticism of work done in various sections.	Art as Imitation II
6. Lecture; analysis of thematic material in *Prometheus Bound;* screening of the Inquisition scene from *The Informer.*	Development of Theme I
7. No meeting; two hours of section work.	Development of Theme II Development of Theme III
8. Lecture-demonstration; theme and variation in music.	Theme and Variations I

Material suggesting principles and procedures:

The organization of Humanities 1-2 is historical and thematic (a "concealed organization" of recurrent themes). The limited number of readings and the eclectic principle of their selection keep the course from being a history of Western thought. The variety of literary types represented makes possible not only such questions as, "how did the Greeks think, how did the Hebrews think," *et cetera,* but also such questions as "what is tragedy, what is philosophy, what is religion?" Recurrent themes appear in questions raised by the problems of free will and necessity as they occur in Greek tragedy, in Augustine, in Luther's *Essay on Christian Liberty,* and in Shakespeare's *Hamlet;* the problem of divine justice as it is raised by Aeschylus' *Prometheus* and the *Book of Job;* the Socratic doctrine of love in the *Symposium* and the Pauline doctrine of love in *I Corinthians XIII.*

The discussions are conducted in small groups of about sixteen students. This is made possible because the course draws in teachers from many departments. Each instructor conducts his discussion groups throughout the course.

In the Humanities Laboratory program an effort is made to unify the program within itself and to set it in meaningful relationship to Humanities 1-2. It is a three-hour course divided into two parts. One hour is work done outside the classroom. Two hours are classroom work given afternoons, one of which is generally a lecture demonstration to a relatively large group, and the other a smaller section meeting. Sections are divided according to different artistic media. The student stays with his chosen medium except for a three-week period when he changes to a second medium for a better understanding of elements common to all art as well as the peculiarities of a particular medium. All students are required to get a passing grade in both courses, and the laboratory grade is computed as 25 percent of the final grade for the two courses.

Wesleyan University has no humanities department. Course 1-2 recruits its instructors from various departments: English, modern languages, classical languages, religion, psychology, anthropology, for example. This policy "reflects the idea that if the Wesleyan faculty expect the student to learn to cross departmental lines in his thinking, they must practice what they preach.

Furthermore, such a staff, widely representative of different departments, enriches itself and the entire academic community by a process of mutual stimulation and assistance. This process of mutual stimulation and assistance is enhanced by the degree of self-governing responsibilities exercised by the staff as a whole. For example, the yearly revision of the course is prepared by a committee of the staff, which is elected by the staff and reports its recommendations back to the staff as a whole for amendment and final approval. An indispensable aspect of the Wesleyan Humanities 1-2 course is the weekly luncheon meeting of the staff at which procedural problems are settled and opinions exchanged on problems of interpretation and pedagogy raised by the current readings. The course has a chairman, appointed by the president, who *primus inter pares,* has to regard the welfare of the course as one of his major responsibilities, thus protecting the course from the danger implicit in the fact that all of the staff have other teaching responsibilities.

The Humanities Laboratory program is staffed by regular members of the departments of art, music, and theater, supplemented by part-time instructors. The program as now established is the result of a great deal of experimentation and theoretical discussion.

(3) Michigan State College[20]

COURSES: History of Civilization. Three quarters. Literature and Fine Arts. Three quarters. These are two of seven required courses in the Basic College.

DISCIPLINES: history, literature, fine arts (music, architecture, sculpture, painting).

OBJECTIVES: These two courses, both oriented from the humanistic point of view, represent still another type of historical-cultural approach. Though the History of Civilization has as its general objective to bring the values of historical study within the educational experience of the student, it is unlike the conventional course in narrative history from which he came away "with a story in mind"; and in which

events and the men connected with them moved from a beginning to a middle, from the middle to an end. Events gave the course its logic; movement gave it life; its meaning was left for the philosopher or "social scientists" to figure out. . . . The student comes away from a course in the History of Civilization with a constructive body of thought. . . . As he proceds from the simpler to the more complex forms of civilization, he begins to catch a clearer and clearer view of the nature of civilization itself and of the privileges and responsibilities of civilized man.

The course Literature and Fine Arts proposes to exhibit "the interrelationships among the arts through historical studies of the arts of literature, of music, and of architecture, sculpture, and painting." Together these courses are mutually complementary undertakings, each reinforcing the other in the common humanistic enterprise of exploring what Rabelais called, in contrast to the order of nature, "that second nature, which is man."[21] Each course

---

[20]H. H. Kimber, "The Humanities in General Education at Michigan State College," *ibid.*, pp. 69-80; John F. A. Taylor, "The Humanities in General Education at Michigan State College," *ibid.*, pp. 80-95.
[21]*Ibid.*, pp. 82, 92.

is guided by a clear cut set of principles in the selection of its materials.

ORGANIZATION: First quarter. History of Civilization: Greek, beginning with Homeric Age; Hellenistic; Roman; Medieval.

Second quarter. Renaissance and Reformation; Eighteenth century.

Third quarter. French Revolution and its aftermath; contemporary civilization of the last hundred years.

First quarter. Literature and Fine Arts: Literature.

Second quarter. Music.

Third quarter. Visual arts.

Material suggesting principles and procedures:

The History of Civilization course is described as not being rigidly fixed. It is the continuing elements of each civilization, or the contributions which one makes to another, which are its primary concern throughout the development.

Contemporary civilization is looked upon as consisting of elements derived from a series of preceding cultures existing within a framework of ideas, institutions, and circumstances peculiar to itself. Each of the component elements which make up the contemporary world must be studied as it existed within its own framework of antecedents, ideas, institutions, and circumstances. The study of each root culture involves the attainment of a lively comprehension of the life of the time as it was lived by men and women in different levels of society; the workings of institutions, political and economic, the role and characteristics of religion, the significant forms of art and letters. The course avoids the superficial and strives to catch for the student the inner mechanism of institutions, the essence of ideas, the spirit of a religion, the soul of an age. Narration of events is reduced to a skeletal minimum; no attempt is made to supply a continuous chronological thread. Civilizations from the Greek age to the twentieth century world are studied in order, but the leading events are subordinated to an attempt to give insight into the character of each one.

An idea of what the course presents may be had from an account of the work of the first quarter, together with some brief summary statements concerning the meanings of the ages considered in the second and third quarters.

First quarter.

The introductory part deals with five topics concerning the nature of civilization and with some early historical examples. The main con-

186

tent of the course begins with a study of Greek civilization, in which the Homeric Age and the nature of the city-states are dealt with, and then Greek philosophy, Greek science, Greek literature, and Greek art are brought into view. This section concludes with a topic on the significance of the Greek achievements for Western civilization. There follows a study of the Hellenistic period which in turn leads to a more extensive analysis of Roman civilization.

Medieval civilization is presented under three major topics. . . . The first topic is concerned with the Church, its foundation, its formation and growth in doctrine and organization, the nature and influence of monasticism, the character of popular religion and the problem of heresy. Medieval political and economic institutions are the subject of the second topic, including feudalism, manorialism, and the life of the medieval town, while the third topic is devoted to intellectual characteristics and achievements of the age.

Second quarter.

The meaning of the age [Renaissance, Reformation, Eighteenth Century] is summed up in the following terms: bankruptcy of the aristocratic ideal, advancing knowledge of the nature of the physical world, belief in reason, beginnings of humanitarianism and development of social idealism, and the spread of material good.

Third quarter.

[The French Revolution and its aftermath, contemporary civilization.] The course concludes with brief consideration of some problems of contemporary civilization. These are stated as threefold: the problem of values, philosophical, religious, and ethical; the problem of government and the social order, raising the issues of security, freedom, and authority; and the problem of world order, involving a realistic approach to the problem of war and peace.

The teaching materials consist of a textbook, a historical atlas, an outline, and a book of collateral readings prepared by two members of the department and published by the college press. . . . Two principles may be said to find expression in the book of readings. The first is wholly orthodox, namely that even in a course of a comprehensive nature 'the study of history by means of a single textbook can only result in inculcating in the student an excessive dependence upon simplified generalizations of dubious accuracy and is a failure to bring to his mind an appreciation of the richness and variety of historical literature.' . . .

There have been brought together in one book, therefore, a number of readings such as might ordinarily be assigned for library reference. . . .

The second principle . . . involves what might be called the heresy of the secondary authority. A good deal of illustrative source material is introduced into classroom work, but the framers of the course quaintly believe that the greatest value to the freshman and sophomore student will accrue if the major portion of his time and energy allotted to historical reading is spent in perusal of the works of the great masters of

187

history and not in trying to dig out a little precious information from some truncated "source"—usually about as common as nails and equally nutritious. An objective of the course is to cultivate an appreciation of historical writing. This means at the very least an introduction, a nodding acquaintance, with adult, mature, serious, scholarly, informed, creative historical exposition. Through the readings provided every student in this course will come into contact with such historians as Bury, Rostovtzeff, Christopher Dawson [philosophical, theological analyst of culture], Foakes-Jackson, Carl Stephenson, Luchaire, Pirenne, Coulton, Lewis Mumford [critic-philosopher], Pollard, Sorokin [sociologist], J. H. Randall [philosopher], to name but a few.

Formal lecturing is discouraged. Each instructor meets his class of from thirty to forty students three times a week and is responsible for the conduct of the entire course. Definitive credit is by comprehensive examination over the entire year's work.

In so far as the course in the History of Civilization achieves meaning, contributes to the student's sense of his own humanity, enables him to see that he stands neither at the beginning nor at the end of the long road of human life on this earth, and gives him a sense of location, direction and proportion by which he may measure and to some extent regulate his own life as an individual and as a citizen, it is indispensable to a program of general education.

(4) Reference is made to a hoped-for "international outlook" as a result of some of the courses described in *The Humanities in General Education,* but none of them undertakes work designed specifically for that end. Is there for the American student, along with the need for a look into the past of his own civilization, also a need for a look at civilizations other than his own? There are those who think so. The present concern will be indicated briefly by a few paragraphs from an article called "Universities for a Global Era" by C. W. De Kiewiet.

The Humanities are not paying enough attention to the history, intellectual activity, influence, and experience of the new magnitudes and multitudes of China, India, the Arab world, which today intimately confront American life. This means bluntly that in the light of the needs of America today there is a disproportionate preoccupation with the history, the intellectual activity, the influence and experience of Western Europe. I am raising a question which can only be acutely controversial.

. . . This is a plea that a resolute effort be made to correct our dangerous illiteracy in the life and thought of great areas of the world where history has begun to roll at such a pace that the things on which

188

we place the greatest value—our security, our way of life, our economic stability—are intimately affected. . . .

Our educational habits and practices have of necessity been deeply influenced by Western Europe. We are an extension of Western Europe. It is there that are the roots of our law, religion, government, and much else. There are big guns that can be brought up to defend the place in the curriculum of the literature, the history, and the art of the different epochs and countries of Western Europe. Some of the subjects they defend are vital and could never be given up. Yet there simply must be room in general education, in the undergraduate curriculum, in the basic instruction of the 2,500,000 students in college, for the opportunity to bring into focus the new world which, if you please, the collapse of Europe has produced. . . .

Reassessment, however, means broadening, not the addition of new specialties; not to see people through the eye of a needle, but to gain a perception of their nature, the flowering of their art, their answers to the problems of good and evil, their careers amid great forces of climate and history, their hopes for the future. It means a respectful making of room, even at the expense of condensation or restriction elsewhere, to enable students to learn some fundamental things about several billion very important human beings. This means less room and time in an undergraduate curriculum for the subjects and materials which are drawn from the nations of Western Europe. Or, better still, it means a skilful selection of what cannot be sacrificed. Of this there is still much.[22]

b. *The Philosophical Approach*

Some institutions regard it as of greater importance that the student in general education be brought face to face with the great issues of living that man has had to confront in the past and must face today, than to be inspired by the historical development of our culture. They turn therefore to great ideas and great books, feeling that the enduring insights of the past have been preserved in the great works of literature and philosophy. They are concerned that students should develop intellectual maturity and a "sustained interest in the problems with which men have wrestled in trying to find meaning and purpose in life."

Haverford College[23]

COURSE: Integration of Life in Western Literature. (A pilot course in the humanities based on the philosophical approach introduced at Haverford in 1947-48.)

DISCIPLINES: philosophy, literature.

---

[22]*Saturday Review Reader No. 3* (New York: Bantam Books, 1954), pp. 150, 153, 154.

[23]J. Glenn Gray, "The Humanities at Haverford College," *The Humanities in General Education*, pp. 1-14

OBJECTIVE:

. . . its most often mentioned aim was to aid and encourage the participating students to build a coherent set of ideals for themselves with which to confront the bewildering present. With that in mind past philosophies were read and discussed from the viewpoint of relevance to today and tomorrow and usually within the framework of student and teacher experience of the Depression Thirties and Warring Forties. We made little attempt to be scholarly. . . .

ORGANIZATION: " . . . no attempt to follow a chronological pattern or to summarize Western intellectual history."

The first semester readings included portions of the *Iliad* and *Odyssey;* Plato's *Apology, Crito, Phaedo, Protagoras* and *Symposium;* Ernst Renan's *Life of Jesus;* the writings of Aquinas; Dante's *Divine Comedy.* The second semester readings included Machiavelli's *Prince;* Descartes' autobiography, the *Discourse on Method* and a few of his *Meditations; Living Thoughts of J. J. Rousseau,* edited by Romain Rolland; Rousseau's *Confessions;* Goethe's *Faust;* Dostoievski's *The Idiot;* Marx's *Communist Manifesto;* Arthur Koestler's *Darkness at Noon;* Santayana's *Platonism and the Spiritual Life* and *Ultimate Religion;* and John Dewey's *A Common Faith.*

Material suggesting principles and procedures:

Socrates' central problem of the individual's duty to his fellows and the laws of his state as opposed to his duty to God or the promptings of conscience brought us to grips with modern realities. The ghost of Socrates continued to crop up in our discussions till the end of the year. . . . We dealt with the figure of Jesus as a Galilean of his time. . . . It was instructive to contrast him and his people with Socrates and the Greeks. We also tried to trace some of our modern concepts and ideals which derive from the Hebraic and Greek sources of our heritage or a combination of both. . . . The supreme synthesis of Greek and Judeo-Christian *Weltanschauungen* occurred in the Middle Ages in the writings of Aquinas and Dante. . . . Differences in Catholic, Protestant, and Jewish concepts of sins and virtues and how these differences [thus] are material of the course. . . . To students acquainted with the machinations of world politics in the last decades, Machiavelli reads like contemporary opinion. Chief topic of discussion was the relation which ought to obtain between political power and ideals. . . . With Descartes we tried to evaluate the wisdom of complete trust in reason as opposed to reliance on feeling and emotion, and found it necessary to distinguish the various senses in which reason had been taken at dif-

190

ferent times in modern history. . . . The problem of the adequacy of scientific method for all aspects of nature and human nature came into our discussion on Descartes with considerable difference of opinion. But the distinctiveness of the Cartesian ideal came rightly into focus only after we had taken up the study of Jean Jacques Rousseau. Opposed as the two men are on their views of reason, nature, society and God, they embody something of the total range of modern thought and its tendency to polar opposites.

The intent was to develop the course for sophomores, but the course reported here was given to a pilot class of eighteen to twenty students mostly juniors and seniors. The final examinations concentrated on testing the student's grasp of ideas dominating the various philosophies of life, rather than on facts or history.

c. The Aesthetic Approach

The University of Chicago[24]

COURSES: Humanities 1. Three quarters. One general lecture, four discussion periods weekly.

Humanities 2. Three quarters. One general lecture, three discussion periods weekly.

Humanities 3. Three quarters. Four periods per week.

(All of the above sequences required during the two years in the College of the University of Chicago.)

DISCIPLINES: literature, the arts, philosophy.

In the preceding approaches to the humanities, the products of the arts were studied as historical evidence or as expressions of philosophical insight; that is, the center of interest was something outside the works themselves. The arts may, however, be studied in another way, namely, as constructs, as created things, with the center of interest within the works themselves. This is not to deny that the former approaches may yield valuable data and understanding. It is noted that *Oedipus*, for example, may provide evidence to the psychologist; the *Areopagitica* to the political scientist; folk music to the sociologist, and so on. Without therefore denying the legitimacy of such interpretation or undervaluing its

---

[24]Russell B. Thomas, "The Humanities Program in the College of the University of Chicago," *ibid.*, pp. 194-206.

191

usefulness, the College of the University of Chicago takes the position that the arts studied as arts, as created or constructed things, is also a necessary discipline, more often than not neglected.

Through the study of disciplines appropriate to the interpretation of poetic construction, students may discover those values in drama, fiction, and lyric poetry which are quite distinct from their capacity to express general truths or to inform us about the past. These values lie in the recognition of works of art as complete in themselves and capable of giving their appropriate kinds of pleasure. Unless such disciplines are taught, the study of the poetic arts tend to drift into a confused discussion that fails to distinguish among several kinds of values.

OBJECTIVE: Humanity 1. "To acquaint the student with a considerable body of the best works in the fields of literature, music and the visual arts."

ORGANIZATION: presentation of comparable aspects of each of the arts in sequence. (Specifics of topics 1 and 2 illustrated below.)

Topic 1. Elements and Form in the Arts

Topic 2. External Factors as an Influence on Works of Art

Topic 3. Types of Art Forms: Principles in terms of which they may be differentiated

Topic 4. Tradition in the Arts: the growth, elaboration, and change in the art forms [not an attempt to give a history of art]

Topic 5. Contemporary Trend in the Arts

Topic 1: "Elements and Form in the Arts." Considers the organization of the elements basic to:

a. visual arts: color, line, volume, mass in a selection of paintings, sculpture, and architectural works.

b. music: the meaning of tone and its organization in terms of melody, harmony, rhythm in some hymns and folk tunes.

c. imaginative narrative: diction, plot, and character in two or three dramas.

Topic 2: "The manner in which the religious needs of a people may serve to explain aspects of a cathedral or temple."

The staff for Humanities 1 is composed of instructors with special training in at least one of the arts. Each instructor directs his discussion section throughout the course, that is, in all three fields. The staff meets weekly for instruction by the specialists in each area. The classrooms are equipped with audio-visual aids, including a piano. Use is made of exhibits in the Art Institute and in other local galleries. Supervised workshop opportunities in the plastic arts and painting and extra listening hours under competent guidance for those interested in music are provided for those who want them. Attendance at certain concerts is required.

OBJECTIVE: Humanities 2.

To develop competence in the arts of interpretation needed for understanding works of history, rhetoric, drama, fiction, and philosophy. For a) History: To provide through the study of the art of historical interpretation a useful foundation for the study of the past; b) Rhetoric: Our effort is to direct attention to the arts of persuasion; c) Drama and Fiction: Primary concern is to present these types as complete and self-contained works of art. Task consists in discovering the organization principle of the work and in understanding how everything in the work is related to it and accounted for by it; d) Philosophy: Concern is to develop those skills by which the validity of general propositions about the nature of things may be tested.

ORGANIZATION: The time for each form is divided approximately as follows: eight weeks for historical writings, three for rhetoric, eleven for drama and fiction, nine for philosophy.

Material suggesting principles and procedures:

Lectures.

These are planned to aid the students by giving them essential data about the historical background of the works read, and demonstrations of methods of analyzing passages. For example, a series of three lectures on rhetorical writing might deal with (1) a historical account of theories about the art of rhetoric, (2) a demonstration of a method of analyzing a rhetorical text, (3) an argument for the utility of the study of rhetoric for the modern student.

Reading. During the study of historical writings, for example, students will read three or four selections from the works of Herodotus, Thucydides, Tacitus, Gibbon, Toynbee, Buckle, Burckhardt, and Taylor. The selection of the texts is based on "their usefulness in demonstrating the essential elements of all historical writing as well as different methods of organizing an account of the past, different theories about causation, and different conceptions about the usefulness of the study of the past."

Discussion. Illustration: Study of text of Herodotus would re-

193

volve around on "how Herodotus' aims have determined the scope of his narrative, the selection of details, and the organization of the work."

OBJECTIVE: Humanities 3. "To develop an understanding of some of the philosophical principles upon which critical judgment and evaluation of works of art are made and to develop some competence in the application of these principles to particular works."

ORGANIZATION: Part I is "devoted to a study of several critical works which establish different but widely held theories about the nature of the arts and criteria for judging them." Kinds of texts: Aristotle, *Poetics;* Plato, *Phaedrus;* Sidney, *The Defense of Poesy;* Hume, *Of the Standard of Taste;* Lessing, *Laocoön;* Reynolds, *Discourse XIII;* Taine, *Introduction to History of English Literature;* Arnold, *The Study of Poetry;* Pater, *The School of Giorgione;* Bukharin, *Poetry.*

Part II "invites the students to make their own critical analyses and evaluations of particular works of art. The students read a selection of contemporary dramas, novels and lyric poems." (Footnote: "In the coming year, 1947-48, we shall try two experimental sections, one of which will direct its study of practical criticism to works of plastic arts, the other to music.")

Examinations . . . at least fifty percent of all examinations in each course is based upon works which students have not discussed in class. . . . On the comprehensive examination for Humanities 3 in June 1947, three of the six hours allowed for the examination were directed to the outside readings of the last quarter of the course.

3

EVALUATION

The foregoing accounts illustrate how under various meritorious points of view the problems inherent in a program of general education in the humanities were being met in 1947-48. The writers freely admit constant re-appraisals and revisions as necessitated by experience, but in no instance among these nineteen reports, is there any disposition to abandon the type. Though one may not

194

accept for oneself the specific proposal of Ernest C. Hassold for meeting the most critical need in the program of his own institution in 1948, one can agree with it as a description both of the problems inherent in such courses and of the faith in their potentialities. "Together with every other program of general education in the humanities, it [the course at the University of Louisville] faces a future far more complex and difficult than anyone could imagine at that time [1932]. The situation today calls for both a critical appraisal of the past and a creative projection of the potential development. To perform this task soundly, it needs a standard of more than merely local acceptance and significance." Because of the alliances to be effected in any general humanities program it will not be beside the point to bring once more into the foreground two general points of view: David H. Stevens says that "the disappearance of historical perspective would be disastrous not only to history as a subject but to every recognized field of learning." Arnold D. Graeffe says, "In the realm of the arts the call for integration is heard louder than in most other areas. This is due to the distinctive property of art by which it addresses the human essence in us. Therein lies its potential educational function."

Throughout the accounts one finds evidence of trends and common problems. There appears to be a general movement away from anthologies, commentaries, and secondary source material, and a corresponding movement "back to the texts" and actual art forms; a tendency to cut across departmental lines in staffing; tendencies toward a considerable enlargement of classroom equipment, toward providing workshop opportunities for all humanities courses which included the fine arts. Proper staffing and proper status for the staff members constitute a vital problem. An all-important factor in the success of the program is the teacher with the necessary faith and perspective. Among the pedagogical problems are those of avoiding the coverage of too much material, avoiding compartmentalization, failing to maintain perspective, failing to relate the materials of the course directly to student need and experience. Considerable time and cooperation are required for the planning of such a course.

195

In commenting on the courses in general education at Colgate University Professor Bewkes has this to say:

Aside from the values these courses have in introducing these students systematically to the basic fields of knowledge and initiating all students into the same educational experience, there are other arguments for making them the central core of an undergraduate's program.

There is a psychological factor brought into being by the survey courses which is a valuable educational asset. They do make the first year of college really something novel and fresh. Instead of college being just more of the same kind of thing the students have had in preparatory school, they are now introduced to the fields of knowledge from a different point of view and in a new way. There is better appreciation of the interrelatedness and significance of the content and nature of the academic pursuits. There is created, in consequence, a zest which is often otherwise absent.[25]

The *Manitou Messenger* for May 6, 1955, expressed itself editorially on the subject of "Educational Integration" at St. Olaf.

Every liberal arts college must teach the humanities. Some colleges make this easier for the student than do others by offering a humanities department filled with good background courses ranging from "The Golden Age of Greece" to "The Twentieth Century—from Eliot to Freud." The program when taken in its entirety is a correlated culture course which deals with important advancements in human understanding. A program of this type offers a firm foundation around which the underclassman can build his entire liberal arts education. Why doesn't St. Olaf offer this stepping stone to better integregation in education?

---

[25]Quoted in Fred B. Millett, *The Re-birth of Liberal Education*, p. 38.

Chapter Ten

General Education
in the
Natural Sciences

THE role of the natural sciences in a college curriculum is a function of the philosophy of education and of life which an institution has consciously or sub-consciously adopted. This same statement could be made of the humanities or the social sciences, but toward those areas of study one rarely finds the extremes of utter distaste or of fawning worship which the natural sciences evoke in academic circles. These misguided attitudes have been classified by Konrad Krauskopf[1] as embodying an outlook either that the scientist is the modern Mephistopheles, the personification of evil in our troubled world, or that he is the high priest of a new religion. Both of these views are alive in minority groups. The anti-science attitude has been reported at Harvard as a vague negativism toward science expressed even by incoming students. This has resulted in almost desperate attempts to sugar-coat the pill enough to make the patient swallow it. A more definite philosophical stand is taken by the other camp in what has been called logical positivism or physicalism. Here all the universe finds unity in scientific language, the reduction of terms to "thing-language" and "observable thing-predicates." It has been the goal of most introductory courses in science to seek a healthy intermediate path which avoids the poles of damnation or deification.

---

[1]Konrad B. Krauskopf, "Science in General Education at Mid-Century," *The Journal of Higher Education*, XXII (February 1951), 59.

A positive and yet restrained view of science with which many educators would agree is expressed by Bertalanffy:

It remains to be seen whether the march of science is triumphal or macabre. One thing, however, is certain. Science is one of those symbolic worlds man has created for mastering the great enigma of the universe, the creation of which is part of his uniqueness. All reasoning consists in the substitution of symbols—concepts, words, mathematical signs—in lieu of reality. Through its immanent logic, this system of symbols gains, as it were, an existence independent of and surpassing the individual life and psychology of its builders. It is in this way that science, in theory, leads to prediction, and, in practice, to the control of nature. The technological mastery over natural events demonstrates that the theoretical system is more than a castle in the air, that it corresponds to certain traits of reality.

"However, none of the world of symbols, the sum total of which is called human culture, is a full presentation of reality. Remember those precious etchings by Whistler: the lagoons of Venice, the bridges, San Marco and its doves—just a few scratches of the needle, giving, nevertheless, an unfathomable perspective of Italian serenity. Whistler called painting the art of omission, representing things by a few characteristic traces. Something similar is true of science. It is not concerned with the innermost core of reality. But it is one of the perspectives of reality, representing, by means of interconnected symbols, certain traces of reality, namely, the orderliness in the relation of things. This, however, is sufficient to allow for theoretical as well as practical mastery of nature.

"It is said, and it is true in a way, that the prelude of Wagner's 'Rheingold' gives a picture of creation, moving upwards from the keynotes of the flowing element to ever higher and more organized, life-imaging melodies, till finally the voice of the elfish daughters of the Rhine emerges. It will be difficult, however, to learn much about the evolution of the vertebrates from Wagner. DaVinci's 'Gioconda' fortunately reveals little of human anatomy, although, incidentally, Leonardo was a keen and quite modern anatomist. What science can do is to symbolize reality in its way, knowing, as its great masters always did, that this is but a humble way to redraw a few traces of the great blueprint of Creation."[2]

[2]"Philosophy of Science in Scientific Education," *Scientific Monthly,* LXXVII (November 1953), 233.

OBJECTIVES IN TEACHING THE NATURAL SCIENCES

From this concept of science as one important view of reality, most natural science courses have derived more specific objectives:

a. *An appreciation of a scientific attitude and of scientific methods*

This is the primary objective in any introductory course in natural science. While there cannot be said to be any series of steps which are *the* scientific method, a student should have a grasp of the meaning and relationship of facts, laws, hypotheses and theories. The unending cycle of experiment, conceptual scheme, and experiment should be illustrated in a general science course by the historical advances of science. The student, himself, should test the methods of science in his reading and in his own laboratory work. The lessons of "ruthless truthfulness" and unswerving logic should be taught as part of a scientific attitude.

One may still ask the question: Can the development of critical judgment and a successful approach to problems be developed only in the natural sciences? The answer, to be sure, is in the negative, but there are advantages even to the non-scientist in the development of reason as it is found in the science courses. The argument is summarized by Hubert Alyea as follows:

. . . the most valuable portions of our education were those which stirred us intellectually, which made us grow beyond the subject matter of the course itself. In trying to meet the challenge which the teacher had put to us we were having intellectual growing-pains. These are the experiences which we all have in common as we look back upon certain courses with admiration and respect. A science course for non-scientists should furnish just such opportunities for individual intellectual growth. But, you will say, these are the aims of any course—in the humanities or social sciences, as well as in natural science. To which I would immediately assent. The value of such training in the sciences, and the advantages it offers over similar training in other fields of endeavor are the simplicity of factors, the limited number of variables, and the elementary nature of scientific reasoning. Science is therefore an admirable medium in which the student can exercise his critical judgment, can feel competent to disagree with and alter some scientific theories under discussion.[3]

---

[3]"The Single-Science Course at Princeton" in Earl J. McGrath, *Science in General Education* (Dubuque, Iowa: Wm. C. Brown Company, 1948), p. 134.

b. *An understanding of the language and basic principles of science*

Most science teachers believe that one must teach science and not merely teach *about* science. The full implications of this area of knowledge on the life of men cannot be understood or evaluated without some comprehension of the basic principles and the language of science. Drill on facts plus rote memorization have often plagued the science student. They should be avoided unless they make a definite contribution to the grasp of basic principles. Nevertheless, to think in science or even *about* science, some of its "jargon" must be mastered like the technical language of any other field.

c. *Relationship between science and society*

Science represents one of the great intellectual achievements of man. As such it has had profound effects on man's thinking in areas outside of the natural sciences. The shift from classical to modern physics is an example of a wave which has sent its ripples into philosophy, religion, and the social sciences. The general education course must make the student aware of the wider implications of science as a part of a culture.

The technological advances which have grown out of science since the time of the industrial revolution have also played an important part in the history of the world. It is a warped picture of sociology, economics, or political science which appears without considering the modes of living which technology has bestowed upon us. Some mention of these effects is inevitable in a science course although many teachers feel that the "gadgets" of science are vastly overstressed in elementary courses and tend to overshadow other more basic purposes of the courses. This is a controversial issue for which one can find a different answer in each college or university. Some basic courses omit the role of technology in our civilization while others are centered around this locus.

d. *Cultivation of intellectual curiosity and creativity*

There is a priceless opportunity in any elementary science course to lay before the student the challenge of a baffling and fascinating universe. What makes an atom bomb work? What is life? What is the evidence for atoms and molecules, believed in, but not seen? There are so many things we do not know in science, so many doors waiting to be opened that it should be possible to arouse through discussion, lecture, and reading, even a very dormant sense of curiosity. If possible this sense of curiosity, once awakened, should be exploited by the use of problems in reasoning plus "discovery" laboratory work in which answers cannot be found in a textbook but must be worked out experimentally by the student. Truly creative research is almost impossible in any elementary course but it can be simulated in the sciences.

2

TYPES OF COURSES

The traditional introductory course in natural science planned primarily for the science major may possibly achieve all of the objectives which have been listed as desirable for a first year course. Nevertheless, a few decades ago, many educators resolved that such courses were too specialized, too loaded with facts and too uninteresting for the average non-scientist. New experimental courses were set up and tested in general education programs. Today the experimentation continues, but certain patterns of organization have emerged. These are summarized below under the titles Survey, Block and Gap, Selected Problems, and Historical. These categories are by no means rigid since there is often overlapping of the different types in one particular course offering.

a. *Survey*

The original general education survey courses were little more than an assembling of diluted versions of introductory courses in a number of sciences. There was usually a different instructor for each part of the course. The resultant compilation was often uncoordinated, very thin in intellectual nourishment, and usually composed of superficial factual knowledge. This type of course still exists with some gestures toward unity and depth. The title "survey" has gradually become anathema in educational circles.

b. *Block and Gap*

The phrase "block and gap" was originated by Eric Rogers of Princeton to describe courses built around a few basic topics which are studied in detail and are interconnected to give an organic structure. The advantage of this treatment is the thoroughness and intensity with which the instruction can be given. The blocks and the gaps may vary from year to year to add interest and variety at least to the instructor's task.

Examples of topics which are commonly used in the physical sciences are: Kepler's laws, Joule's work, the concept of atoms and molecules, and the concept of ions. An integrated use of the block and gap procedure is illustrated by a course in biology at the University of Florida which lists the following topics:

1. The isolated individual organism
2. The organism as a link in a sequence of generations
3. The organism as a product of evolution
4. The organism as a unit in a social economic complex

The topical pattern of teaching has been so successful that there are few introductory science courses which do not at least pretend to its use. There are two common problems which arise. The first consists of using too many topics in a course, thereby changing it to a survey course. The second problem is caused by a lack of adequate links between topics, thus destroying the unity of a course. Neither weakness is basic but is more likely the result of failure by the instructor to see an overall course objective.

c. *Selected Problems*

The problem approach to organization has received its greatest impetus from the successful pioneering work at Colgate University. At that institution all of the usual course trappings have been dropped in favor of concentrating the attention of the students on a few select problems in the physical sciences and the biological sciences. Typical problems are, "Does the earth travel around the sun or the sun around the earth?" and "How does life depend on light?" These problems are treated mainly in discussions sections but with some lectures and demonstrations plus laboratory experience and field trips.

202

In such a study an effort is made to jolt the student out of authoritarian learning, to teach him to examine the world around him with open eyes and to grasp in a vivid personal way how science works. Although the purpose of the course is not to give a comprehensive view of science, the students are said to have a surprising store of scientific information at the end of a year.

Some weaknesses are reported such as a lack of quantitative thinking, a too limited use of the laboratory, and a failure to make the course meaningful in terms of everyday life and thought. These difficulties are not considered basic by the instructors at Colgate, and some of the defects can probably be corrected. More important is the apparent success in teaching critical thinking in the natural sciences.

d. *Historical*

The history of natural science has not received much support as an adequate fulfillment of a general education requirement in this area. This does not mean that the history of natural science cannot be a meaningful course offering, nor does it imply that it does not have a place in an introductory course. But most scientists feel that the history of science is only a partial introduction to science and that a more direct contact with scientific thinking and working is needed.

A variation of the historical approach is the use of historical cases as has been proposed and worked out by Conant and his colleagues. Some of the great crucial problems in the natural sciences are studied as a method of obtaining an insight into "scientific thinking." Examples of such case histories are: "The Overthrow of the Phlogiston Theory" and "Robert Boyle's Experiments in Pneumatics." These problems are presented in their philosophical, economic, and social background. The set-backs and the advances in each case portray the frailties and the genius of the scientists involved. Original papers are scanned and the spirit of the original investigation is recaptured as nearly as possible. This may also be said to be a problems approach with a variation in the way critical thinking is presented.

Criticism of the case history method is that when used as a sole introduction to natural science it loses much of the drama and

203

excitement of modern science which is with us in our daily lives. It discloses the methods, but it does not give the sense of personal participation and delight which is said to be gained from a course which is actually *in* science.

Each of the above methods of teaching natural science is used either in a mixed-science or in a single-science course. The mixed-science course contains material from two or more sciences. Examples would be a typical physical science course containing astronomy, chemistry, geology, and physics, or an earth science course containing astronomy and geology, or a biology course containing zoology and botany. This kind of general education course is more widely used than the single-science course and is found in each of the above categories.

The single-science course is not just another name for the elementary course given to majors. Is is designed as a terminal course and it attempts to avoid a narrow view by drawing extensively on all other areas of natural science. Indeed, if it is properly taught, many instructors feel that it is hardly distinguishable from the mixed-science course. The advantages claimed for the single science course are that it gives greater intellectual depth, that it involves less of a problem in staff training as well as less dislocation of the normal instructional program, and that it conserves the time of the student and instructor because it eliminates the need to correlate the specific substances of several fields. It is maintained that the basic objectives of learning, namely, critical thinking and the scientific method, can be taught without loss when the facts and principles are centered around a single field rather than around many fields.

Most general education programs have preferred the wider scope which a mixed-science course can lay before the student, but there has been a growing movement toward the single-science course in the past few years. This probably stems as much from the administrative headaches of the mixed-science course as from anything else.

SOME ISSUES IN TEACHING BASIC COURSES IN NATURAL SCIENCE

The present day areas of agreement and disagreement with regard to course content and methods of instruction in general education courses in natural science have been summarized by Krauskopf.[4] A few explanatory sentences have been added to parts of Krauskopf's outline.

a. *Areas of agreement on course content*

1. There should be some emphasis on teaching the scientific method and developing a scientific attitude.

2. The "block and gap" approach is better than either the usual orthodox first-year course or the superficial survey course.

3. Physical sciences are better taught separate from biological sciences or by separate men in different terms of the same course. There are a few schools such as Stephens College and Boston University which have a completely integrated course in the natural sciences, but these are a small minority.

b. *Areas of disagreement on course content*

1. Can the scientific method actually be taught in an elementary course? Is actual research in an advanced course or in graduate school the only true means of coming to grips with the scientific method?

2. How much mathematics, history, philosophy, *etc.*, should be included in the courses?

3. Shall the mixed-science or the single-science approach be used?

c. *Areas of agreement on methods of instruction*

1. Guidance of a lecture section or a discussion section should be done by one man per term. It is acknowledged that when a mixed-science course is first set up, the temporary use of more than one individual may be necessary until the instructors become familiar with teaching outside of their specialty

---

[4]"Science in General Education at Mid-Century," pp. 59-61.

2. Small discussion sections are highly desirable. In some types of organization such as the "problems" course, classes of 15 to 25 are required. Even where primarily the lecture method is used, large classes are thought to be undesirable. An example of recent experimentation in class size is given by P. A. Davies, Chairman of the Division of the Natural Sciences at the University of Louisville:

> It is a mistaken idea that a large number of students can be handled effectively at one time in introductory courses of this type. We have experimented with classes of more than a hundred students and with small classes. If large lecture classes are supplemented by small discussion and quiz groups, a fair return in student achievement is obtained. We have found, however, that about forty students is an ideal size class. This number may be seated close enough to the instructor to see clearly the demonstrations; it is large enough to develop a spirit of competition between students and to retain the enthusiasm of the instructor, yet small enough for personal attention in class discussion and question answering. Smaller classes lack competition and enthusiasm necessary for maximum achievement.[5]

3. Individual laboratory experience is desirable although not indispensable. A few years ago there was great strength in the movement to eliminate the laboratory from general education courses. The pendulum is now swinging in the other direction with a growing emphasis on student participation. Rogers says:

> Most of us feel that some laboratory work is essential. "Learning by doing" goes much deeper than "learning by listening," and for some students actual laboratory experimenting is the only way of giving an understanding of scientific work. It gives them a feeling of familiarity and respect for the foundations of science. Without it, texts, original writings, and even teachers take on an air of sacred authority.[6]

The interest in laboratory training by no means indicates a complacent acceptance of the usual laboratory course. Dull "cookbook" following of a manual of recipes does little to arouse the curiosity of the student or to increase his respect for the natural sciences. Some colleges, like Bard, have gone over completely to the "discovery" experiment, in which the student must make a genuine investigation to obtain results which are not merely copied from a convenient sourcebook.

[5]P. A. Davies, "Science Introductory Courses for General Education in the University of Louisville," in Earl J. McGrath, *Science in General Education*, p. 308.
[6]"Science in General Education," *ibid.*, p. 18.

d. *Areas of disagreement on methods of instruction*

1. What shall be the relative distribution of instruction time between lectures, discussions, laboratory, demonstration, and visual aids?

2. Shall objective or essay examinations be given? The common compromise is to give both.

3. Can success in teaching the primary objectives be evaluated?

e. *Other unsettled questions* lie in the realm of administration. Some of these have been listed by Krauskopf.

1. How shall staffs be obtained for inter-departmental terminal courses in the natural sciences? Shall the instructors teach these courses plus some work in their departments or shall a separate staff for general education be set up? The former pattern is most common since there is usually a desire to have top-flight, enthusiastic scholars participate in the program. Unfortunately the time demands of a general education course rarely permit the research minded individual to stay long with such a course. Nor does this individual usually have the broad background necessary for the general education program.

Another peculiar dilemma has developed. With few exceptions, the inauguration of general education courses has been the product of college presidents and deans and not of scientists themselves.[7] Despite this administrative blessing, the majority of the teachers of these courses are in the lower professorial ranks and have poorer professional training than others in their field of specialty. These instructors also find themselves less favored in salary raises and promotions. This mixed attitude toward general education on the part of administrators and departmental aversion have often completely disrupted the general education development.

2. Shall any students be permitted to substitute the conventional introductory courses in a particular science to satisfy the basic natural science requirement? There is general agreement that separate general education courses in science should exist for the non-major. Whether or not the usual first-in-a-sequence science

---

[7]Robert A. Bullington, "Summary of a Study of College Science Courses Designed for General Education," *Association of American Colleges Bulletin*, XXXVI (May 1950), 266.

course fulfills the same mission for the science major (or for any other student), is a point of contention.

3. Shall the general education courses be limited to the freshman and sophomore levels or should advanced courses in science be offered to upperclassmen as well? There are only a relatively few institutions such as Harvard that now offer upper division courses for the non-science major.

Perhaps a fourth question should be added to Krauskopf's list.

4. How much work in the natural sciences should be required?

A survey made in 1950 of 720 colleges and universities indicated that 50% require one year of natural science and 50% require two or more years, usually covering both the biological and the physical sciences. In *Science in General Education* edited by McGrath one can get a better idea of what the schools interested in general education have done. Three-fourths of the nineteen schools reporting in this book require two or more years of natural science, and perhaps even more significant is the fact that in only two of the nineteen schools does natural science constitute less than twenty-five percent of the required core curriculum. The usual problem faced by a faculty is stated by Earl Wallace of the Pennsylvania College for Women:

> Science cannot, of course, occupy the whole of the college curriculum, and the faculty limited the time for natural science to fourteen semester hours. Such an amount may seem too small to the teacher of science, too large to the teacher of French, yet it should enable the instructor to present an adequate view of the world of science without specialization in any one field. Naturally, a number of us in the sciences felt that not enough time was given to what we regarded as the most important of human developments; at the same time, some of our colleagues thought that the time given to science could be spent much more wisely in considering the glory of Greece and the grandeur of Rome. The compromise in allotted time forced upon the committee the question of selection of material.[8]

4

EVALUATION

Despite the many differences of opinion as to how best to teach natural science in higher education, there is general agree-

[8]"Natural Science at Pennsylvania College for Women," in Earl J. McGrath, *Science in General Education*, p. 286.

ment that it has a proper and a necessary place as part of general education. There is further agreement that the courses to be taught in this common educational core should be different in content and in method from the orthodox introductory course for the major. Beyond these two general propositions, each college must work out its own program to fit its peculiar goals and within the limits of the training and competence of its teaching staff.

Chapter Eleven

General Education
in the
Social Sciences

1

OBJECTIVES IN TEACHING THE SOCIAL SCIENCES

OCIAL scientists have been more enterprising than any
other academic group in meeting the demand for instruction adapted to the needs of the nonspecialist student, that is, the
student who does not expect to devote his life to the study of one
of the social science disciplines. Perhaps that is because of the
sense of urgency which members of that professional group feel
about preparing this generation of youth to understand and act
intelligently about the complex problems of their time."[1]

If the champions of general education in the social sciences
were asked what they hoped to achieve by their educational reforms
they would undoubtedly place as their first objective the training
of citizens more capable of grappling with the complex problems
of modern life.

Intelligent citizenship is the primary objective of liberal education.
Consequently, whenever and wherever a revision of the curriculum of
the College of Liberal Arts is discussed, courses in social science are
likely to be a center of attention. If students are to decide wisely and
well on matters affecting the social good, modern education must

---

[1]Earl J. McGrath, "Trends in Social Science in General Education," *Social
Science in General Education* (Dubuque, Iowa: Wm. C. Brown Company, 1948),
p. 272.

develop minds disciplined to promote the general welfare. In this sense, a major share of the responsibility for general education must fall within the confines of courses in social science.[2]

The reformers argue that the traditional departmentalization of knowledge makes it impossible for the students to get an intelligent grasp or understanding of the problems which beset our age.

Amid present-day confusion and conflict it is a gross understatement to say that it is difficult for a young citizen to see his world with any clear perspective. Yet, in our democratic society, in order to attempt a fair solution of our problems, it is imperative that a majority of our citizens have an over-all understanding of the problems of the whole social order. The sociologist would say that we need to "become aware of the culture as a whole." It is part of the obligation of a general educational program, therefore, to give our student citizens the broadest and most penetrating understanding of the social-political-economic aspects of the civilization in which they will be forced to live.[3]

The advocates of new approaches in the social sciences contend that the economic and political crises which have struck the country during the last generation have found the American people woefully unprepared to understand or analyze the problems confronting them. A large share of responsibility for this unpreparedness, they say, must be laid at the door of our social science teaching. Writing in 1934, Professor John M. Gaus said:

One of the . . . . aspects of public opinion during the depression is the highly particularistic and separatistic nature of the views and proposals of people; their lack of any common agreement, for example, concerning the meaning or implication of terms such as "freedom" or "regimentation" essential for political communication, their ignorance of the facts essential to any most elementary statement of problems confronting us all. This suggests that social scientists in particular have been living in a fool's paradise.[4]

World War II found the Americans as confused as did the depression, according to the critics. The Americans knew how to run the new mechanical devices which technological science put into

[2]Jack T. Johnson, "Core Courses in Social Science at State University of Iowa," *Social Science in General Education,* p. 75.

[3]John A. Decker, "The Contemporary Social Issues Course at Stephens College," *Social Science in General Education,* p. 211.

[4]"The Relation of the Social Sciences to General Education," *General Education, Its Nature, Scope, and Essential Elements,* Wm. S. Gray, ed. (Chicago: University of Chicago Press, 1934), p. 76.

their hands, but, it is maintained, they were absolutely bewildered by all the questions forced upon them largely as a result of the impact of the machine upon modern civilization. If the war found us provincial and immature in outlook, the peace finds us possibly even worse prepared to grapple with the more subtle questions which now confront us.

We debate the Marshall Plan in terms of dollar costs and fail to appreciate what the economic collapse of Western Europe would mean to the general democratic power position. We invent an atomic bomb, which could turn the clock back to the stone ages in the course of a few weeks' time, but the general public refuses to be depressed by the delay in working out satisfactory international machinery to control atomic experimentation. We give lip service to the principles of the United Nations, but remain unshaken in our devotion to the unrestricted national sovereignty.[5]

To remedy this weakness in our national character we are told that we must break away from the narrow departmentalization, especially in the social sciences, and introduce a system which will help the students see the world and its problems in broader perspective. "We know that democracy requires that every citizen be able to make decisions required for the solution of local, national, and world problems, but our educational system has neglected this phase in an overemphasis on vocational specialization. Specialization is necessary for the citizen's economic contribution to the welfare of the group, but general education is equally necessary for his contribution as the source of sovereignty in a functioning democracy."[6]

Besides their main aim of introducing the students to "the origin, complex nature, and possible solutions of fundamental social, economic, and political problems which confront man in the twentieth century," the advocates of general education also list as common objectives "preparation for fuller living," "giving insight into the methods of the social scientists," and equipping young people with a "common core" of knowledge, "an integrated view of life," which will make it easier and more pleasurable for them to communicate with each other.

[5]John A. Decker, "The Contemporary Social Issues Course at Stephens College," p. 216.

[6]John Stover Welling, "General Education in Social Studies at Colorado College of Education," *Social Science in General Education*, p. 144.

If any doubting Thomas should ask whether it is possible to give an integrated course in the social sciences the answer from the reformers is absolutely definite:

This question is predicated upon the assumption that each of the collegiate departments (anthropology, economics, political science, sociology, and geography) studies a different subject matter. Nothing could be further from the truth. All the social science disciplines investigate the same basic material: the study of man as a member of a group. Thus, there is no point in asking: What is the integrating factor in the social sciences? Such a question is based upon a false premise. It presupposes that each of the social sciences is different in subject matter and in methodology. However, these differences are not differences in fact; they are a division of labor. What is already a single whole cannot be integrated. And without engaging in a dispute with the purists, there is social science and not social sciences. . . . Social science is a tool for the solution of problems. And everyday problems do not follow the lines of demarcation set by academicians. Social problems are what they are. In this sense a course in social science is not only possible, it is an imperative![7]

The study of society is a unique discipline, so it is argued, because it is the field in which all students in adult life will exert direct influence on what happens in state, nation, and the world at large. We employ specialists to build bridges and heal diseases; here general education may be of little direct instrumental value, but in dealing with social problems every citizen is expected to take a hand. Scientists invent atom bombs, but it will depend largely upon John Q. Citizen if and when we are to use them. Because of their training and the position they usually attain in the community, college graduates are especially influential in moulding opinion and forming public policies. Hence it is maintained that general education in the social sciences is especially urgent—education in this area is of direct practical importance.

Precisely because the social studies are so highly charged with controversial material, they are a difficult field to teach, especially in a period like the present when there are fears of "isms" on every side, and particularly when taught from the point of view of general education which aims specifically at arousing the students to analyze their fundamental beliefs and standards of judgment. Furthermore, students usually come to the social studies

---

[7]Jack T. Johnson, "Core Courses in Social Science at State University of Iowa," p. 77.

with their minds fairly well made up about the problems, big and small, which will confront them in class and in society. Their opinions about such matters as political parties, race questions, religion, capital, and labor are likely to be those of their home and community, probably reinforced by a civics course in high school. Very few students come to the physical sciences and the humanities with as many preconceived notions and as much cock-sureness as they do to the social sciences where the ideas of "Tom, Dick and Harry," in popular opinion at least, are supposed to be more sound than those of "high brows" and "egg heads." "Hence, a major part of our effort consists of making the students aware of their biases and of the presuppositions derived from their cultural heritage with which they come to us. This exposes us frequently to the charge of indoctrination. The only answer we can make to this charge is that we are constantly making efforts to discover our own biases, and that nothing is more dangerous to assume in the social world than that we have arrived at absolute and final truths in which our own interests have played no role."[8]

2

TYPES OF COURSES

It is very difficult to describe the general education programs set up in the social science field in many American institutions because very seldom are any two programs identical. The various plans worked out are influenced by local conditions and traditions and by the individuals who are responsible for their inception. Usually, also, the programs are subject to change from year to year. What was true of the courses at one time may not be so at present. Despite the similarity of the avowed objectives of the various programs, uniqueness, experimentation, innovation, and reform seem to characterize almost all the new ventures. With time some of them have taken on the semblance of permanency through the appearance of syllabi, textbooks, anthologies, and bibliographies. But when they have assumed these signs of rigidity,

---

[8]Louis Wirth, "Nature, Scope, and Essential Elements in General Education," *General Education, Its Nature, Scope, and Essential Elements*, p. 33.

they seem to be viewed with suspicion by the genuine devotees of general education.

Despite this rich variety, the workers in the field have tried to classify the programs under various main headings, some of which may be discussed as follows.[9]

a. *History of Civilization Course.* Under this general heading a great number of varieties could be listed, depending on such factors as the time and area covered, themes selected for discussion, relative emphasis placed on the chronological or problem approach, *etc.* In general it can be said that the aim of these courses is not to teach history in the traditional way of "covering" a certain era but rather to unearth the "constants of history," those forces which, in changing forms, have always been at work in society. By examining these forces in various periods of history, it is hoped that the student will be better able to understand the problems of his own age.

One of the best known programs taking an historical approach is the Contemporary Civilization course at Columbia University, which analyzes the development of European ideas, ideals, and institutions from about the end of the eleventh century up to the present.

The course is concerned with showing the changing attitudes of Western civilization toward revealed religion and the search for salvation, the concept of the state, the idea of natural law, the use of the scientific method, the creation of free associations, and the like. All, however, within an historical frame of reference, for the Middle Ages, the mercantilist epoch, and our own modern times have offered various explanations and cultivated different attitudes toward human strivings and social institutions. Each epoch, as it were, has its own time spirit. Nevertheless, out of the experiences of all of them a set of values emerges which may properly be regarded as our heritage from the pains, the yearnings, and the achievements of the past. There have been transmitted to us both means and ends; and these the student is taught to keep ever in sight as he examines the problems of our own day.[10]

This course is followed by a second-year course dealing with the United States. About one-third of the course is given to an his-

---

[9]For such attempts at classification, see *Social Science in General Education*, pp. 88-90, 159-161, 276-284.

[10]Harry J. Carman, "General Education in the Social Sciences at Columbia College," *Social Science in General Education*, p. 19.

torical survey of American ideas and institutions, "presented as problems." The rest of the year is devoted to an analysis of the development and the nature of the economic, social, and political problems of the present.

> The materials of this part of the course are economic and political; but the methods of treating these materials do not correspond to those ordinarily used in introductory courses in economics and government. At no point, to any significant extent, is there developed a theory of the state, for example. The method actually employed is that of analytical description of going institutional affairs in terms which seem to present the most fruitful and provocative set of relationships among the various institutions under examination.[11]

Practically all institutions include more or less historical material in their general social science courses. Among these can be mentioned Dartmouth, Wesleyan University, University of Louisville, University of Kansas, University of Oregon, Pennsylvania College for Women, Michigan State College, and many others. Some institutions, like Chicago and Wisconsin, take, in part, an historical approach but classify history with the humanities. Even in those courses where the outlook is focused strictly on the present, it is recognized that the present has its roots in the past and that man's thinking is related to experience derived both from the present and the past.

The criticism usually levelled against the "History of Civilization" course is that it does not devote enough time to the problems of today. It merely brings the student up to the threshold of the present, the critics say, and hence leaves him as much as ever a stranger in his own house. The student does not get enough "training for citizenship," in other words, unless the historical course is followed by another course, as at Columbia, devoted almost exclusively to the contemporary scene.

b. *Problems Course*. In recent years many institutions have begun to offer courses which plunge the student directly into the maelstrom of contemporary issues such as race relations, civil liberties, capital and labor, crime and the maladjusted, marriage and divorce. They consider that this is one way of shocking the students out of their lethargy and making them more aware of and

---

[11]*Ibid.*, p. 23.

interested in the pulsating life about them. They feel also that the problems course offers a good pedagogical approach, because discussions of live issues "have the genuine ring of reality" and give the student "the feeling of having been admitted to a ringside seat near the center of social conflict." Furthermore, its proponents argue that it gives the prospective citizen training in democratic thinking, since their biases and presuppositions are continually put through the fiery ordeal of actual debate. The participants in the discussion soon discover how little they usually know concerning subjects which they approach with great self-assurance. Thus they may learn that "a little knowledge is a dangerous thing" and that it may be well for them to drink deeper of the Pierian spring before passing judgment on profound issues. Another virtue claimed for the problems course is that it serves as an excellent integrator of knowledge because important social issues are no respecters of academic demarcation lines; such a question as the race issue, for instance, can not be confined within the walls of either economics, sociology, political science, anthropology, philosophy, religion, or history. All these disciplines, and others, can shed some light on the subject, but none is "sufficient unto itself" if full clarity is sought. Practically every issue of any importance, so it is argued, may serve to prove the interrelatedness of all the social sciences and other fields of knowledge as well.

Despite the challenging nature of the problems course it has been subjected to considerable criticism. According to one observer there is a "constant tendency for both the instructional staff and the students to emphasize more and more the data and facts of the problems and, as a result, to drift away from a conscious development of a social perspective that will grow and expand as the student matures."[12] Another observer says that his institution rejected the problems approach decisively, and for many reasons. "We felt that too frequently these problems were considered as separate and isolated parts, that they were not presented with sufficient anthropological and historical background, that in actual practice they often degenerated into mere chitchat about current events. More, we felt that they emphasized marginal and peripher-

---

[12]Arthur Naftalin, "The Minnesota Approach to the Basic Social Science Course," *Social Science in General Education*, p. 88.

al questions at the expense of leading and central trends."[13] The main objection against the problems course seems to be that it may excite the students—at least for a while—about the issues of the day but that it fails to introduce them to the grand sweep of human experience and the lasting cultural heritage of the race.

c. *Case Method.* This type can be defined as a narrowed problems approach to the study of human relations. It is an outgrowth of the case method developed at the Harvard Graduate School of Business Administration, which again was an outgrowth of the case method long applied in American law schools. The case method in the social sciences has also been likened to the clinical method used in medical schools. It is "an attempt to capture a segment of reality and transfer it inside the classroom for clinical observation on the part of the student."[14] Actual problems which have occurred in the life of human beings are written up with great fidelity, giving sufficient detail to explain how the quandary or perplexity developed. The cases selected are problems which may arise in the life of the ordinary citizen and will, therefore, only incidentally touch upon great social, historical, national, or international issues. These bigger issues may be brought into the discussion, but this is not the prime objective in the case method as it is in the regular problems course. The main aims of the case approach can be summarized as follows: (1) To help the students understand their relationship with others in society. "And we believe that that help can come best when students address themselves to concrete problems from our social life today."[15] (2) To help students acquire the ability to analyze and see relationships between factors that would have little or no meaning for the untrained intellect. "In attaining skill here there is so far no known substitute for the clinical method—the repetitive study of problem situations in as full complexity as feasible." (3) To help students acquire information. Though it is regarded as a purely incidental by-product, "there is some evidence to indicate that even with this

[13]William G. Carleton, "The Social Science Comprehensive at the University of Florida," *Social Science in General Education,* p. 160.

[14]H. Gibson and W. Sandelius, "General Education in the Social Sciences at the University of Kansas," *Social Science in General Education,* p. 150.

[15]S. J. French and W. H. Bash, "General Education in the Social Sciences at Colgate University," *Social Science in General Education,* p. 189.

treatment information has not been lost—they may even be learning more facts."

According to reports, the case method met with immediate student approval both at the University of Kansas and Colgate University, two of the first institutions to introduce such courses in their liberal arts offerings. "The university is completely embarrassed by its inability to provide the trained personnel for the number of sections which should be given," says the Kansas report. "As contrasted with a survey type course, there is an upward jump of student interest, quantitatively and qualitatively. More students participate in the discussions voluntarily and they become more interested in the outcome of the discussion," says the Colgate report. But there are also reports to the effect that the students find "little to put in their notebook" in these courses, which seems to indicate that they find little real substance in them. The discussions stir up student interest, so it is said, because very live issues and dramatic situations are taken up for debate. The participants have to "think on their feet" and draw on knowledge gathered both in school and in "life." But students also seem to find that these courses frequently take on the nature of a "bull session" with much triviality entering into the discussion.

d. *Survey Course.* This is one of the oldest and most widely used types of general education courses in the social sciences. As offered at Oregon University[16] it begins with *Background Studies:* geography, human biology, psychology, anthropology, after which it moves on to *Descriptive Studies:* political science, economics, sociology, and concludes with *Interpretative Studies:* philosophy, history, religion, fine arts, and aesthetics. Other survey courses follow roughly the plan just outlined but introduce more history by tracing the development of political, economic, social, religious, and educational institutions as well as by taking up for consideration such fields as philosophy, ethics, and aesthetics. The aim of the survey course is presumably to introduce the student to the various social sciences, give him some insight into the methodology of the social scientists, and to indicate the interrelatedness of the various fields.

---

[16]Quirinius Breen, "Social Science: A Liberal Arts Course at the University of Oregon," *Social Science in General Education,* pp. 100-112.

The survey type was very popular during the thirties and is still quite common, but is gradually becoming an extinct species. "Scholars generally agree that in a field in which the subject matter is so vast as it is in social science, any attempt to survey the constituent disciplines must necessarily result in superficiality."[17] It is criticised as being almost wholly descriptive rather than analytic. "At best it confronts the student with a series of brief digests of several different introductory courses which in themselves are brief digests. The result is likely to be a scattering and smattering of information and principles."[18] Also, it is argued, the survey course fails at the job of integration. It merely gives "a brief dip into the nature and problems of history, then a brief dip into the nature and problems of political science, then economics, then sociology, then psychology, then geography—each discipline in a given number of pages presenting its case."[19] In commenting on the Oregon survey course, Professor Breen says: "In our effort to integrate we have had little of a common conviction about the integer. We have so long dealt in fractions that we have little certainty about a whole. We have therefore contented ourselves with putting our subjects together so as to suggest the unity provided by a string of pearls."[20]

e. *Area Study.* Another approach which has found favor with many educators and was widely adopted during World War II to train young Americans for possible service in foreign countries is the area study. A study of this type draws upon the resources of a wide variety of disciplines which may help throw light on the country or area taken up for consideration. It would logically begin with an inquiry into the physical aspects of the area, its geography: what attracted people to the region; what are the natural bases for the sustenance of life, the development of agriculture, mining, industry, and communication system; what were the "challenges," to use a Toynbeeism, which the inhabitants had to meet, and how did they influence the culture of the region. All

---

[17]Earl J. McGrath, "Trends in Social Science in General Education," p. 279.
[18]Arthur Naftalin, "The Minnesota Approach to the Basic Social Science Course," p. 88.
[19]William G. Carleton, "The Social Science Comprehensive at the University of Florida," p. 160.
[20]"Social Science: A Liberal Arts Course at the University of Oregon," p. 101.

these considerations would, of course, involve study of the historical development of the region, its changing political, social, religious, and economic institutions, and finally its achievements in such realms as science, literature, and the fine arts. Obviously this would be attempting integration on a rather ambitious scale, since practically all fields of learning would be taxed in a definite endeavor to see man in nature and society. How successful the integration would be in actual practice would, of course, depend on the teachers and students involved.

The advocates of area studies argue that by their method the student is introduced to problems "that will increasingly be most urgent to him as a person, as a citizen, and as a worker, and problems that reveal interdependence and change."[21] Furthermore, it is claimed that this approach helps solve the difficulty of motivation because "the student can be made to understand and to be responsive to the variety of interests, opportunities, and challenges which an evolving society possesses, and can begin to search for those particular ones in which he himself will want to participate."

The "types" discussed above by no means exhaust the subject. Many others could be added, but it is hoped that enough has been said to give some idea of what is meant by general education courses in the social sciences. It must be emphasized that institutions which have introduced general education usually do not limit themselves to one course or to one division but try to build up a sequence of courses covering the main areas of human knowledge. Thus, at Pennsylvania College for Women a required curriculum consisting of the following studies was introduced:

1. A one-year course in the study of the human organism and its development
2. A two-year course in the natural sciences

[21]John M. Gaus, "The Relation of the Social Sciences to General Education," p. 78. Professor Gaus worked with Professor Alexander Meiklejohn in the experimental college at the University of Wisconsin, one of the earliest and best known adventures in general education in this country. As consultant of the St. Olaf Self-Study Committee, Professor Gaus made the interesting suggestion that St. Olaf might initiate studies covering the Scandinavian countries and part of the Midwest. This would offer opportunity (1) to compare an old European society with a comparatively new American society, (2) to study the transplanting of peoples and cultures from one area to another, and (3) to compare the manner in which the two areas were affected by and attempted to solve the problems of our industrial age.

3. A two-year sequence in the arts
4. A two-and-a-half-year sequence in the social sciences (Western civilization, Modern Society, World Culture)
5. A one-year course in philosophy of life

These courses, together with requirements in composition and speech, constituted a total of 63 semester hours out of the total 120 needed for graduation.[22]

At Michigan State a Basic College was organized and assigned the task of developing a general education program for the freshman and sophomore years. It consists of seven departments, each responsible for one basic course: written and spoken English, biological science, physical science, social science, effective living, history of civilization, and literature and fine arts.[23]

At the State University of Iowa the students are required to take a minimum of 32 semester hours in general education divided as follows: (1) literature, (2) social science (the student has a choice between three courses in this field: Political Society, Introduction to Social Science, Man and Society) (3) natural science, (4) historical and cultural studies.[24]

At the University of Wisconsin a voluntary program of Integrated Studies was set up a few years ago covering the first two years of college. The courses were arranged as follows:

Humanities:
1. Classical Culture
2. Medieval and Renaissance Culture
3. Modern European Culture ("The literature of ideas and values of England and the Continent, 1750-1850")
4. American Culture, 1850 to the present

Social Studies:
1. Early Man and His Society
2. Transition to Industrial Society
3. Modern Industrial Society, U.S.A.
4. International Scene

Science:
1. Introduction to the Physical Universe
2. Earth Science
3. Biology: The adaptation of animal life to changing environments and the development of functional variations

---

[22]*Social Science in General Education*, p. 130.
[23]*Ibid.*, p. 113.
[24]*Ibid.*, p. 76.

222

4. Biology, a continuation with the introduction of psychology and heredity

Composition:
1. Theory and Practice of Writing
2. Nature and Functions of Language

Electives:
10 to 13 hours in language, mathematics, or other subjects.[25]

The above examples, chosen almost at random, will indicate that in general education programs attempts are made to fit the individual courses into a well-articulated plan of studies which, it is hoped, will help the student see the interrelatedness of the various fields of knowledge.

3

SOME ISSUES IN TEACHING BASIC COURSES IN
SOCIAL SCIENCE

a. *Lecture or Discussion.* Despite the fact that the general education movement has not developed any set methods of instruction, there seems to be remarkable agreement upon certain points. Thus, practically every institution offering general education courses in the social sciences stresses the importance of class discussions. The following are typical statements: "Every opportunity is given for student participation and discussion" (Boston University). "The division of time between lectures and conference periods with small sections of students has been a subject of much discussion and experimentation. Our conclusion is that one lecture and two or three conference sessions a week is more effective than two or three lectures and one conference. The personal element is important with immature students" (University of Arizona). "Classroom work is devoted almost exclusively to discussion based on the assignments" (Columbia University). "At Chicago we have chosen discussion as our primary instrument of instruction."

The general arguments in favor of the discussion method is summed up as follows by one observer:

The lecture method . . . is not encouraged. It is believed that the student should be required and trained to participate in class discussion.

[25]*Ibid.*, p. 200.

In order that student contributions may not degenerate into random expressions of opinion and prejudice, emphasis is given to the necessity of knowing the pertinent facts, analyzing their significance, then considering the implication of such data for the vital issue under consideration. The student is as often as possible placed in a position of intellectual responsibility where he must present data in support of his views and support them in logical fashion. In this line of procedure, the student can be made clearly responsible for the soundness of his own thinking. He is doing exactly what the citizen should do when he is called upon to decide difficult and controversial issues as a part of his civic responsibilities.[26]

Lecturing has not been abandoned entirely. Most programs call for one or two lectures per week to bind the material together, but never are they depended on as the sole method of instruction.

b. *Sections.* It logically follows that the sections must be kept rather small. In most institutions they run from twenty to thirty-five students per group. If the sections are much larger than this the method will defeat itself, because only a small percentage of the class will participate in the discussion and the teacher-student relationship will not become as intimate as it ought to be.

c. *Instructional Responsibility.* In most programs it has been found advantageous for the same instructor to be in charge of the course throughout, instead of putting it into the hands of a series of specialists in the various disciplines involved. "The task of synthesis, the importance of showing continuing interrelations among the several social science fields in any realistic study of important contemporary issues, and the determination not to allow the course to become fragmented on the basis of the specialized knowledge of the instructor require, in our judgment, that each staff member consider the entire area of the course as his field of responsibility."[27] A cooperative study of general education which was carried on in twenty-two colleges during the years 1939-1944 came to the same conclusion:

The most important type of integration at the general education level is that which comes through the process of teaching. There is need for a real rapport between the student and the instructor in the classroom situation, and the personality and the basic frame of reference of the

---

[26]Walter R. Fee, "A General Education Course in Social Science at Michigan State College," *Social Science in General Education*, p. 124.
[27]*Ibid.*, p. 122.

instructor as revealed to students over an extended period of time constitute an integrating principle for classroom instruction. Consequently, we have insisted that each instructor teach the entire two-year course. This makes it possible to approach unfamiliar topics in terms of a frame of reference with which the students have been previously familiar.[28]

d. *Materials.* There is also a decided tendency in general education to abandon textbooks, wholly or in part, and rely largely on source materials and outstanding secondary works in the field of human society, past and present.

Most textbooks deprive the student of the opportunity to exercise just those habits of thought which it is the end of general education to develop. They present him with highly simplified summaries of results and practically no insight into the methods and processes by which these results were arrived at. They seldom communicate to the student any of that passionate sincerity or integrity to be found in original works. They do not really contain knowledge but a kind of conventionalized gossip about knowledge which is thought to be sufficient for beginners. . . . In reading originals, on the other hand, the student has an opportunity to watch first-rate minds at work and to retrace the development of a significant idea or theory.[29]

It is, of course, recognized that source material must be carefully selected, because the mere fact that a document is original does not guarantee that it will stimulate thought or discussion. Certain selections may also be too obscure or deal with such esoteric material that it is beyond the comprehension of immature students. The general observation, however, seems to be that freshmen and sophomores are able to grapple more successfully with original sources than they are usually given credit for. And it must again be emphasized that general education programs usually assume that most of the instruction will take place in small sections where obscurities in thought or language can be clarified through intimate discussions between students and teachers.

In order to acquaint the students with the latest thinking in the field of human relations, the most noteworthy works of recent years are also read in whole or in part. Thus, by comparing the sources with later works the students have an opportunity to

---

[28]Albert W. Levi, *General Education in the Social Studies* (Washington, D. C.: American Council on Education, 1948), p. 309. Chapter XI of this report describes in detail a suggested two-year general education course in the social studies.

[29]Milton B. Singer, "The Social Sciences Program in the College of the University of Chicago," *Social Science in General Education*, p. 43.

observe the development of human thought and the adaptation of ideas to changing social conditions. Many champions of general education, furthermore, plead for more use of literature in the social studies courses—for a closer affiliation with the humanities.

Both the humanities and social science deal with man. The humanities offer the richest suggestion for interpreting man. How can they, in all good conscience, be separated from social science? . . . the great cultural documents—philosophical, historical, poetical, fictional—are the very ones also needed for the understanding of man and society. . . . We have too long kept them out of social science. The great literature of mankind can wonderfully excite one to great thinking, for it is the creation of man at his best. Again, the document is a whole thing, a complete entity, which crosses our departmental lines without apology and often wanders beyond them all. The document sometimes mirrors the very integer of integration, when its content evokes that enjoyment which we take in the union of truth and beauty.[30]

Another observer finds that we suffer from a "rationalistic fallacy" in social science instruction. We assume that knowledge is acquired solely through the laborious process of scientific inquiry. Without in any way minimizing the importance of scientific research, it is pointed out that social awareness and "social sensitivity" are aroused especially by emotional contact with social situations.

The process of acquiring social sensitivity demands that students have the kind of experiences which compel them to identify themselves with individuals in situations of social maladjustment, unfamiliar as these situations may be. It is just at this point that novels and fictional materials have their greatest value. They enable an individual to gain experiences (albeit vicariously) which would be totally inaccessible on the basis of direct participation. Thereby fiction opens up new worlds and provides the possibility for enlargement of what had previously been a provincial point of view.[31]

A statistical survey of the distribution of our national income can be highly informative, it is argued, but it cannot arouse a student's interest as will a reading of such novels as John Steinbeck's *The Grapes of Wrath* or Michael Gold's *Jews Without Money*. In this connection it may be apropos to remind ourselves of the impact upon the social thinking of the nineteenth century made by such poems as Hood's "The Song of the Shirt," Elizabeth Barrett

---

[30]Quirinius Breen, "Social Science: A Liberal Arts Course at the University of Oregon," p. 111.
[31]Albert Levi, *General Education in the Social Studies*, p. 311.

226

Browning's "The Cry of the Children," Shelley's "The Men of England," the various novels by Dickens and Zola, and the dramas of Ibsen and Strindberg. Not only may literary works portray vividly social conditions but they may themselves become documents of great historical and social significance.

e. *Instructional Staff.* There seems to be absolute unanimity of opinion that a general education program places extraordinary responsibility upon the teachers and that its success or failure depends upon the instructional staff. "The one indispensable condition for the success of a general course is a staff of capable teachers with a deep conviction that it can and should be developed. Without such a staff all the other factors are fruitless. This statement may appear self-evident, but it cannot be overemphasized. One corollary is that the administration of the college and those who formulate its curricula must be prepared to work vigorously for the plan" (University of Arizona). "The effectiveness of this type of course depends, more than on any other one factor, upon the teaching personnel. The teacher in an introductory survey course must be able to see the broad implications of the materials and must have the gift of making the problems seem vital and real to his students. . . . There is no substitute for inspired teaching and good classroom teachers do not grow on every graduate bush" (Stephens College). "One of our greatest difficulties is in securing competent teachers. . . . What is needed is a specialist *plus,* specialists with a flair for vivid teaching and meaningful generalization. One of our staff members once remarked that what we wanted was not teachers but angels" (University of Florida). "A general education program must rely for its success primarily on excellence of instruction. Unimaginative and routine teaching, unfortunate at any level, is completely unacceptable in this type of program" (Michigan State College). "Great care is exercised in selecting the staff, and only men of outstanding personality and teaching ability who have been willing to give up part of their interest in specialization and to do a great deal of painstaking and diligent study in order to acquaint themselves with such a diversified field have been invited to cooperate in the course" (Columbia University). Thus the comments run, and they might discourage any in-

227

stitution from ever attempting a general education program since "angels" or supermen are not plentiful on any faculty. Nevertheless, practically all the institutions which have described their programs maintain that the faculty problems can be solved. Competent teachers can be obtained, and they can be developed, it is claimed, provided there is enthusiastic leadership and faith in the venture. Most of the institutions declare that the participating teachers usually find the general education courses stimulating and that they are glad to stay by the program at the sacrifice of specialization and research if they are not penalized as far as advancement is concerned.

4

EVALUATION

Judging by reports from institutions which have experimented with general education in the social sciences, the programs seem to have met with success though the degree of endorsement varies from the enthusiasm of Columbia University to the rather non-committal attitude of Harvard. Numerous attempts have been made to evaluate general education but as yet no specific results have been achieved. The difficulties in the way of obtaining anything approaching "scientific accuracy" are legion. There is, for instance, the question of objectives. "Goals in general education have often been expressed in such fine-sounding generalizations that our colleagues in traditional curricula have wondered whether general courses differ only in the selection of facts to be emphasized."[32] As the Self-Study Committee at St. Olaf discovered, most departments in any American college will claim to have practically the same objectives as the general education programs. The next question will then be under which systems are these objectives best obtained? It is obviously quite impossible to devise rigorously valid evaluation tests to answer questions concerning which program most effectively produces "good citizens," "well-balanced personalities," "integrated views of life," "satisfactory emotional ad-

---

[32]George W. White, "Improving an Established General-Education Program," *Addresses on Current Issues in Higher Education* (Washington, D. C.: Department of Higher Education, National Education Association of the United States, 1951), p. 170.

justment," "independent thinking," and the numerous other declared objectives of American education, "general" or "traditional." In this connection one evaluation committee comments as follows: "A number of studies about the development of good citizenship characteristics were noted. None of these has satisfactorily defined what good citizenship actually is. Defined one way, good citizenship consists merely of the practice of certain rudimentary mechanisms incident to democratic government. . . . If good citizenship were defined narrowly, the only possible measure of achievement would be to obtain evidence of how many times graduates voted, went to town meetings, contributed blood, or wrote to editors."[33] This particular committee decided that the evaluation of good citizenship would involve a battery of tests covering such a wide variety of subjects (knowledge, attitudes, value judgments, beliefs, etc.) that their mere development was clearly beyond its competence.

Various tests have been given to measure the development of "critical thinking" in different types of courses. About the only conclusive results obtained from these tests seemed to be that the ability of the teacher was a highly important factor and that there is a close but not absolute relationship between knowledge of the social sciences and critical thinking in matters involving that field.[34]

The committee referred to above seems to conclude that it is too early as yet to pass definitive judgment on the general education movement. "With the term general education applied to a wide variety of educational experiences from rechristened but still inviolate liberal arts programs, through vocational and home-making courses in junior colleges, to a 'hitch' in the service, it is manifestly impossible either to commend or condemn general education."[35] The very title of the report (says the foreword to the study) with its emphasis upon the *exploratory* nature of the work, indicates that we still have far to go in finding ways of appraising more surely what needs to be done in the classroom. Evaluation regarded as a

---

[33]Paul L. Dressel and Lewis B. Mayhew, *General Education, Explorations in Evaluation* (Washington, D. C.: American Council on Education, 1954), p. 35. This volume is the final report of a cooperative committee which studied evaluation in general education in a number of American institutions during the years 1950-1954. The study was sponsored by the American Council on Education.

[34]*Ibid.*, Chapter III, *passim.*

[35]*Ibid.*, p. 9.

judgment of the worth of general education was deemed premature since most of the committee members felt that "the full significance of general education objectives was not yet realized and that certainly the means for appraisal of their achievements was not yet available."[36]

---

[36]*Ibid.*, p. 18.

Chapter Twelve

Integrative Studies
in the
Senior Year

1
THE SENIOR YEAR

CURRICULUM" means "course." If the term "course" is used to designate one or two semesters' study of a subject, "curriculum" would mean a "course of courses." The four-year curriculum or course of study should, therefore, be characterized not only by *quantity* (four years, 128 semester hours) but also by *qualities* such as excellence in units of study (passing grades), levels of difficulty (advanced work), intelligible coherence through understanding of relatedness of studies, and climactic consummation in the senior year.

A curriculum or whole course is an entity with a beginning, middle, and an end. Without minimizing the middle sophomore and junior years, one may justifiably maintain that the freshman and senior years are of critical importance in that they are the beginning and conclusion of the four-year course. It is reasonable that students enter college with the expectation of something more than an additional year comparable to high school study. The college student's less clear expectation that the senior year ought to be more than merely additional work similar to that of the preceding semester is even more justifiable, because the fourth year is the conclusion of sixteen years of schooling for most seniors. Although the freshman year in college is generally distinguishable from the senior year in high school because of higher standards, greater independence and responsibilities for the student, and some new subject areas and approaches, many colleges and universities are expending considerable thought and effort to develop a freshman or lower division program more commensurate with both the students' high expectations and the objectives of liberal education. The complementary task of providing an adequate senior program has received somewhat less attention.

One symptom of deficiency in the concept and use of the senior year is the too prevalent, though not universal, "senior slump." This academic disease is comparable to the pointlessness and inattentiveness of a lame-duck congress. In the absence of a better concept, the senior year is easily thought of as being a "last year" rather than a climactic conclusion pointing beyond itself in both directions. If no distinguishing expectation is engendered by the plan and kind of study in the senior year, it is too readily thought of as being the final addition of more courses to fulfill the arithmetic requirement of "hours for graduation."[1]

If the teaching task of the college is regarded as a whole and likewise the learning career of the student is regarded as a whole, the senior year should be a point of special qualitative concern for both teachers and students. The earlier years should come to fruition in depth and comprehensiveness. The senior year ought to be the highest intellectual level in that educational responsibility is placed more than ever on the student through a plan of work requiring mastery in depth of penetration and coherent inclusiveness in understanding. The startling fallacy of the additive approach is that it frequently is not even additive, except in the registrar's office: the earlier courses have been taken and put behind and more are added in the senior year. Far more effective educationally would be a program consciously intended to draw together and to deepen the work in a major field and to integrate the student's studies in diverse areas.

---

[1] Cf. A. E. Sevringhaus, H. J. Carman, and W. E. Cadbury, *Preparation for Medical Education in Liberal Arts Colleges* (New York: McGraw-Hill, 1953), chapter VII, "Majors and the Culminating Year."

The desirability of making the senior year more than chrono-logically unique has evoked a number of study plans. There is, however, no universality in practice, partly because the plans, however educationally helpful, do usually entail some additional work and even additional funds in some instances. A study of senior plans in operation and the judgment of those involved suggest, however, that the educational values far outweigh the moderate expenditures. The problem is essentially one of educa-tional aims and of value judgments in the use of means. The pos-sibility of doing uniquely significant work in the senior year justifies consideration of the plans which seem to be within reach for the concerned liberal arts college: honors work, comprehen-sive examinations, and capstone senior studies.

2

HONORS WORK

The definition of "honors work" varies throughout the country. In some colleges it means independent study; elsewhere it signifies independent study culminating in an honors thesis and a com-prehensive examination; in still other institutions it denotes a quali-ty of work throughout the student's career. For the sake of clarity in this discussion, "independent study" will refer to supervised individual work. "Honors work" will refer to supervised individual study or restricted seminar studies culminating in a thesis and a comprehensive examination departmental or interdepartmental. The usual practice at graduation time is to designate successful "honors work" students as graduating with "honors in a field" and to list the thesis titles; high ranking students without honors work or irrespective of honors work are then designated as graduat-ing with "distinction in a department."

The primary reason for an honors work program is that it helps prevent the sacrifice of better students to a group-leveling process. There is in this no disparagement of the average student—if he is actually average in capacity. It does, however, aim to draw the apparently average and obviously superior students out of a ten-dency to develop lazy habits and intellectual lukewarmness by involving them in work more commensurate with their capacities.

One other aspect of honors work is especially important. Given a cumulative grading system, the arithemetic grade average of a student may camouflage the kind of thing teachers covet for students: the awakening of a slow-starter who becomes converted to education, who comes to know the excitement of learning as he grows in penetration and understanding. Not infrequently a student in the last two years redeems an unspectacular beginning. Honors work gives him an opportunity to work on the level of newly discovered powers and interests and at the same time provides that this be shown on the record apart from his cumulative class standing and arithmetic average. For this reason the tendency in a student's record is of greater importance in establishing eligibility for honors work than is the flat grade average. This kind of work should not be reserved for the very small upper level of a class reckoned on grade averages. If practicable, a fairly large number of students should be doing this kind of studying. At Amherst, Professor Marsh reports, " . . . we . . . have been well pleased with the progress of the integrated curriculum and I am sure the plan has provoked a real effort on the part of our students, as we find nearly 50% of our Juniors and Seniors involved in an honors program."[2]

In addition to calling the superior students to work qualitatively more suitable to their capacities, and to recognizing the possibility of intellectual awakening in students with less spectacular early records, this sort of program has something to do with intellectual pursuits after graduation because it is more independent, more penetrating, and more coherent. Professor Brooks, writing of honors work at Swarthmore, points out the long-range importance of this type of studying:

Perhaps the most practical single advantage resulting from the method of self help is the conviction it stamps upon the student's mind that, given an intellectual interest on his part, he does not have to ask a professor to offer a course on it but can find in the library the books dealing with it, appraise their value quickly, and then draw from the few best of them the knowledge he desires, criticizing and classifying it as he reads. Observers of our academic institutions are much given to noting the fact, and it is undeniable, . . . that the education of so many college men and women ends with the college. Why should this not be the case, since they are no longer in reach of courses to continue

[2]Allison W. Marsh, Professor of Physical Education, in a letter, April 12, 1955.

their intellectual work, and are not habituated to any other more independent method of carrying on the study of subjects in which they may be interested? Self educated men have acquired such a method, usually at the cost of an excessive amount of floundering, but the important point is that they do know how to teach themselves. It is precisely because they are capable of self instruction that men of this type usually continue their education throughout life, often outstripping in middle age the intellectual acquirements of the ordinary or even of the superior college graduate. College men and women who go to a graduate school also acquire, under direction, the method of independent study, but post-graduate study is so costly in time and money that it is open to a very small fraction of the total college output. Certainly one of the most urgent needs of American undergraduate instruction at the present time is that of a system which will ground in all students capable of acquiring it the habit of independent study.[3]

Although these various claims are made for the value of honors work and evidence can be produced to justify them, there are objections, the main one of which is that it is expensive and therefore impracticable for all but the extraordinarily endowed colleges. This objection cannot be eliminated categorically. Yet some replies can be made which restore the plan to the realm of possibility for almost any college. First, the plan is quantitatively flexible. If teaching loads are high, honors work will be restricted to those students of unusually high ability and who can be advised by instructors interested enough to assume an additional task. The disadvantage of this is the overburdening of the willing and the confinement of the program to very few students, for which few the honors work retains the values inherent in the plan. This objection, is, therefore, not an argument against the plan but merely a statement of one of its less-than-fatal difficulties. Second, if the plan includes a departmental seminar approach, the group of honors work students may well be as large as many advanced classes, so that the honors work group could administratively be reckoned in the teaching load without making any concessions, however educationally legitimate such concessions are. Third, if, in accordance with standard practice, departmental chairmen have somewhat reduced loads, this reduction would coincide with the quite natural role of the chairmen as the likely ones to supervise a disproportionate number of students doing honors work.

[3]Robert C. Brooks, *Reading for Honors at Swarthmore* (New York: Oxford University Press, 1927), pp. 25-26.

Fourth, it is entirely conceivable that a moderate honors program in a department would make possible dropping some upper division course. In form, intention, and substance the honors work would not necessarily replace the course, but quantitatively it could, and thereby part of the economic argument would be answered.

A second objection is that honors work is discriminatory, aristocratic. This is frankly admitted. But further analysis reveals that ignoring the superior students and the awakened average students is discriminatory against them. Why should they be penalized by concentration on the middle group, or why should the poor students be the object of discriminatory extra help and the superior students ignored? Insofar as there are distinguishable levels of capacity, the upper group justly deserves appropriate attention in terms of time, money, and persons just as do the middle and lower groups. It may also be pointed out that the honors work program, given faculty interest and an educational view in the use of funds, is good educational stewardship for both students and college. Furthermore, honors work is not intended for merely the rare student. If practical difficulties do not determine educational policy, the honors work plan envisages a majority of upper division's students doing this independent work. At some institutions honors work or some variation of it (like the Senior Essay at Notre Dame) is required of all students. It is desirable, therefore, that honors work not be conceived *a priori* as an extraordinary permissive program, but rather as a kind of work imperative for the more able student and valuable for as many students as the faculty can handle properly.[4]

3

COMPREHENSIVE EXAMINATIONS

Although honors work as outlined includes a departmental or interdepartmental comprehensive examination, such an examination is used in many colleges for every candidate for graduation. At Swarthmore experience with comprehensives in honors work

---

[4] Cf. Robert H. Bonthius, F. James Davis, and J. Garber Drushal, "Independent-Study Programs, *The Journal of Higher Education*, XXV, 8 (November 1954).

led to an extension of the examination because of the integrative effect—upon both faculty and students.

Thus the advantages of comprehensive examinations as employed in the latter [honors work] have made a deep impression not only upon the faculty but upon the undergraduate body. Representatives of a recent senior class expressed themselves as dissatisfied with the type of final examinations given them, differing as the latter did in no whit from those they had been taking with monotonous regularity for four years. They concluded their statement with a request that tests of a broader scope be substituted. With the annual demonstration of the success of honors examinations in compelling students to correlate the knowledge gained in various fields, it is increasingly easy to perceive the defects of the old "class, course, unit and examination" system. The comparatively meager results obtained from ordinary methods of teaching make it apparent that students are being trained "to take such short steps as to prevent many of them from ever getting into any long intellectual stride. They learn some tidbit of knowledge, are examined on it, and forget it, and by repeating this process a sufficient number of times are supposed to have acquired an education. . . . They do not learn to plan, to coordinate, to organize, to deal with the content of a subject; their attention is limited to single courses, to short steps; they tend to feel that the whole duty of the undergraduate is obedient submission to a fixed academic routine." In accordance with this new point of view a number of departments are planning to introduce final comprehensive examinations for regular Seniors. Unlike the final honors tests these examinations will be given by resident professors, but in all other respects they will be modelled as closely as possible upon the former. Of course it is not intended or desired to make them quite so severe, but they will be sufficiently broad and searching to secure a degree of organized and coordinated study at present unthought of by the regular undergraduate simply because it is not demanded of him.[5]

The above statement gives some of the essential rationale of the comprehensive examination. The objectives could be formulated briefly as follows:

a. The examination should test the student's understanding of general principles, not merely his possession of facts.
b. The examination should be an incentive to the student to bring together into an integrated and intelligible whole the knowledge acquired in his major field and in other relevant areas.
c. The examination should help the student develop maturity of thought and independence of judgment.

These aims of the comprehensive examination plan seem to be educationally unexceptionable. Again the objections are mostly

[5]Robert C. Brooks, *Reading for Honors at Swarthmore*, pp. 72-74.

of a practical kind. Frequently essential faculty interest in the plan founders on the concentrated demands made upon the faculty members towards the end of the second semester each year. "Inasmuch as our teaching loads are heavy now, how can we add this extra burden?" constitutes a common dismissal of the plan. Not a few institutions with funds for this purpose (at Swarthmore the reported annual cost was about $1,500 for a hundred seniors a few years ago) invite outside examiners to do this work. Such a method answers the load problem, but it is aimed primarily at a lifting of the quality of examining and a shifting of the relationship between student and instructor away from the examined-examiner pattern. In one Midwest college which recently inaugurated the comprehensive plan, the concentrated task was faced squarely by the faculty and was judged to be educationally worth the added effort. After a few trial years there is unusual faculty consensus on the positive value of the program, the extra work notwithstanding.

It has been the experience of some that more intrinsic problems arising in comprehensive examinations are a result of revelation rather than of creation by the examination plan. In this category are such difficulties as the incoherence of courses in and between departments, departmental personnel problems, and excessive informationalism in teaching and memorization at the expense of understanding. The emergence of such problems is one of the dividends the plan pays to the faculty in its own task of continued self-education and pedagogical improvement.[6]

The most important intrinsic criticism of comprehensives is that they are usually of departmental character and thereby accentuate a specialist approach which many educators consider to be too strong already. This objection is not implicit in the comprehensive examination but rather in its limitation to single departments—it may not be comprehensive enough. The essential values of the plan can be achieved more widely by an interdepartmental comprehensive covering the core work of the students as well as the

[6]Cf. Fred B. Millet, *The Rebirth of Liberal Education*, pp. 57-58.
[7]R. H. Knapp and H. B. Goodrich, *Origins of American Scientists* (Chicago: University of Chicago Press, 1952), pp. 75-76.
"One of the most striking features of the honors program has been the system of examinations. Honors students are not required to take regular course examina-

work in a major area.[7] This could be done by using the Graduate Record Examination General Education Tests, if funds are available, or by locally prepared and graded examinations. The latter alternative seems to be insurmountable wherever the more limited comprehensive examinations are desired but even they seemingly cannot be instituted because of teaching loads. Experienced proponents of the plan do not insist that it be confined to single departments, but they point out that it is more likely to be successful if a beginning is made at the point where all faculty members participate with greatest concern and competence: in their own departmental work. They would add that the intellectual toning-up resulting from just the departmental comprehensives have a good effect on the intellectual climate of the entire campus.

4

SENIOR STUDIES

Honors work and comprehensive examinations may well be carried on by a portion of the Senior class or of the Junior and Senior classes. Senior Studies courses or Senior Capstone courses are usually taken by all seniors. Such courses are not, however, as common as honors work and comprehensives are. Perhaps this is because the latter two plans are aimed at a number of persistent educational goals, including a pulling together of various strands of college work; whereas Senior Studies are an attempt to meet this particular need which has been more acutely felt in the past generation, especially in the past decade.

During this period Senior Capstone courses have been introduced in many colleges and great interest is shown in them by many others. Hugh Stickler in a recent study found that "more

---

tions beyond the sophomore year but must meet a single exhaustive honors examination at the end of their senior year. This is given by outside examiners, brought in from other colleges and universities to design and administer the examinations. This program was intended to encourage fellowship in learning between teacher and student. It has provided strong motivations for students and teachers alike and incidentally has served to cultivate intimate relations between the college and the graduate schools at which Swarthmore students have frequently pursued their advanced studies.

"The curriculum for the remainder of the students, not enrolled in the honors program, varies somewhat from department to department but follows essentially that prescribed in most liberal arts colleges. A fairly heavy schedule of generalization courses is required in the first two years, and the fulfilment of major requirements is commonly accomplished in the last two years. Since about 1930 comprehensive examinations have been required of all students not engaged in the honors program."

239

senior integrative courses are in operation today than ever before. Many other colleges and universities have such programs in the blueprint stage or are giving serious consideration to the launching of such programs. During the period of this study [1954] the author again and again received comments such as this: 'Although we do not have such a course at present we are greatly interested in such a project and are, in fact, giving serious consideration to establishing a similar course. Please let us know what you find in your study.' "[8]

Some of the Senior Studies courses recently offered are these:

Allegheny College .... Senior Seminar in General Education
Colgate University........ The American Ideal in the Modern World
College of the Ozarks.................................. Great Issues
Colorado State Coll. of Ed................. Philosophy of Education
Cornell College (Iowa)
.... Senior Colloquium: The Crisis in Human Values
Dartmouth College.................................... Great Issues
Denison University........... Basic Philosophic and Religious Ideas
Eastern Kentucky State College
.... Ideological Foundations of Western Civilization
Fisk University .... Great Issues
Guilford College.................... Basic Religious and Philosophic
Thought: A Record of Human Points of View
Knox College...... American Civilization: A Seminar on the Midwest
Mary Baldwin College.......... Problems in the Philosophy of Life
Northwestern University................... Contemporary Thought
Oberlin College......................... The Humanistic Tradition
Pennsylvania College for Women................ Philosophy of Life
Reed College.................................... Senior Symposium
St. Louis University........................ Survey of Philosophy
Sarah Lawrence College.............. Studies in Reality and Values

However varied these courses may seem to be (and the variety is wider than this brief list indicates), there is a common purpose encompassing all of them. Henry Wriston writes of "reflective synthesis"—this is the primary aim of Senior Studies.

The final discipline which I wish to discuss is the discipline of reflective synthesis. This is the highest of all the disciplines essential to general education. It looks to the validity of the intellectual experience itself. It has in common with the discipline of opinionation the creation of patterns and hypotheses. Its distinguishing difference is that the data have to do not so much with observed phenomena of an objective, tangible, and external character as with the ideas and concepts them-

---

[8]Hugh Stickler, "Senior Courses in General Education," *Journal of Higher Education*, XXV (March 1954), 146.

selves. It is the synthesis, if one may so speak, of all the patterns built up through opinionation. It is the effort to give reality not merely to observation but to experience itself. It is an effort to find meaning not only in the world about us but in life. Montaigne in one of his essays said: "What he shall learn, make him look at it in a hundred aspects and apply it to as many different subjects, to see if he has fully appreciated it and made it his own."[9]

Looking at American higher education in a broad way, Stickler corroborates Wriston's analysis of this kind of need and affirms the strategic function of Senior Studies in meeting this need. "Fragmentation and overspecialization still characterize the undergraduate curriculum in the typical American college and university. As countermeasures to these weaknesses educators committed to general education have long thought that broad-area courses were needed, especially senior integrative courses that would serve as capstones for the entire undergraduate experience."[10] "Within the diversity of educational patterns there is a dominant unity of purpose—a common resolve that the undergraduate experiences of the Senior shall be more meaningfully integrated and that he shall be better prepared to accept the adult responsibilities of after-college life which lie immediately ahead. In spite of the variety of approaches, these senior courses in all of these colleges and universities seem to be making substantial progress: They constitute the positive side of the situation regarding senior courses in general education."[11]

The common purpose of reflective synthesis is illustrated by Senior Studies courses in two small liberal arts colleges: Cornell and Bucknell. At Cornell the Senior Colloquium has been centered around the issue of "The Crisis in Human Values." The basis and objectives of the Colloquium are:

The desirability of giving the students in their senior year an integrating intellectual experience.

The need of making clear that there are many problems which present themselves in all areas of human experience, not solely in one of the divisional areas.

The desirability of bringing into contact with each other intellectually students who have been separately working in their respective fields of concentration.

---

[9]Henry Wriston, "Nature, Scope, and Essential Elements in General Education," in *General Education*, ed. by W. S. Gray, p. 14.
[10]"Senior Courses in General Education," p. 139.
[11]*Ibid.*, p. 145.

Exploration of the possibilities of more informal and free procedures than are customarily followed in typical classroom operations.[12]

At Bucknell the University Course is likewise centered around specific yet wide-ranging questions: "Science and its impact on modern life, Historical process and perspective. The humanities, Philosophy and religion as pre-eminent fields of integration." Again the course has the aim of reflective synthesis: "a theoretic fundamental understanding of the fields of knowledge, of the individual and society, and of their functional, integrative relationships."[13]

The substance of Senior Studies is usually a root issue requiring philosophical analysis and drawing upon historical and descriptive material from all areas of college study. The questions about which the work centers have, therefore, an inclusiveness of range and depth of penetration which make possible a focusing of the student's studies (in this sense the question is an occasion) and the treating of a perennially important issue (in this sense the question is intrinsically significant). The steering committee for the Dartmouth Great Issues course, in changing the specific concern of the course from year to year, has used a concept which "automatically tends to eliminate the ephemeral, however noisy, and emphasize the abiding, however inconspicuous. It implies that issues can be grasped in their ultimate fundamentals only in terms of history and philosophy and of men's hopes and fears."[14]

The New Program in Yale College also emphasizes the philosophical level at which relational understanding is sought. Although the following description is of work for the first two years, the problems and objectives are essentially the same except that the difficulties ought to be lessened in the senior year.

The first year of work consists of five courses: Science I (a combination of chemistry and physics); a special course in mathematics of a historical and philosophical character; a special course in literature; a foreign language; and, at the center, a discussion course in philosophy which attempts to tie together the other courses the student is taking and to analyze the natures of scientific, mathematical, linguistic, and literary truth. The discussion courses in philosophy are small, and the teacher is in the position of the commentator in Thornton Wilder's "Our

[12]Mimeographed material on the Cornell Senior Colloquium.
[13]Preston Warren, "Concepts as Integrators," *Bucknell University Studies* III (March 1952), 56.
[14] Wilson, "The Great Issues Course at Dartmouth," *The Journal of Higher Education*, XXV–5 (May 1954), 232.

Town," as he points out the implications of what is happening. We are now in the middle of the first year of this program; and all seems to be going very smoothly.

We are at work at present upon the courses of the second year, in which the student will take Science III (a combination of botany, zoology, and psychology) and new courses in Studies in Society and in History, continue his foreign language, and again take a discussion course in philosophy. During this year, the philosopher directs the student's attention to biological, social, and historical aspects of truth by the same methods as those employed in the first year. In the work of each year, philosophy is the binding element, and the attempt is made to achieve a modern integration of the studies involved.[15]

The same approach is also reflected in the University of New Hampshire's Senior Synthesis course which grew out of " 'a need [felt by] many, especially Seniors, for a chance to stand, if only briefly, within the temple of philosophic thought, perhaps to integrate the scattered impressions of their four years of separate courses, perhaps to glimpse the outlines of a personal philosophy of life which each might appropriate and adapt to himself.' "[16]

If the core of Senior Studies is a root issue with substance drawn from all relevant fields, and if the basic approach is philosophical analysis, the aim of Senior Studies involves still more than the analysis of an inclusive, important problem. The aim includes a clarification of presuppositions and a coherent interpretation of the clustered data and partial interpretations. This, too, is a philosophic task, the work of philosophical synthesis, incomplete, no doubt, but moving in the direction of intelligible wholeness.

A very important part of the varied material brought to bear upon the central question would be a religious understanding of human existence and reality. In the interpretive synthesizing task, the substance of Christian theology would have even greater significance. The Harvard study eliminated religion as an integrating factor.[17] But in the Christian liberal arts college Christian theology

[15]William Devane, "The New Program in Yale College," *The Journal of Higher Education*, XVIII–4 (April 1947), 192.

[16]Quoted in Hugh Stickler, "Senior Courses in General Education," p. 145.

[17]*General Education in a Free Society*, p. 39. "This, then, or something like this, is the present state: an enormous variety of aim and method among colleges as a whole and much the same variety on a smaller scale within any one college. This condition, which seemingly robs liberal education of any clear, coherent meaning, has for some time disturbed people and prompted a variety of solutions. Sectarian, particularly Roman Catholic, colleges have of course their solution,

and the Christian faith are at least live options and have a primary contribution to make to the constructive work of the Senior integrative course. Therefore, in a genuine though undogmatic sense such a course could quite properly be regarded as a religion course concerned with the relevance of the faith to our culture.

The operational details of Senior Studies are not unimportant. The course should continue throughout the senior year to allow for adequate treatment of the issues, the inclusion of contributory materials from many areas of study, and the direct participation of all members of the class. The sections themselves should not be very large, about twenty, in order that full discussion may be customary rather than exceptional. There should also be considerable individual writing for class presentation, criticism, and discussion. An imperative is interdepartmental faculty participation. Most of the lecturing should be done by instructors not directly responsible for the sections. An extremely important by-product of this mode of working is mutual self-education within the faculty. Responsibility for a section should be delegated to a single instructor to ensure greater continuity in planning and discussion. Over-all responsibility for Senior Studies would most effectively be lodged in a steering committee appointed by the Dean of the College with a Director of Senior Studies to make necessary arrangements for the program and to continue an evaluation of the work in terms of its objectives.

Every new program has special pitfalls because of newness itself. In addition an educational plan with objectives beyond the course itself and beyond a single department has its unique hazards. These are brought out in a review of the well-known, extremely effective senior course at Northwestern: Contemporary Thought.

For twenty years it flourished under the wise leadership of Baker Brownell. Through all the years it was offered, the purposes of the course remained the same: to integrate the materials of the student's college work, to acquaint the student somewhat with the frontier

which was generally shared by American colleges until less than a century ago: namely, the conviction that *Christianity* gives meaning and ultimate unity to all parts of the curriculum, indeed to the whole life of the college Yet this solution is out of the question in publicly supported colleges and is practically, if not legally, impossible in most others. Some think it the Achilles' heel of democracy that, by its very nature, it cannot foster general agreement on ultimates, and perhaps must foster the contrary. But whatever one's views, religion is not now for most colleges a practicable source of intellectual unity."

problems of modern interest, and to help him find an adequate relationship with the world in a modern *Weltanschauung*.

The public was invited to participate in the course, and the audiences for noted guest lecturers frequently numbered fifteen hundred to two thousand. Student and public support was enthusiastic. Nevertheless, after twenty years Mr. Brownell elected to discontinue it. Two factors seem to have been instrumental in his decision: " . . . I was not able to build up men who could take over in my place. I had several opportunities to hire excellent young men who were interested in carrying on the work, but I was unable to [do so] because of administrative difficulties, objections, and lack of budget.

"Courses *de novo* in integration face the resistance of those faculty members who resent intrusion into their sacred groves. They see the ark defiled at the hands of the unanointed. They strike in priestly rage at those who do not recognize the rituals of approach and procedure. 'Are not these men,' they ask, 'outsiders, untrained in the specialties of the field and beyond departmental control? Why should they not be smitten down when the academic order of precedence and departments is threatened by them? This was the cause in part of the endless sabotage of the experiment by Meiklejohn at Wisconsin, of the endless sabotage of the course in Contemporary Thought at Northwestern, of the deadly attack on the Campus Course at Iowa, ..."[18]

Mr. Stickler sounds two warnings in connection with a Senior Studies plan. "Mr. Brownell's comments should give us pause. They bring into sharp focus the two conditions necessary for the launching and continuance of a senior integrative course: First, adequate and enthusiastic leadership is indispensable. It usually will come from a broadly trained individual or from a steering committee. For competent leadership in this kind of work there is no substitute. Second, firm administrative support from the president and deans is essential to the success of such a course. These officers must be unequivocal in their basic commitments, for strong administrative support is a *sine qua non* for the success of any program of this type. The college or university which lacks either of these conditions should never attempt a senior integrative course such as we have been considering. . . . [19]

These problems, although weighty, are not insurmountable, as is shown by the fair number of colleges and universities now conducting integrative studies for seniors. They are conditions to be met rather than reasons for not entertaining the initiation of a program with indisputable educational values as its goal. Senior

---

[18]Hugh Stickler, "Senior Courses in General Education," pp. 145-146.
[19]*Ibid.*, p. 146.

Studies are the way most within the reach of the small liberal arts college to remedy a serious lack in the curriculum and in most students' educational development. Both in theory and in practice the Senior Studies plan seems to be worthy of the effort necessary to launching and continuing it.

Today college curriculums are more fragmented than ever before. For that reason the idea of general integrative education engages the minds of leading educators throughout the nation. The lack of integration in the culture of the colleges and universities is so deep-seated that fundamental re-examinations of objectives, methods, curriculums, materials, and the training programs of college teachers will have to be made. In the final analysis it may matter little what else colleges and universities do if they do not produce graduates who are well-integrated, dedicated human beings of high moral character, capable of meeting their responsibilities as citizens in a democratic society of our time. The need for integrative senior courses is so apparent and so great that they will probably increase in number in spite of the difficulties involved.[20]

[20]*Ibid.*, pp. 146 and 171.

Chapter Thirteen

Curricular
Proposals

1

A COLLEGE AND ITS CURRICULUM

No curriculum is ideal in theory or in practice. Quite properly, therefore, every educational institution repeatedly scrutinizes its educational plan and its educational work in the light of its conscious intentions. Even though an inferior curriculum taught by unusually good teachers on behalf of extraordinary students would in practice no doubt be superior to a better planned course in the hands of less able faculty and students, good teachers and good students will do still better with an improved curriculum. A curriculum is a means and not an end, and better means can improve the results sought by a good workman. In addition, a curriculum is symbolic of the objectives of a college and should embody, for faculty and students, these objectives as clearly as possible in its structure and substance.

Apart from the curriculum there are many possibilities for a faculty which values educational integration and seeks to develop this in the faculty as a community of scholars.

A. Faculty community an indispensable factor in educational integration
   1. Educational integration the student's task; yet the necessary role of faculty and curriculum
   2. Faculty community as
      a. Awareness of relationship of courses, department, and one's teaching to the objectives of the whole college

247

To change a curriculum has been asserted to be "as difficult as moving a graveyard. Everyone is sentimental about what is on the surface and no one cares about what is underneath." Nevertheless American colleges have in the past twenty years been particularly concerned about curriculum, perhaps to the point of under-valuing the significance of motivation and quality in teaching and learning. All these concerns may, however, be concurrent and together express the studied resolution to improve the educational yield. The purpose of proposals to revise a curriculum is basically justified only on this ground, although some educators recommend occasional change for the sake of refreshing and de-rutting the on-going teaching within the college.

The norms of curricular revision are at heart the objectives of the college, in this case of the Christian liberal arts college (cf. Chapters V, VI, VII). Most simply these could be stated as being: education of the person by helping each student to grasp human experience and reality intellectually in the context of a Christian understanding of the world and human destiny. College is not less college by being Christian, and therefore the Christian college

---

    b. Some knowledge of and respect for the substance of the teaching in other areas
    c. Interchange (mutual education); criticism
    d. Unity of objective and large understanding together with relative autonomy and freedom

B. How may integration as scholarly community be better achieved?
    1. Common faculty reading (Book of the Year); discussions
    2. Departmental in-service training
    3. Faculty retreat. Value of faculty lounge
    4. Appointments: requisite of experience in, knowledge and appreciation of Christian liberal arts college
    5. Attendance in each other's courses
    6. Inter-departmental teaching in appropriate ways
    7. Role of administration in educational thinking

C. How may integration as scholarly community be made manifest?
    1. Advising students: A college course rather than a collection of courses; concomitant courses; interpretation of Christian liberal arts college
    2. Suggestive allusions in lectures and discussions
    3. Measure of appropriate interdepartmental teaching
    4. Attendance in each other's courses

does not minimize the intellectual enterprise without which the liberal arts college may be many things, but it would no longer be a college. Thus the goal of the curriculum could be formulated in this way:

1. Development of powers of intellectually disciplined judgment:
   a. Understanding and habits of valid critical thinking
   b. Careful, effective use of symbols—native language, foreign language, the language of mathematics, the symbolic world of the arts, and the special languages of the various areas of liberal education
   c. Discriminating discernment of values—truth and falsity, beauty and ugliness, good and evil, holy and unholy
   d. Synoptic interpretation—apprehension of relationships, a more coherent grasp of the whole

2. To teach fundamental truths about nature, man, and God, in accord with the best learning possible, and from the theological and philosophical viewpoint of Christian thought. Such a statement implies that a theological centering of the intellectual life of the student and of the curriculum itself is possible, as well as a synoptic (historical and philosophical) grasp of the interrelationship of all areas of knowledge. Every study has its intrinsic value and can be the occasion for a wider, coherent view which is essentially theological-philosophical-historical.

These intellectual goals—mental development, vigor, and vision, together with a body of significant knowledge—have fundamental relevance to the student as an individual and as a social being. Liberal education seeks to free the mind of the person. A Christian college, with its concern for spiritual and moral truth, ought, with a suitable curriculum and qualified teachers, to be able to accomplish these aims to an eminent degree.

2

SPECIFIC PROPOSALS

The proposed curriculum does not represent a shift from the generally accepted objectives of the Christian liberal arts college, nor does it represent anything strikingly unique in contemporary educational practice. It is based on a study of liberal education as practiced in colleges and universities of high standing in America, of serious educational thought past and present, of educational experience at St. Olaf College, and of educational judgment by

St. Olaf faculty and seniors. Certain conclusions stand out. The purpose of these curricular proposals is to meet with a fair degree of adequacy the general objectives stated above and to give expression to specific corollary judgments of special relevance to the present state of American higher education.

Wholeness and coherence of knowledge and understanding are very important in the aims of Christian liberal arts education. There may be disputes about specific means for achieving this aim, but there is almost unanimous agreement that integration of teaching and learning are of great significance and that the task involves curriculum, teaching, and student learning. At the same time that it is generally urged that all standard studies of the college, properly taught, can contribute greatly to more significant educational integration, a larger responsibility is legitimately placed on theology, philosophy, and history. Therefore, we recommend courses for all students in (a) Western Civilization, (b) Biblical Studies, (c) Christian Doctrine and Ethics, and in (d) Senior (capstone) Studies (theological-philosophical in approach, drawing on all areas of college studies in substance, and integrative in purpose).

While recognizing the educational values through mastery and depth in major studies, in recognition also of the need for a more common core of studies in basic areas, we recommend for all students courses in: (a) written and oral expression (present requirement); (b) coherent valid thinking (Systematic Thinking), fundamental to all studies as are grammar and high proficiency in the use of our native language; (c) natural science, aimed at rigorous knowledge of man's physical world and at a way of knowing to be grasped by historical and analytical-synthetic understanding (Single Science and Introduction to Science courses); (d) social science, concerned with man's intellectual grasp of social life (Political, Social, and Economic Institutions); and (e) man's creative symbolic world, interpreting man's understanding, intuition, and vision of man as man (Humanities). These courses have as their aim, not an introduction to a departmental sequence, however valuable they are for this, too, but rather a coherent introduction to the intelligible world common to every man as his humane inheritance and his inescapable context of thought and life.

250

PROPOSED PLAN OF STUDIES

Freshman Year

	Sem. Hours
Written and Oral Expression[1]	6- 8
Biblical Studies[1]	6
Systematic Thinking; Introd. to Science[1]	6
Western Civilization[1]	6
Electives	6-10
	30-34

Sophomore Year

	Sem. Hours
Humanities[1]	8
Single Natural Science[1]	8
Political, Social, and Economic Institutions[1]	6
Electives	8-12
	30-34

Junior Year

	Sem. Hours
Foreign Language and Literature[2]	0-15
Christian Doctrine and Ethics[3]	6
Major Studies	12-16
Electives	0-16
	30-34

Senior Year

	Sem. Hours
Major Studies	12-16
Senior Studies (capstone)	6
Electives	12-16
	30-34

PRESENT PLAN OF STUDIES

Freshman Year

	Sem. Hours
Written and Oral Expression	6- 8
Religion	4
Natural Science	8
History and/or Philosophy	6
Electives	6-10
	30-34

Sophomore Year

	Sem. Hours
Fine Arts	3
Nat. Science or Math.	0- 8
Social Science	6
Religion	4
Electives	9-21
	30-34

Junior Year

	Sem. Hours
Foreign Lang. or Lit.	0-15
Christian Doct. or electives	6
Major Studies	12-16
Electives	0-16
	30-34

Senior Year

	Sem. Hours
Major Studies	12-16
Electives	18-22
	30-34

Organization.

It is proposed that the all-college courses of obviously inter-departmental character (see next paragraph) be taught by capable teachers from throughout the faculty. An interdepartmental Steer-

---

[1]These all-college courses should be taken by students in the year designated in order to give a basic background which can be presupposed in other courses and also to provide an important common substance for all students at a given level.

[2]Foreign language and literature may be taken in the freshman, sophomore, or junior years as desired and as schedule permits.

[3]May be taken, if necessary, in the senior year.

251

ing Committee should be appointed by the Dean of the College, which committee shall be responsible for further policy formulation and evaluation of the all-college courses in light of the objectives of the program. Administration of all-college studies should be the responsibility of the Dean of the College or a Director appointed by him.

Order of going

It is proposed that the plan of studies be approved in principle by the faculty and that appropriate interdepartmental working committees be established (by the Dean of the College in consultation with the Steering Committee) for the following courses: Western Civilization; Systematic Thinking; Introduction to Science; Humanities; Political, Social, and Economic Institutions; and Senior Studies. These committees should include persons selected from the faculty to participate in the offering of such courses and others concerned with the role of these courses in the whole work of the college. These committees would have the task of preparing the appropriate syllabi to fulfil the objectives of such courses.

It is further proposed that the new portions of the plan be initiated as requirements in a series of steps:

First Year: Biblical Studies for Freshmen; Christian Doctrine and Ethics for Juniors; Senior Studies

Second Year: Western Civilization for Freshmen; Humanities for Sophomores

Third Year: Political, Social, and Economic Institutions for Sophomores; Systematic Thinking for Freshmen; Introduction to Science for Freshmen

252

Date Due

MAY 3 - '58			
JUL 2 6			
MR 5 '58			
AG 6 '58			
JY 20 '59			
AG 5 '59			
NO 20 '61			

NO. 340   PRINTED IN U.S.A.   BECKLEY - CARDY CO.